13

THE FORGOTTEN
WRITINGS OF
BRAM STOKER

The FORGOTTEN WRITINGS *of* BRAM STOKER

Edited by John Edgar Browning
Foreword by Elizabeth Miller
Afterword by Dacre Stoker

palgrave
macmillan

THE FORGOTTEN WRITINGS OF BRAM STOKER
Copyright © John Edgar Browning, 2012.

First published in 2012 by
PALGRAVE MACMILLAN®
in the United States—a division of St. Martin's Press LLC,
175 Fifth Avenue, New York, NY 10010.

Palgrave Macmillan is the global academic imprint of the above companies
and has companies and representatives throughout the world.

Palgrave® and Macmillan® are registered trademarks in the United States,
the United Kingdom, Europe and other countries.

ISBN 978–1–137–27722–0

Library of Congress Cataloging-in-Publication Data is available from
the Library of Congress.

A catalogue record of the book is available from the British Library.

Design by Newgen Imaging Systems, Ltd., Chennai, India

First edition: December 2012

10 9 8 7 6 5 4 3 2 1

Printed in the United States of America.

For Harry Ludlam, Jeanne Youngson, and the Stokers

CONTENTS

**Part VII   Catalogue of Valuable Books,
Autograph Letters, and Illuminated and
Other Manuscripts, Including The Library of the
Late Bram Stoker, Esq. and Associated Press (1913)**

ILLUSTRATIONS

A NOTE ON THE TEXTS

T he edition of each text, as well as any textual variations, is covered in the endnotes, and volume and issue numbers are given where available; British or American spelling has been kept depending on the country of origin of the edition being reproduced. Minor typographical errors and misspellings have been silently corrected; in the case of "Old Hoggen" (1893), missing text is designated by an ellipsis enclosed in rectangular brackets ("[...]"); missing text that can be reasonably inferred is enclosed in rectangular brackets ("[text]"); partially obscured text is designated in italics ("[...]*rts*"); and in the few instances in which variant capitalization or spacing is given—like "cousin Jemima" and "old Hoggen" instead of the more regularly seen "Cousin Jemima" and "Old Hoggen," or "coastguard" instead of "coast guard"—the text has been altered for uniformity.

For the Companion.

ONE THING NEEDFUL.

In Martha's house the weary Master lay,
Spent with His faring through the burning day.
The busy hostess bustled through the room
On household cares intent; and at His feet
The gentle Mary took her wonted seat.
Soft came His words in music through the gloom.

Cumbered about much serving, Martha wrought,
Her sister listening as the Master taught,
Till something fretful an appeal she made:
"Doth it not matter that on me doth fall
The burden? Mary helpeth not at all.
Master! command her that she give me aid."

"Ah! Martha, Martha, that art full of care,
And many things thy needless troubles share,"—
Thus with the love that chides, the Master spake—
"One thing alone is needful,—that good part
Hath Mary chosen from her loving heart,
And that part from her I shall never take."

*   *   *   *   *   *   *

One thing alone we lack! Our souls, indeed,
Have fiercer hunger than the body's need.
Oh! happy they that look in loving eyes!
The harsh world round them fades; the Master's voice
In sweetest music bids their souls rejoice,
And wakes an echo there that never dies!

London, England.   BRAM STOKER.

ABASHED.

Figure F.1 Bram Stoker's first known published poem, "One Thing Needful," with punctuation that differs slightly from the two subsequent printings.

(From *The Youth's Companion* [December 10, 1885]: 522)

BRAM STOKER, HIS LIFE AND WORKS

Elizabeth Miller

Abraham (Bram) Stoker was born on November 8, 1847 in Clontarf, on the outskirts of Dublin, Ireland. He was the third of seven children born to Charlotte Thornley (1818–1901) from western Ireland and Abraham Stoker (1799–1876), a civil servant in Dublin. He was a sickly child, practically bedridden during his early years. During this time, his mother entertained him with stories and legends from Sligo, which included supernatural tales and accounts of death and disease. This may have helped lay the foundation for some of the gothic motifs to be found later in his fiction.

By the time he entered Trinity College in 1864, he had fully recovered from his mysterious (and undiagnosed) illness. Indeed, he was a strong young man who excelled at athletics, winning several awards for prowess in football, racing, and weightlifting. He followed in his father's footsteps and joined the Civil Service at Dublin Castle. During the 1870s, he worked on what would be his first book *The Duties of Clerks of Petty*

Sessions in Ireland (1879) and penned several short stories, as well as theatre reviews written gratis for the Dublin *Evening Mail*. It was one of his reviews (of *Hamlet*) that brought him into contact with the British actor Henry Irving. A close friendship developed between the two men that was to last until Irving's death in 1905. In 1878, Irving invited Stoker to join him in London as business manager of his Lyceum Theatre.

Just before leaving Dublin, Bram married Florence Balcombe, reputed to be one of Dublin's most beautiful women. The couple had just one child, a son named Irving Noel Thornley, born in December 1879. Stoker's work at the Lyceum made great demands on his time. His responsibilities included arranging provincial seasons and overseas tours, keeping financial records and acting as Irving's secretary. He organized the Lyceum's eight North American tours, during which he met and befriended Walt Whitman (whose poetry he had defended as an undergraduate at Trinity) and Mark Twain. His association with Irving brought him into contact with many of the leading figures of his day, such as Alfred Lord Tennyson, Franz Liszt, Richard Burton, Henry Morton Stanley, Lord and Lady Randolph Churchill, and William Gladstone.

Stoker continued his writing, publishing numerous short stories as well as novels. He began work on what would become *Dracula* early in 1890. His working notes for the novel (now available as *Bram Stoker's Notes for Dracula: A Facsimile Edition*) provide much information about the development of characters, settings, and elements of the plot, as well as the nature of his research. The town of Whitby, which Stoker visited with his family in the summer of 1890, had a significant influence on the shaping of his book. In fact it was at the library in Whitby that he came across the name "Dracula," which he quickly appropriated for his vampire. Earlier vampire literature, most notably Sheridan Le Fanu's "Carmilla" (1872), also likely helped him develop his own story.

As a writer, Stoker was best known in his own day for *Personal Reminiscences of Henry Irving* (1906). Some of his lesser-known works include the novels *The Snake's Pass* (1890), *The Shoulder of Shasta* (1895), *The Jewel of Seven Stars* (1904), *Lady Athlyne* (1908), *The Lady of the Shroud* (1909), and *The Lair of the White Worm* (1911). Also of note are two collections of short stories—*Under the Sunset* (1881) and *Dracula's Guest and Other Weird Stories* (1914)—as well as the nonfictional *A Glimpse of America* (1886).

He died in London on April 20, 1912. His ashes are located at Golders Green Crematorium. But he left behind copious writings including novels, short stories, poetry, theatre reviews, newspaper/magazine articles, a two-volume biography, and a journal.

The pioneer in the field of Stoker bibliography was Richard Dalby, who published *Bram Stoker: A Bibliography of First Editions* in 1983. Building on that foundation, he joined forces with William Hughes in 2004 to produce a much more complete listing of Stoker's work—*Bram Stoker: A Bibliography* (Desert Island Books). This has been and still is regarded as the standard record of his literary production. But 100 years after Bram Stoker's death, the list of published works is expanding. Scholars are still unearthing obscure writings, the most recent being his missing journal, edited by Elizabeth Miller and Dacre Stoker. The publication of his journal, written for the most part while he was still living in Dublin during the 1870s, provides a clear sense of the extent of his versatility as a writer.

The challenge now is to compile a complete bibliography of Stoker's writing. New technology has allowed for more digitizing of newspapers and magazines, so that dozens of stories and articles both by and about Stoker are resurfacing and changing the face of Stoker studies. Leading the field is John Edgar Browning who has prior to this present work succeeded in finding dozens of previously unknown reviews and notices about *Dracula* from 1897 (its date of publication) to 1913 (the year following Stoker's death). This body of material forces us to challenge the long-held notion that the early critical reception of *Dracula* was "mixed," an error in judgment resulting from reliance on a limited sample of reviews.

Browning's continued research has yielded a bumper crop of Stoker's published writing that is only now coming to the surface. He divides his findings into 4 categories: poetry, short stories, journalistic prose, and period writings (1896–1912) about Stoker.

Stoker's first known published poem was "One Thing Needful," published in *The Youth's Companion* in December 1885 and reissued in *A Volunteer Haversack* in 1902 and in *The Queen's Carol* in 1905. Several other poems by Stoker appear in his journal, though there is no indication that any of them were ever published (see Journal, Chapter 1). Browning, however, has discovered at least two more: "The Member for the Strand" (lyrics for a song, 1890) and "The Wrongs of Grosvenor Square" (1892). In addition, Browning has unearthed six short stories (mostly from the 1890s), five articles, six period writings about Stoker (1896–1912) and a few miscellaneous items. Of special import for scholars is the inclusion in this volume of the contents of the "First Day's Sale: The Property of Bram Stoker, Esq." from the *Catalogue of Valuable Books, Autograph Letters, and Illuminated and Other Manuscripts, Including the Library of the Late Bram Stoker, Esq., and Associated Press* (1913).

This volume helps to resolve a problem that has nagged Stoker scholars for decades: the serialization of *Dracula*. In 1926, Florence Stoker wrote a foreword for a serialization in *Argosy*, stating clearly that this was the first appearance of the novel in that form. Yet references to a serialization in 1899 sent scholars (including myself) scurrying to find the first such publication—but to no avail. Now thanks to Browning, along with David J. Skal who will present his findings in his forthcoming book (2013) *Bram Stoker: The Final Curtain*, this mystery has been solved. *Dracula* did indeed appear in serial form in 1899. In fact, Stoker arranged for the serialization of at least two of his other novels: *The Gates of Life* (1908) and *Lady Athlyne* (1909).

One wonders how much more Stoker material is out there. But with eager young scholars such as John Edgar Browning on the trail, we may rest assured that any further hidden treasures will someday be uncovered.

ACKNOWLEDGMENTS

As the wise and ever kind Carol A. Senf said of her *Bram Stoker (Gothic Authors: Critical Revisions)* (2010), the present book on Stoker could not have been "Without the help and support of numerous people around the world." The world enjoys a love affair with Stoker, but it is certainly not a new one. Indeed, newspapers and journals throughout much of the English-speaking world have been Stoker crazy since at least the 1880s. Today, his allies don many languages and abound from many cultures. This book owes everything to you, and we owe everything to Stoker. Contrary to surviving photos, the *Blackburn Weekly Standard and Express* said of Stoker on April 22, 1899 that he "flattered everybody with his irresistible smile" (12)—this is how I like to think of him if he could read this book here and now.

I would like to start by thanking a crew of very dedicated graduate students who helped me to complete in record time the transcriptions of the works collected here. They include (alphabetically): Ronan Crowley (SUNY-Buffalo), Justin De Senso (SUNY-Buffalo), Kyle Fetter (SUNY-Buffalo), Juliette Highland (Louisiana State University), Chelsea Jones (SUNY-Buffalo), Jennifer Loft (SUNY-Buffalo), Monica Miller (Louisiana State University), Conor Picken (Louisiana State University), and Rachel Van Sickle (Louisiana State University). Digital Humanities is rarely easy work, but these burgeoning scholars performed brilliantly. They have my infinite gratitude.

The inclusion of many of the illustrations reproduced herein was made possible by the following kind people, institutions, and organizations: Logan Rath, Drake Memorial Library, SUNY-Brockport; Melissa

S. Mead, Rush Rhees Library, University of Rochester; Rockefeller Library, Brown University; the University of North Texas Libraries; the Lockwood Memorial Library, Libraries Annex, and the Teaching & Learning Center, SUNY-Buffalo; *British Periodicals* and ProQuest, The Quorum, Barnwell Road, Cambridge, CB5 8SW, UK Tel: +44 (0) 1223 215512, Web page: http://www.proquest.co.uk; the National Library of Australia; the British Library Board; and the California Digital Newspaper Collection, Center for Bibliographic Studies and Research, University of California, Riverside, htttp://cdnc.ucr.edu.

Finally, I would like to extend my personal gratitude to David J. Skal, the Bram Stoker Estate, Dacre Stoker, Elizabeth Miller, Carol J. Senf; to my terrific editors at Palgrave who believed in this project—Brigitte Shull and Maia Woolner; and most especially to Michael Agan.

JOHN EDGAR BROWNING
Buffalo, New York

Figure I.1 Photograph of Sir Henry Irving (1905) addressing crowd at unveiling of the tablet placed at the residence of famous eighteenth-century Irish actor James Quin, by Walter G. Lewis, showing Bram Stoker peering down behind Irving.

(National Library of Australia)

Figure I.2 Photograph of Sir Henry Irving (1905) unveiling the tablet placed at Quin's residence, by T. C. Leaman, with Bram Stoker emerging from behind Irving.

(From *Black & White* [February 25, 1905]: 258)

Introduction

A PERIODICAL PORTRAIT OF THE "AUTHOR OF DRACULA"

John Edgar Browning

After two years of intense archival inquiry, I have the pleasure of presenting in this collection, for the first time[1] since their publication over a century ago, twelve previously unknown published works of fiction, poetry, and journalistic writing by Bram Stoker, in addition to three works by Stoker never before reprinted, twelve relatively unglimpsed period writings about Stoker, including three interviews with Stoker himself, and finally a facsimile of the exceptionally rare 1913 estate sale catalogue of Stoker's personal library. To look upon the pages contained here will be, I suspect, as close as someone living today may come to the experience of living at the turn of the century and purchasing and reading "new" writings by Stoker during his lifetime. To be sure, this discovery underscores Richard Dalby's assertion, shared too by his co-author, William Hughes, in *Bram Stoker: A Bibliography* (2004), that "more of [Stoker's] ephemeral stories and articles may still be awaiting discovery in obscure newspapers and magazines."[2] But more still, for one like Stoker whose shorter literary works, outside of "Dracula's Guest" (1913), lie on the periphery of a legacy that for many offers little distinction from the world's greatest of vampire narratives, the necessity to examine his periodical writings is twofold. For one, it will aid in the task of elucidating Stoker-as-writer; but more critically, it will allow us to engage in dialogue with scholars like Dalby and Hughes, Carol A. Senf,[3] Lisa Hopkins,[4] and a host of other dedicated scholars who aptly call into question our insistent tunnel view of *Dracula* as Stoker's only legacy worthy of consideration. At the same time, it is only natural that several of the writings collected here should offer new avenues from which we may scrutinize *Dracula* and the genesis of its composition. That nearly all of Stoker's friends,[5] even Stoker himself,[6] and "without exception," notes Nina Auerbach, literature treating the affairs of Lyceum Theatre, are eerily "silent about *Dracula*,"[7] we must look then to the intricacies of his extraordinary professional and literary life if we are to uncover more clues.

The first part in this collection includes previously undocumented poetry by Stoker. The first selection, "The Member for the Strand" (1890), published in *Judy: Or The London Serio-Comic Journal*, is a song celebrating Sir Henry Irving's mock candidacy to Parliament, and the second selection, "The Wrongs of Grosvenor Square" (1892), published in *The Speaker*, is a political poem. Both are especially interesting finds, being that they are now only the second and third works of verse Stoker is recorded ever to have published. Of particular interest is "The Wrongs of Grosvenor Square," which appeared in print just three years before another of Stoker's works to appropriate the use of a Scottish dialect, *The Watter's Mou'* (1895), wherein, according to Hughes, "The sporadic dialect...received a less favourable reception"[8] from language-conscious reviewers[9] than Stoker's previous novel, *The Snake's Pass* (1890).

Part II, "Unknown Fiction by Bram Stoker (1893–1908)," comprises the collection's largest number of writings by Stoker that have until now eluded bibliographers, or in the case of "A Baby Passenger" (1899), escaped reproduction and examination. Verging on the Gothic as well as the comedic, the first selection, "Old Hoggen: A Mystery" (1893), is by far the collection's most peculiar addition. The story's protagonist, Augustus, to appease the finicky appetites of his mother-in-law and cousin by marriage, goes out searching for crabs early one morning along the English coast. What he does not expect to find is the drowned body of town patriarch and eccentric Old Hoggen floating along the shore, for whose disappearance Augustus and his household, being relative newcomers to town, have been suspect for several weeks. Eventually, Augustus, afraid that an eminent storm will draw the body further out to sea, resolves to convey the body to safety, a task of no short distance. Unfortunately, the body of Old Hoggen is in a state of advanced decay, so Augustus begins to shed body parts one by one along the way, until finally all that remains is the head, which he carries under his arm. Before so Augustus abandons the torso, however, two crabs emerge from its chest cavity, which he quickly pockets in his "shooting jacket," intending to feed them later to his mother-in-law and cousin. It is interesting to note here that Stoker was himself no stranger to carrying lifeless bodies to safety. In 1882, the Royal Humane Society bestowed upon Stoker a medal for jumping overboard from a steamer into the Thames to save a drowning suicide victim; Stoker conveyed, to his private residence, the body of the elderly man (who unfortunately had already expired) in the futile hope that Stoker's brother, George, a surgeon, might revive him.[10] Also of note, there is a striking parallel between Old Hoggen, whose coat hid—and subsequently poured forth—a fortune in bank notes, and Count Dracula, whose clothing produces more or less the same effect during an encounter in London with Stoker's "Crew of Light":[11]

[Harker] had ready his great Kukri knife, and made a fierce and sudden cut at [Dracula]. The blow was a powerful one; only the diabolical quickness of the Count's leap back saved him. A second less and the trenchant blade had shorne through his heart. As it was, the point just cut the cloth of his coat, making a wide gap whence a bundle of bank-notes and a stream of gold fell out.[12]

The next three selections, "When the Sky Rains Gold" (1894), "Bengal Roses" (1898), and "A Young Widow" (1899), are love stories. As with "Old Hoggen," we may see in these three tales points of intersection with Stoker's private life and other of his published works. In "When the Sky Rains Gold," for example, which appeared in two serial installments in *The Boston Sunday Herald*, we see, as in *Dracula*, traces of Stoker's love for maps; his love of the sea, which, in life, Stoker made no effort to hide; a self-referential nod, perhaps, in the characters of the "red-haired, big-bearded, brawny giants who spoke in Gaelic"; and, most striking of all, not only do we encounter in the story an American frontiersman brandishing a bowie knife (like Quincy in *Dracula*), but in the protagonist's love-interest, Riddy, who in the story exudes only love and purity, the description of her mouth, "like pearl and ruby where the white teeth shone through the parted lips," bears remarkable resemblance to her antithesis in *Dracula*, the three Brides, who "had brilliant white teeth that shone like pearls against the ruby of their voluptuous lips."[13] The similarity is made all the more intriguing by the fact Stoker was busy researching *Dracula* at the time he published this story. The next selection, "Bengal Roses," which appeared in two serial installments in *Lloyd's Weekly Newspaper* (London), begins with a short prologue in which the protagonist, Edward, a gentleman of about 32, encounters the scent of Bengal roses in his study and is reminded by them of the adolescent love he, as a sickly boy many years earlier (Stoker had himself been a sickly boy for much of his childhood[14]), shared for an orphaned girl 5 years his senior named Arabella Devanti. The name "Arabella," Stoker aficionados will recall, is given also to the villainess "Lady Arabella" in *The Lair of the White Worm* (1911). (Curiously, Arabella Devanti becomes, by the end of "Bengal Roses," a countess, i.e., "Lady Arabella.") For the remainder of the story, Edward recounts, as a young boy, both his affections for "Bella" and his subsequent heroic efforts to thwart a devious marriage plot against her. We also encounter, along the way, traces of Stoker's interest, again, in maps, physiognomy, and it is impossible not to see, in the character of the "tall, powerful.... athletic young parson," some of Stoker's college-day brawn. The last of the three love stories, "A Young Widow," appeared in *The Boston Sunday Herald*. Of the story's young heroine, again it is worth noting that the protagonist's affectionate description of her "full lips showing scarlet against her white teeth" mirrors that of Dracula's three Brides. Thus, the once clear demarcation in *Dracula* between heroine and villainess is made uncomfortably fluid by Stoker's parallel descriptions in these love stories.

Finally, "A Baby Passenger" (1899), "Lucky Escapes of Sir Henry Irving" (1900), and "What They Confessed: A Low Comedian's Story" (1908) cap off Part II. First appearing in *Lloyd's Weekly Newspaper* (then rehashed as "Chin Music" nearly a decade later in *Snowbound: The Record of a Theatrical Touring Party* [1908]), "A Baby Passenger" became, at the time of its publication and in the years that followed, Stoker's most prolific short story (as I will discuss at length momentarily). In it are subtle traces of the Gothic, coupled with elements of Stoker's travels in America and, again, his keen interest in physiognomy. Written in the form of successive anecdotes, "Lucky Escapes of Sir Henry Irving" is a fictionalized self-narrative in which Stoker describes "potential" disasters that *could* have befallen the Lyceum Theatre Company at its various destinations in America. Finally, "What They Confessed: A Low Comedian's Story," a variant version of Stoker's "In Fear of Death" (which he published the same year in *Snowbound: The Record of a Theatrical Touring Party* [1908]), is—like "A Baby Passenger"—another of Stoker's "tales told on the train," this time about a passenger car full of actors who are tricked into confessing their sins for fear of a natural disaster they are told is about to befall the train.

Part III, "Unknown Journalistic Writings by Bram Stoker (1891–1908)," brings together four selections. The first is an obituary article entitled, "Recollections of the Late W. G. Wills" (1891), in which Stoker recounts some of his fondest memories of the dramatist who brought Irving his most financially successful play, *Faust*. The next two selections underscore Stoker's devotion to Irving, beginning with "Sir Henry Irving: An Appreciation by Bram Stoker, His Longtime Friend" (1904), an article that appeared in the *New-York Daily Tribune*. The next selection is a popularly reprinted eulogy entitled, "12,000 Miles of Irving's Audiences" (1906), which Stoker gave at the Westbourne Park Institute. While the earliest edition I have been able to locate appeared in *The Des Moines Daily News* (reprinted herein), it was printed as far and wide as New Zealand (as I show later). Finally, completing this section is "Where Hall Caine Dreams Out His Romances" (1908), a *The New York Times* article in which Stoker describes the life and daily rituals of his dear friend and celebrated author Hall Caine at his home on the Isle of Man.

Part IV, "Unknown Interviews with Bram Stoker" (1886–1890), offers three relatively short interviews with Stoker. The first, "Irving and Hudson: Bram Stoker Tells What He Thinks About the Controversy" (1886), printed in *The Boston Herald*, and second, "A Chat with Mr. Stoker About Irving" (1886), printed the same day in *The New-York Daily Tribune*, both concern an incident with a former member of the Lyceum Theatre Company by the name of Hudson; additionally, the latter reveals Stoker's thoughts about some new stage effects scheduled for implementation in *Faust*. Finally, the third interview, "The Gangway Seats at the Lyceum" (1890), appeared in *The Era* and concerns the London County Council's ruling to abolish the Lyceum's gangway seats.

Part V, "Rare and Uncollected Works by Bram Stoker (1896–1906)," reproduces for the first time since its initial publication a souvenir booklet entitled, *Sir Henry Irving and Miss Ellen Terry in Robespierre, Merchant of Venice, The Bells, Nance Oldfield, The Amber Heart, Waterloo, etc.* (1896), which is among the rarest of Stoker's works that may be found today. Also included in this section is the rare article, "Henry Irving's Fight for Fame" (1906), which appeared in *Success Magazine*, and in it Stoker spends considerable time discussing the tenacity of Irving's dedication to the art form during his youth. Irving's tenacity to learn the role—to *become* the part—is, interestingly, reflected also in the way Stoker characterizes Dracula's obsession with "sounding" and "becoming" English before his journey across Europe to London.

Seven "Period Writings about Bram Stoker (1896–1913)" comprise Part VI. First among them is "To Bram Stoker" (1893), Hall's Caine's heartfelt dedication to his friend in *Capt'n Davy's Honeymoon* (1893). Afterwards follows an extract from "Green Room Gossip" (1896), an article printed in the *Daily Mail* (London) that boasts of Stoker's "Herculean" talents among theater managers. Next is a poem from *The Brooklyn Daily Eagle* entitled, "Night with Sir Henry Irving: With Intimations That Bram Stoker Was Also in the Neighborhood" (1900), by R. M. Field, in which the speaker, addressing "Bram," recounts the joy of staying up all night talking with Irving and other like company—mostly more admirers of Irving's. The whole episode is slightly reminiscent of Jonathan's (forced) ritual of having to stay up all night talking with the Count in *Dracula*. The next selection, an article from *The Boston Sunday Herald* entitled, "Actor-Manager and Author: Bram Stoker Finds Recreation in Writing Romances" (1902), offers a cursory historical sketch of Stoker's personal, professional, and literary life. Then follows the "Story of Senator Quay" (1904), a charming short short story printed in the *Oswego Daily Palladium* (New York) about the time a keg of reeking sauerkraut arrived for Stoker's consumption during one of his visits with Irving to Philadelphia. The section then concludes with two articles *in memoria*. The first is an American obituary from the *Cleveland Plain Dealer*, titled, simply, "Bram Stoker" (1912). In it is produced one of the more eloquent, yet informed obituarial notices for Stoker I have ever encountered. Whereas a number of such notices will downplay some aspects of Stoker's life and laud others, this obituary speaks favorably about numerous facets of Stoker's life and career. In short, it is unlike many of the obituaries one will encounter, particularly because it reads like a more "modern" perception of Stoker's achievements. Following it is an article published in *The Irish-American* entitled, "Bram Stoker, Irishman" (1913), in which the author declares—nay, celebrates—Stoker's "Irishness" after a recent article about the sale of his personal library called Stoker a celebrated "*English* author and scholar [emphasis added]."

Concluding, Part VII, "Catalog of Valuable Books, Autograph Letters, and Illuminated and Other Manuscripts, Including the Library of the Late Bram Stoker, Esq. *and* Associated Press (1913)," opens with the incredibly rare catalog, "First Day's Sale: The Property of Bram Stoker, Esq. (Deceased)." Reproduced in facsimile, the catalog details the sale of Stoker's personal effects. Afterwards follow three articles associated with the sale: "Bram Stoker's Valuable Library to Be Sold," published in *The Sun* (New York) prior to the sale in order to advertise some of the items expected to fetch the highest sums; then "Low Prices for Americana: Library of Late Bram Stoker Sold in London" in *The Sun* (New York), and "Whitman Writings Sold: Lecture on Lincoln Brings $25 at Bram Stoker Library Sale" in *The New York Times*, both published at the close of the sale to lament the unexpectedly low prices at which the hammer fell for much of Stoker's library.

The sheer number of periodical writings collected here is by itself no small feat, but that most of them are new and thematically diverse is profound. For, in the context of the Stoker himself—an extraordinarily busy man who, because he supplied the world's most prolific vampire narrative, has come under such incredible scrutiny as to make it exceedingly difficult to realize anything new about him—these writings, indeed, speak voluminously. Yet, also, they comprise only one dimension of Stoker's literary career that still has much to tell us.

Through his unparalleled office as business manager to Irving, Britain's most celebrated stage actor, clearly Stoker was no stranger to the limelight. Yet, new evidence suggests that he, at some point, came to understand the value of distribution, as well as media coverage.[15] An example worth consideration is *Dracula*'s serial publication, a mystery which is only now beginning to tell its secrets. Stoker's widow, Florence, reported in a foreword to *Dracula*'s reputed first serial installment in *Argosy* magazine in 1926 that she was there presenting for the first time ever in serial form her late husband's most famous novel. However, according to The Bram Stoker Estate, the *Washington Times* printed a complete newspaper serialization of the 1899 Doubleday & McClure edition of Stoker's novel, under the title "Dracula, or The Vampire," from September 13, 1917 to January 21, 1918. Even still, earlier newspaper articles—like the review ("A Grewsome Tale") reproduced online by The Bram Stoker Estate, in addition to (from what I have been able to ascertain independently) at least six other articles[16] printed between September 1899 and October 1902—purport that *Dracula* had indeed been serialized in newspapers considerably earlier. At last, the answer came when friend and comrade-in-arms David J. Skal reported to me that he had unearthed one of these alleged early serials in the *Charlotte Daily Observer*. Printed there under the title "Dracula: A Strong Story of the Vampire," the serial ran from July 16, 1899 to December 10, 1899.[17] Almost immediately following Skal's report, I, too, located, in two identical newspaper ads printed in the *Fitchburg Daily Sentinel* and the *Lowell Sun*,[18] positive proof of *Dracula*'s serialization prior to the *Argosy* run, only this time under the simple title "The Vampire," in the morning and Sunday editions of the *Boston Advertiser* in May 1921. Also of note, *Dracula* saw a lengthy excerpt in *The Cabinet of Irish Literature: Selections from the Works of the Chief Poets, Orators, and Prose Writers of Ireland* (1906), from just into "5 May. *The Castle*" through to the end of Chapter One;[19] and "Dracula's Guest" (1914) as well was likely reprinted in a January 1917 issue of *Short Stories* (Doubleday, Page, and Co.).[20]

Apparently Stoker was not content to restrict serialization or excerptation of his novels to *Dracula* alone. In fact, he began doing so with his very first book-length work of fiction, *Under the Sunset* (1881). The chapter entitled, "The Castle of the King," appeared as a lengthy excerpt (incorrectly labeled as "The Shadow Builder") in *The Supplement to the South Bourke & Mornington Journal* (Richmond, Victoria, Australia) (1882).[21] Further, *The Snake's Pass* (1890) appeared as a weekly serial in *The Newcastle Courant* (Newcastle upon Tyne, England) between September 27 and December 27, 1890, and in the *Weekly Mail* (Cardiff, Wales),[22] which, according to my colleague Paul McAlduff, occurred between July 19 and November 29, 1890.[23] What is more, an excerpt entitled, "The Night at the Shifting Bog," appeared in *Current Literature* (January–April 1891),[24] and chapter three was published as "The Gombeen Man" in *Irish Literature* (1904).[25] Also in *Current Literature* (July–December) appeared an extract from *The Watter's Mou'*, entitled, "At the Watter's Mou': Between Duty and Love."[26]

At the start of the new century, Stoker apparently authorized as well the serial reproduction of both *The Mystery of the Sea* in *The Denver Post* between April 10 and April 13, 1902, and *The Jewel of Seven Stars* (1903), starting in late-January of 1903, in the *Sunday Chronicle* (Manchester).[27] Later that same decade, his novel *The Gates of Life* appeared in serial form in the *Poughkeepsie Daily Eagle* (New York), from approximately May 1 through June 30, 1908; in *The Daily Picayune* (New Orleans), from May 1, 1908 to June 23, 1908; in the *Baltimore American*, as "Through the Gates of Life," from May 27 to July 10, 1908; in *The Montgomery Advertiser* (Montgomery, AL), from May 1, 1908 to June 30, 1908; and in the *Evening Post* (Charleston, SC) and *The Morning Leader* (Regina, Saskatchewan) during approximately the same time as the New Orleans, New York, Montgomery, and Baltimore runs, in all six cases being nearly two months before the book's American edition on July 11, 1908. His *Lady Athlyne*, too, appeared in serial form in the *Utica Daily Observer* (New York), from approximately March or April through May 1909, and in the *Fort Worth Star-Telegram* (Texas), from approximately April 26, 1909 to June 2, 1909, some eight months before the book's American edition in November 1909.[28] Thus, that Stoker did not restrict serialization to *Dracula* alone, particularly during the last few years of his life, lends itself to an assertion made by Hughes: that, whereas Stoker's reasons for writing and publishing early on in his career were not purely economic, this may well have changed for an author who, following Irving's death in 1905, was in the decline of his literary prominence.[29]

Other of Stoker's periodical works for which I have located new information include several shorter works as well. For example, while "Bengal Roses" was appearing in *Lloyd's Weekly Newspaper*, it saw a simultaneous run in *The Boston Herald*.[30] Another short story, "Our New House," is generally cited in *The Theatre Annual*, which, according to E. L. Blanchard in "A Chain of Memories" (1887), saw print in November 1886.[31] In actuality, however, Stoker's short story appeared a full year earlier on December 20, 1885 in *The Boston Herald*.[32] Further still, Stoker's short story resurfaced again, this time several months before *The Theatre Annual* printing, in a February edition of the *Utica Daily Observer*, and again (the precise month unknown) in the *Clinton Courier* (New York), in both instances being misprinted under the authorship of a "Bram Stokes [*sic*]." Additionally, "Crooken Sands," which Dalby and Hughes cite in *The Illustrated Sporting and Dramatic News* (1894),[33] was excerpted in *The Capricornian* (Rockhampton, Queensland, Australia) on July 25, 1896 and in *The Morning Bulletin* (Rockhampton, Queensland, Australia) on July 29, 1896. His short story "A Yellow Duster" appeared on May 7, 1899 in *The Boston Sunday Herald*[34] and, according to McAlduff, saw a simultaneous printing in *Lloyd's Weekly Newspaper*.[35]

Newspapers also readily excerpted from Stoker's journalistic writings. Stoker's interview with Sir Arthur Conan Doyle, which Dalby and Hughes cite in *The World* (New York) (July 1907) and two other reprintings in 1908,[36] also appeared in excerpted form in the *Daily Kennebec Journal* (Augusta, ME) on September 2, 1907; in *The Daily News* (Perth, Western Australia) on November 23, 1907; in *The Star* (Auckland, New Zealand) on December 9, 1907; and in the *Examiner* (Launceston, Tasmania) on January 1, 1908.[37] Stoker's interview with W. S. Gilbert, too, which Dalby and Hughes cite in the *Daily Chronicle* (London) (January 1908),[38] appeared as a lengthy excerpt under the title, "Our Comedians Better Than Our Tragedians," in the *Evelyn Observer and Bourke East Record* on February 28, 1908.[39] Finally, Stoker's article "Mr DeMorgan's Habits of Work" saw a lengthy excerpt in *The Daily News* (Perth, Western Australia) on September 10, 1908.[40]

As I hinted earlier, "A Baby Passenger" seems also to have enjoyed a longer, and more far-reaching print life than previously documented. The earliest printing, as Paul Murray was first to point out, appeared in *Lloyd's Weekly Newspaper* on February 19, 1899.[41] However, unbeknownst to scholars, the story resurfaced in news print at least twelve other times in a span of just four years, in the United States, Australia, and New Zealand. These reprintings include: *The Boston Sunday Herald* on February 19, 1899; the *Daily Iowa State Press* (Iowa City) on April 26, 1899 (reprinted herein); *The Aspen Tribune* (Aspen, CO) on May 2, 1899; *The Victoria Advocate* (Victoria, TX) on May 6, 1899; *The Liverpool Herald* (New South Wales, Australia) on May 20, 1899; as an unsigned piece in *The Northern Advocate* (Whangarei, New Zealand) on May 27, 1899; *The Western Mail* (Perth, Western Australia) on June 2, 1899; *Des Moines Gazette* on June 8, 1899; *The Lexington Gazette* (Lexington, Virginia) on June 14, 1899; *The Shenandoah Herald* (Woodstock, VA) on June 23, 1899; *The Cedar Rapids Republican* (Cedar Rapids, Iowa) on July 8, 1899; and *The Bruce Herald* (Tokomairiro, New Zealand) on July 14, 1903. Also, Stoker's "12,000 Miles of Irving's Audiences," as I indicated earlier, was reprinted far and wide: as "Irving's Audiences Would Cover 12,000 Miles If Placed Together" in the *Supplement to the Poverty Bay Herald* (Gisborne, New Zealand) on November 24, 1906; and under the title "Irving as an Educator: Tribute Paid to Great Actor by his Lifelong Associate" both in *The Mt. Sterling Advocate* (Mt. Sterling, KY) on January 23, 1907 and in *The Montgomery Tribune* (Montgomery City, MO) on January 4, 1907.[42]

Finally, "The Coming of Abel Behenna," another of Stoker's periodicals, appeared in his posthumous collection *Dracula's Guest and Other Weird Stories* (1914), reputedly as a reprint according to Florence Stoker; but from where it was reprinted we have never been sure, until now.[43] In *From the Shadow of Dracula: A Life of Bram Stoker* (2004), Paul Murray is not far off the mark when he writes that Stoker found inspiration for the story while on a walking tour near the village of Boscastle during Holy Week in 1892.[44] For, indeed, the story did appear a year later in *The New Haven Register* (New Haven, CT) in March 1893 and in *Lloyd's Weekly Newspaper* in April 1893. Additionally, it appeared thirteen years after *Dracula's Guest*, in *Argosy* magazine around the same time *Dracula* was being serialized there. Similarly, Stoker's "The Burial of Rats" also appeared in *Dracula's Guest and Other Weird Stories*, but from where it was reprinted has until now remained unknown. Indeed, as McAlduff also notes,[45] the story appeared simultaneously, in two serial installments, in *Lloyd's Weekly Newspaper* and *The Boston Herald* on January 26 and February 2, 1896.

Florence Stoker also asserted that at the time of her late husband's death in 1912, he had been planning to publish three collections of his short fiction that had appeared previously in various periodicals.[46] From these periodical writings, Florence Stoker publishes posthumously, together with Stoker's unpublished "Dracula's Guest," *Dracula's Guest and Other Weird Tales* (1914). On the subject of the other two collections mentioned by Florence Stoker, Albert Power aptly concludes, in "Bram Stoker and the Tradition of Irish Supernatural Fiction" that it is difficult to surmise which of Stoker's other, multifarious periodical writings would have comprised the remaining two volumes.[47] It is not unthinkable, then, that the writings that follow may have been among these mystery works. Of this we may never be certain. However, we *can* amply conclude that Stoker's periodical writings do indeed denote a much greater force in his literary repertoire than previously accepted, and when examined in more depth will undoubtedly yield further insight into a man whose hitherto underestimated work frequently bestows upon scholars the task of rethinking both his accomplishments and his enigmatic persona.

PART I

UNKNOWN POETRY BY
BRAM STOKER (1890–1892)

Figure 1.1 Illustration, "A First Night at the Lyceum" (1890), by George C. Haite. (From *The Strand Magazine: An Illustrated Monthly* 1 [January–June 1891]: 12)

Chapter One

THE MEMBER FOR
THE STRAND (1890)[1]

BRAM STOKER

YE *actors, play a tune upon the trumpet,*
  Batter forcibly the parchment of a drum;
Get a table and incontinently thump it;
  For the moment of your victory has come.
The reward of merit reaches the deserving;
  There is joy in ev'ry corner of the land
That the doyen of the mummers, Henry Irving,
  Is about to sit as Member for the Strand.
Ev'ry fashion of improvement he will dish up;
  All varieties of hobbies he wil [sic] run;
He will move that Edward Terry shall be bishop,
  And retiring Mary Anderson a nun;
He will tell the House that all the world a stage is,
  Its inhabitants a histrionic band;
And he'll move for raising histrionic wages,
  If you'll vote for him as Member for the Strand.

He will talk about the "mission of the drama,"
  And expound it with an unction, you may bet!
He will posture, self-important as the Llama,
  Who is worshipped in the uplands of Thibet.
With the truculent McDougall he will grapple;
  He will drive him to some very distant land;
Or confine him in his own dissenting chapel,
  When he sits, at last, as Member for the Strand.

Chapter Two

THE WRONGS OF GROSVENOR SQUARE (1892)[1]

BRAM STOKER

[*Indignation grave and deep has been existent for some time past with regard to the running of omnibuses through Grosvenor Square, and it is rumored that an indignation meeting of the servants of that aristocratic neighborhood is shortly to be held.*]

Brother footmen! met together, I address you from the chair
On the subject of the Omnibus that desecrates our Square.
In the past our 'appy Hengland 'ad one jewel in her crown
Which your Bradlaughs and your Gladstones dar'sn't wenture to pull down!
There was one spot in our Island where wulgarity was rare!—
Need I trouble you by mentioning the name of Gruvnor Square?

Oh! 'ere indeed was manners! In the land it stood alone
For its genooine secloosion and the 'ighness of its tone.
It was 'ealthy! it was 'appy! It was priviledge to stand

On the doorsteps of the 'aughty and the 'ighest in the land!
And the British public knowed it, for their tone was lowered when
Their heyes beheld the gorgeous mansions of the Hupper Ten!
Even the cabbies when they entered on our precincts ceased to swear
And with bated breath the growler meekly crorled along our Square
We 'ad chariots, we 'ad britskas. We was strong and could assume
Toleration for the later hinnovation of the brougham!
But, as yet, we 'adn't 'ansoms, much less what is even wuss!—
We was mercifully spared the degradation of the 'Bus,
With its "cads" and its "conductors," and its knife-board full of Gents:
I 'ope I ain't a-flyin' in the face of Providence—
But wotever sins we're guilty of, full penalties we bear
When 'Im 'as plagued Egyptians sent the 'Buses to the Square!

When the Serpent came to Heden for to give the primal cuss,
He forestalled our present ruing; he was bodied like a 'Bus!
He was blue and he was yaller; he was red and he was green!
He was all that was horrific; he was all that was obscene!
And they wrote upon 'im "Oundsditch," "Ampstead," "Ighgate"—even wuss!
You might read the foul word "Chelsea" wrote out brazen on the 'Bus!

We, too, 'ad our little Heden, for our Square it blossomed then
With the mansions of our greatest and our 'ighest noblemen,
Till there came the fell disaster what 'as brought us to our knees
With a hominous beginning in the presence of M.P.'s;
With their pockets full of money an aggression they would dare
And would join the Aristocracy by living in our Square!

Even brokers now and jobbers, when they're rich by selling shares,
Tries to make theirselves respectable by coming to our squares,
Little thinking of our feelings or what tender chords they shock
When they quit their foul secloosion in the wilds of Bedford Pawk!
But there's justice in the Hupwards, and they'll meet it sure as Fate!
Their presumption will be punished, for we shan't associate!
Brother footmen! wake your thunder; and don't do the thing by halves!

Tear the knots from off your shoulders! pull the padding from your calves!
Take the curl from out your whiskers! dust the powder from your hair!
Doff your buckles and your buttons! show the depths of your despair
At the outrage put upon you by the 'Buses in the Square!

Let us gather in our thousands! Let us deputate our Queen!
Let us throw ourselves upon her—on her sympathies, I mean.
She, at least, will understand us and our troubles with the 'Bus
When we wenture to remind her—Mr. Brown was one of Us!
Let us make a hardent protest! Let us say, with one accord,
"Gracious Queen! there is a something what your servants 'as haborred!
Give us back our hancient Heden as a hanswer to our prayer,
And make 'appy loyal Hengland in the pusson of the Square!"

If 'Er Majesty makes answer that she will, upon that day
We shall tell 'er with our blessing 'er petitioners will pray!—
If there isn't such a answer, we will tell her we deplore
That the glory of our nation has departed evermore!
Welcome then the fell invader! Revolution, hurry up;
For you cannot add a single drop of bitter to our cup.
We shall fly from outraged London unto London-super-Mare,
Crying, "Ichabod! The glory has departed from the Square!"

Figure 2.1 Illustration, "Mr. Henry Irving Unveiling the Marlowe Memorial at Canterbury" (1891), with Bram Stoker appearing far right.

PART II

UNKNOWN FICTION BY BRAM STOKER (1893–1908)

Chapter Three

OLD HOGGEN:
A MYSTERY (1893)[1]

BRAM STOKER

"If he had half the spirit of a man in him, he would go himself," said my mother-in-law.

"Indeed, I think you might, Augustus. I know I often deny myself and make efforts to please you; and you know that my dear mamma loves crabs," said my mother-in-law's daughter.

"Far be it from me to interfere," said Cousin Jemima, as they call her, smoothing down her capstrings as she spoke. "But I do think that it would be well if Cousin Kate, who, like myself, is not at all so strong as she looks—could have something to tempt her appetite."

Cousin Jemima, who was my mother-in-law's cousin, was as robust as a Swiss guide, and had the appetite and digestion of a wild Indian. I began to get riled.

"What on earth are you all talking about?" said I. "One would think you were all suffering some terrible wrong. You want crabs—and you are actually now engaged on bolting one of the biggest crabs I ever saw. What does it all mean? Unless, indeed, you want merely to annoy me!"

Here my mother-in-law laid down her fork in a majestic way and glared at me, saying:

"If there are no crabs nearer than Bridport, then you must go there," while her daughter began to cry.

This, of course, settled the matter. When my mother-in-law has a go in at me I can—although it makes me uncomfortable and unhappy—stand it; but when her daughter cries, I am done; so I made an effort by an attempt at jocularity—feeble, though, it was—to grace my capitulation and go out with the honors of war.

"I shall get you some crabs," said I, "my dear mother-in-law, which even you will not be able to vanquish—or even, Cousin Jemima, with her feeble digestion."

They all looked very glum, so I made another effort.

"Yes," I went on. "I shall bring you some giant crabs, even if I have to find old Hoggen first."

The only answer made in words was by my mother-in-law, who cut in sharply: "If Old Hoggen was as great a brute as you, I don't wonder that he has got rid of—"

Cousin Jemima indorsed the sentiment with a series of sniffs and silences, as eloquent and expressive as the stars and negative chapters of Tristram Shandy. Lucy looked at me, but it was a good look, more like my wife's, and less like that of my mother-in-law's daughter than had hitherto been, so tacitly we became a linked battalion.

There was a period of silence, which was broken by my mother-in-law: "I do not see—I fail to see why you will always introduce that repulsive subject."

As she began the battle, and as Lucy was now on my side, I did not shun the fight, but made a counter attack.

"Crabs?" I asked interrogatively, in a tone which I felt to be dangerous.

"No, not crabs—how dare you call the subject of my food—and you know how delicate an appetite I have—disgusting—"

"Well, what do you mean?" I inquired, again showing the green lamps.

"I call 'disgusting' the subject of conversation on which you always harp—that disreputable old man whom they say was murdered. I have made inquiries—many inquiries—concerning him, and I find that his life was most disreputable. Some of the details of his low amours which I have managed to find out are most improper. What do you think, Cousin Jemima—"

Here she whispered to the other old dear, who eagerly inclined her ear to listen.

"No, really! seventeen? What a wretched old man," and Cousin Jemima became absorbed in a moral reverie.

My mother-in-law went on:

"When you, Augustus, bring perpetually before our notice the name of this wicked man, you affront your wife."

Here the worm, which had hitherto been squirming about trying to imagine that it was built on the lines of a serpent, which can threaten and strike, turned, and I spoke.

"I do not think it is half so bad to mention a topic of common interest, and which is forced upon us every hour of every day since we came here, as it is for you to make such a charge. I respect and love my wife too much"—here I pulled Lucy toward me, who came willingly—"to affront her even by accident. And, moreover, I think, Madam, that it would be better if, instead of making such preposterous and monstrous charges, you would give me a little peace to my meals by holding your tongue and giving yourself an opportunity of getting tired and sick of crabs. I have not sat down to a meal since I came here that you have not spoiled it with your quarrelling. You quite upset my digestion. Can't you let me alone?"

The effect of the attack was appalling.

My mother-in-law, who by this time had finished the last morsel of the crab, sat for a moment staring and speechless, and for the only time in her life burst into tears.

Her tears were not nearly so effective upon me as Lucy's, and I sat unmoved. Cousin Jemima, with an inborn tendency to rest secure on the domineering side, said, audibly:

"Served you quite right, Cousin Kate, for interrupting the man at his supper."

Lucy said nothing, but looked at me sympathetically.
Presently my mother-in-law, with a great effort, pulled herself together and said:

"Well, Augustus, perhaps you are right. We have suffered enough about Old Hoggen to make his name familiar to us."

Indeed we suffered. The whole history of old Hoggen had for some weeks past been written on our soul in the darkest shade of ink. We had come to Charmouth hoping to find in that fair spot the peace that we yearned for after the turmoil and troubles of the year. With the place we were more than satisfied, for it is a favored spot. In quiet, lazy, Dorsetshire it lies. Close to the sea, but sheltered from its blasts. The long straggling village of substantial houses runs steeply down the hillside parallel to the seaboard. Everywhere are rivulets of sweet water, [and] everywhere are comfort and seeming plenty. [The] smiling and industrious peasantry are the normal inhabitants among whom the good old customs of saluta-tion have not died away. A town-made coat enacts a bob curtsey from the females and a salute in military fashion from the men, for the young men are all militia or volunteers.

We had been at Charmouth some three weeks. Our arrival had caused us to swell with importance, for, from the time we left Axminster in the diurnal omnibus till our being deposited at our pretty cottage, [fl]owered in enticing greenery and rich with [...] world flowers, our advent seemed to [in]cite interest and attention. Naturally I surmised that the rustic mind was overcome by the evidence of metropolitan high [...]*m/ne* manifested in our cloths and [...]. Lucy put it down—in her own mind which her mother kindly interpreted [fo]r her—to the striking all-the-world-over effect of surpassing loveliness. Cousin Jemima attributed it to their respect for blood; and my mother-in-law took [it a]s a just homage to the rare, if not [uni]que, union of birth, grace, gentleness, [bre] eding, talent, wisdom, culture and [po]wer—as embodied in herself. We soon [fou]nd, however, that there was a cause different from all these.

There had lately come to light certain circumstances tending to show that we [ar]e objects of suspicion rather than veneration.

Some days before our arrival great ex[cite]ment had been caused in Charmouth [at] the disappearance, and, consequently, [depl]ored murder, of an old inhabitant, one Jabez Hoggen, reputed locally to be of vast wealth and miserly in the extreme. This [...] reputation brought him much esteem, [not i]n Charmouth alone, but through [whol]e country round from Lyme Regis on the one hand even as far as distant Bridport on the other.

When inland the trumpet note of old Hoggen's wealth sounded to Axminster [and] even to Chard. This good repute of wealth was, however, the only good repute he had, for his social misdoings were so [two] fold and continuous as to interest [all] the social stars of Lyme. These are [the l]adies who inhabit the snug villas in [the u]plands at Lyme, and who claim as [their] special right the covered seats on the [...]rts walk of that pretty town, and who [are s]o select that they will not even associate with others except in massed groups [...]stulm. Old Hoggen's peccadilloes afforded them a fertile theme for gossip. [...] was an inexhaustible store of minute [...] wicked details of this famous sinner. [Yea]r after year old Hoggen moved [amon]g the law-abiding inhabitants of Charmouth, wallowing in his wickedness [...]ding to his store of goods in the here [and] in the hereafter.

[Str]ange to say, all this time not once—[not] even once—did the earth yawn and [swall]ow him. On the contrary, he flour[ished.] No matter what weather came [alway]s benefited. Even if the rain did [...] y one of his crops, it made [...]r to flourish exceedingly. When [there] was storm he accumulated sea rack; [when t]here was calm he got fish. Many of [his nei]ghbors began to have serious doubts [of] the earth ever yawning and swallowing [...]*t* all; and even the old ladies in [Lyme] Regis—those who had passed the age [...]*p*osals and begun to regret, or at least [to pon]der, their youth, sometimes thought [that p]erhaps immortality was a little too [...]y condemned after all.

[Sudd]enly this old man disappeared, and [Charm]outh woke up to the fact that he was [the be]st known, the most respected, the [most i] mportant person in the place. His [...]*o*g sank into insignificance, and his [...]*t*ood revealed in gigantic propor[tion.] Men pointed out his public spirit, [...]*a*rms he had instituted, the powers [he had] developed; women called attention [to the t]enderness he had always exhibited [to each] sex, unworthy as had been the ex[...] of the same that had darkened the [...] of his life. More than one wise matron was heard to remark that if his lot in life had been to meet one good woman, instead of those hussies, his manner of life might have been different.

It is a fact worthy of notice that in the logic of might-have-been, which is pitying woman's pathway to heaven, the major premise is pitying woman.

However, were his life good or ill, old Hoggen had disappeared: and murder was naturally suspected. Two suppositions—no one knew whence originating—were current. The most popular was that some of his unhappy companions, knowing of his wealth and greedy of his big gold watch and his diamond ring, had incited to his murder other still more disreputable companions. The alternative belief was that some of his relations—for he was believed to have some, although no one had ever seen or heard of them—had quietly removed him so that in due time they might in legal course become possessed of his heritage.

Consequent upon the latter supposition suspicion attached itself to every new comer. It was but natural that the vulture-like relatives should appear upon the scene as soon as possible, and eager eyes scanned each fresh arrival. As I soon discovered, my respected connection by marriage, Cousin Jemima, bore a strong resemblance to the missing man, and drew around our pretty resting place the whole curiosity of Charmouth and concentrated there the attention of the secret myrmidons of the law.

In fact, the Charmouth policeman haunted the place, and strange men in slop clothes and regulation boots came from Bridport and Lyme Regis, and even from Axminster itself.

These latter representatives of the intellectual subtlety of Devon. Dorset and Wilts were indeed men full of wile and cunning of device. The bucolic mind in moments of unbending, when frank admission of incompleteness is a tribute to good fellowship, may sometimes admit that its workings are slow, but even in the last stage of utter and conscious drunkenness one quality is insisted on—surety.

Of surety, in simple minds the correlative is tenacity of purpose and belief.

Thus it was that when once the idea of our guilt had been mooted and received, no amount of evidence, direct or circumstantial, could obliterate the idea from the minds of the rustic detectives. These astute men, one by one, each jealous of the other, and carrying on even among themselves the fiction of non-identification, began to seek the evidences of our guilt. It struck me as a curious trait in the inhabitants of the diocese of Salisbury that their primary intellectual effort had one tendency, and that all their other efforts were subordinate to this principle. It may have been that the idea arose from historical contemplation of the beauty of their cathedral and an unconscious effort to emulate the powers of its originators.

Or it may not have been.

But, at all events, their efforts took the shape of measuring. I fail myself to see how their measurements, be they never so accurate, could in anywise have helped them. Further, I cannot comprehend how the most rigid and exact scrutiny in this respect could have even suggested a combination of facts whence a spontaneous idea could have emanated. Still, they measured, never ceasing day or night for more than a week, and always surreptitiously. They measured one night the whole of the outside of our cottage. I heard them in the night, out on the roof, crawling about like gigantic cats, and, although we learned that one man had fallen off the roof and broken his arm, we were never officially informed of the fact. They made incursions into the house, under various pretexts, there to endeavor to measure the interior.

In every case a ruse was adopted. One morning, while we were out bathing, a man called to measure the gas pipes, and, after going through several of the rooms taking the dimensions of the walls, was informed by the servant that there was no gas, not only in the house, but in the village. Not being prepared with a further excuse, he said, with that nonchalance he could assume, that "it was no matter," and went away. Another time a British workman, as he styled himself, arrayed in cricket flannels and a straw hat, came to look at the kitchen boiler for the landlord, and asked that he might begin on the roof. I saw the inevitable rule and tape measure, and told him that the landlord's house was next door, and that he would find the boiler buried in the garden. He withdrew, thanking me with effusion, and making a note of the words "buried in the garden" in his notebook.

Another day a man called with fish—he had only one sole and that he carried in his hand. The cook was out and I told him we would have it. He asked if he might go into the garden to skin it. I told him he might, and went out. When I came back in about an hour's time, I found him there still, measuring away. He had got all the dimensions of the garden and the walls, and was now engaged on the heights of the various flowers. I asked him what the dickens he was doing there still, and why he was measuring. He answered vaguely that he was not measuring.

"Why, man alive," said I, "don't tell me such a story—I saw you at it—why, you are doing it still," as indeed he was.

He stood up and answered me: "Well, sir, I will tell you why. I was looking to see if I could find room to bury the skin of the sole."

He had not skinned the sole, which lay on a flag in the hot sunshine, and was beginning to look glassy.

They even measure as well as they could the height of the members of the family. When any of us passed a wall where any of these men were, he immediately spotted some place on the wall of equal height: and the moment we passed, out rule and measured it.

Our cook was asked one night by a tall man to lay her head on his shoulder. She did so, as she told us afterward being so surprised that she did not know what to do. When she came in we saw on her black stuff bonnet a series of reversed numbers in chalk dying away over the temple with ·uɪʐ⁄19 ·ɟϛ.

Cousin Jemima, who was of a full habit of body—to say the least of it—was one evening stopped in the lane by two men, who put their arms round her waist from opposite sides. She distinctively said that they had something that looked like a long rope marked in yards, or, as she persisted, in chains, which, when she had escaped from them, they examined with seeming anxiety, and made some entry in books which they carried, laughing all the time heartily and digging each other in the ribs as they pointed at her.

Our dog was often measured, and one afternoon there was a terrible caterwauling, which we found to arise from a respectable man trying to weigh out cat in an ouncel, borrowed from a neighboring shop.

My mother-in-law, who had no suspicion whatever that she was an object of suspicion, waxed at times furiously indignant at the rudeness of the loiterers round our door, and now and again comported herself so violently as to cause them serious fright. I was unaware during the time of my courtship that this remarkable woman possessed such a power of invective. She certainly proved herself a consummate actress in concealing it as she did: for during that time of rapture and agony I enjoyed the contemplation and experienced the practical outcome of a sympathy and sweetness as ripe as unalloyed. My wife and I both understand the motives of the local detectives, and always recognized them under their disguises. It was a never ending source of mirth to us to enjoy the spectacle of Cousin Jemima's ungratified curiosity, and of my mother-in-law's periodic anger. For the purposes of our own amusement we filled up the daily blanks caused by the slackness of the executive in keeping perpetually before them the theme of old Hoggen. I amused myself by keeping a little note book in which I jotted down all kinds of odd measurements for the purpose of leaving it about sometime to puzzle the detectives.

Thus it came about that the repulsive individuality of old Hoggen became, in a manner, of interest to us, and his name to be interwoven in the web of our daily converse.

I knew that to mention old Hoggen to my mother-in-law, when previously influenced by hunger or any collateral vexation, would have the effect of a red rag on a bull, and, as has been seen, I was not disappointed.

Now, however, that supper was over and the crab had been all consumed, I found myself pledged to discover by the morrow a full supply of that succulent food. I did not let the matter distress me, as I anticipated a delightful walk by the shore to Bridport, a walk which I had not yet undertaken. In the morning I awoke early, just a little after daybreak, and, leaving my wife asleep, started on my walk.

The atmosphere of the early dawn was delightful and refreshing, and the sight of the moving sea filled me with a great pleasure, not withstanding the fact that an ominous shower on the water and a cold wind foretold a coming storm.

At this part of the Dorset coast the sea makes perpetual inroads on the land. As all the country is undulating, the shore presents from the sea an endless succession of steep cliffs, some of which rise by comparison to a scale of moderate grandeur.

The cliffs are either of blue clay or sandstone, which soft or friable material perpetually gives way under the undermining influence of the tides assisted by the exfiltration of the springs, causing an endless series of moraines. The beach is either of fine gravel or of shingle, save at places where banks of half-formed rock full of fossils run into the sea.

The shingle, which forms the major portion of the road, makes walking at times trying work.

I passed by the target for a rifle practice, and the spot reserved tacitly as the bathing place for gentlemen, and so on under the first headland, the summit of whose bare yellow cliff is fringed with dark pine trees bent eastwards by the prevailing westerly breeze.

Here the shingle began to get heavier. It had been driven by successive tides and storms into a mass like a snow drift, and it was necessary to walk along the top of the ridge whence the pebbles rolled down every step.

The wind had now begun to rise, and as I went onward the waves increased in force till the whole shore was strewn with foam swept from the crests of the waves. Sometimes great beds of seaweed—a rare commodity on the Dorset coast—rose and fell as the waves rolled in and broke.

On I went as sturdily as I could. The blue black earth of the Charmouth cliffs had now given place to sandstone, and great boulders shaped like mammoth bones—as indeed they probably were, cumbered the foreshore. I stopped to examine some of these, ostensibly from scientific interest, but in reality to rest myself. I was now getting a little tired, and more than a little hungry, for when starting I had determined to eat my breakfast at Bridport, and to test the culinary capabilities of the place.

As I sat on the stones looking seaward I noticed something washing in and out among the boulders. On examination it proved to be a hat—a human hat. I hooked it in with a piece of driftwood. I turned it over, and in turning it saw something white stuck within the leather lining. Gingerly enough I made an examination, and found the white mass to be some papers, on the outside of one of which was the name "J. Hoggen."

"Hullo!" said I to myself. "Here is some news of old Hoggen at last." I took the papers out, carefully squeezed the wet out of them, as well as I could between flat stones, and put them in the pocket of my shooting jacket. I placed the hat on a boulder and looked round to see if I could find any further signs of the missing man. All the while the breeze was freshening and the waves came rolling in in increasing volume.

Again I saw, some twenty yards out, something black floating, bobbing up and down with each wave. After a while I made it out to be the body of a man. By this time my excitement had grown to intensity, and I could hardly await the incoming of the body borne by the waves.

On and on it came, advancing a little with each wave, till at last it got so close that reaching out I hooked part of the clothing with my piece of timber, and pulled the mass close to the shore.

Then I took hold of the collar of the coat and pulled. The cloth, rotten with the sea water, tore away, and left the piece in my hand.

With much effort—for I had to be very careful—I brought the body up on the beach, and began to make an accurate examination of it.

While doing so I found in the pocket a tape measure, and it occurred to me that I must fulfill all the requirements of the local police, and so began to take dimensions of the corpse.

I measured the height, the length of the limbs, of the hands and feet. I took the girth of the shoulders and the waist, and, in fact, noted in my pocketbook a sufficiency of detail to justify a tailor in commencing sartorial operations on a full scale. Some of the dimensions struck me at the time as rather strange, but having verified the measurements I noted them down.

On examination of the cloths and pockets I found the massive gold watch hanging on the chain and the big diamond ring, to whose power of inspiring greed local opinion had attributed the murder. These I put in my pocket together with the purse, studs, papers and money of the dead man. In making the examination the coat became torn, revealing a mass of bank notes between cloth and lining: in fact, the whole garment was quilted with them. There was also a small note case containing the necessary papers for a voyage to Queensland by a ship leaving Southampton the previous week.

These discoveries I thought so valuable that I felt it my duty to try to bring the body to the nearest place of authority, which I considered would probably be Chidiock, a village on the Bridport road which I had seen upon the map.

It was now blowing a whole gale, and the waves broke on the beach in thunder, dragging down the shingle in their ebb with a loud screaming. The rain fell in torrents, and the increasing of the storm decided me in my intention to carry the body with me.

I lifted it across my shoulder with some difficulty, for at each effort the cloths, already torn in the extrication of paper money, fell to pieces. However, at last I got it on my shoulder, face downwards, and started. I had hardly taken a step when, with an impulse which I could not restrain, I let it slip—or, rather, threw it—to the ground.

It had seemed to me to be alive. I certainly felt a movement. As it lay all in a heap on the beach, with the drenching rain sweeping the pale face, I grew ashamed of my impulse, and, with another, effort, took it up and started again.

Again there was the same impulse, with the same cause—the body seemed alive. This time, however, I was prepared, and held on, and after a while the idea wore away.

Presently I came to a place where a mass of great boulders strewed the shore. The stepping from one to another shook me and my burden, and as I jumped from the last of the rocks to the smooth sand which lay beyond I felt a sudden diminution of weight. As my load overbalanced, I fell on the sand higgledy piggledy with my burden.

Old Hoggen had parted in the middle.

As may be imagined, I was not long getting up. On a survey of the wreck I saw, to my intense astonishment, some large crabs walking out of the body. This, then, explained the strange movement of the corpse. It occurred to me that the presence of these fishes was incontrovertible proof that crabs did exist between Bridport and Lyme Regis, and not without a thought of Cousin Jemima and my mother-in-law, I lifted two or three and put them in the big pocket of my shooting coat.

Then I began to consider whether I should leave the departed Hoggen where he was or bring him on.

For a while I weighed the arguments pro and con, and finally concluded to bring him on with me, or it, or them, or whatever the fragments could be called. It was not an alluring task, in any respect, and it was by a great effort that I undertook the duty.

I gathered the fragments together, and a strange looking heap they made—waxen limbs protruding from a wet heap of dishevelled rags.

Then I began to lift them. It had been a task of comparative ease carrying the body over my shoulder, but now I had to pick up separate pieces and carry them together in my hands and under my arms. Often I had laughed, as I went through Victoria street, to see people of both sexes, worthy, but deficient of organizing power and system, coming forth from the co-operative stores bearing hosts of packages purchased without system in the various departments. Such an one I now felt myself to be. Do what I would, I could not hold, all at one time, the various segments of my companion. Just as I had carefully tucked the moieties of old Hoggen under my arms, I spied some of his clothing on the shore, and in trying to raise these also lost a portion of my load. What added to the aggravation of the situation was that the wear and tear began to tell upon the person of the defunct. Thus while I was lifting the upper section, an arm came away, and from the lower a foot.

However, with a supreme effort I bundled the pieces together, and, lifting the mass in my arms, proceeded on my way. But now the storm was raging in full force, and I saw that I must hurry or the advancing waves, every moment rushing closer to the cliffs, would cut me off. I could see, through the blinding rain, a headland before me, and knew that if I could once pass it I would be in comparative safety.

So I hurried on as fast as I could, sometimes losing a portion of my burden, but never being able to wait to pick it up. Had my thoughts and ejaculations been recorded they would have been somewhat as follows:

"There goes a hand; it was lucky I took off the ring."
"Half the coat; well that I found the bank notes."
"There goes the waistcoat; a fortunate thing I have the watch."
"A leg off—my! will I ever get him home?"
"Another leg."
"An arm gone."
"His grave will be a mile long."
"We must consecrate the shore that he may lay in hallowed ground."
"The lower trunk gone, too. Poor fellow; no one can hit him now below the belt."
"An arm gone, too; he would not be able to defend himself if they did."

"Murder! but he's going fast."

"The cloths all gone, too—I had better have left him where he was."

"Ugh! there goes the trunk; nothing left now but the head."

"Ugh! that was a close shave anyhow. Never mind, I will keep you safe."

I clung tight to the head, which was now my sole possession of the corpse.

It was mighty hard to hold it, for it was as slippery as glass, and the tight holding of it cramped my efforts and limited me as I leaped from rock to rock or dashed through the waves, which now touched in their onward rush to the base of the cliff.

At least, through the blinding rain, I saw the headland open, and with a great rush through the recoil of a big wave I rounded it and rested for a moment to breathe on the wide shore beyond.

Then I tried for a while to collect my scattered faculties, such being the only part of the goods scattered in the last half-hour which could be collected.

I felt ruefully that my effort to bring to the rites of burial the body of old Hoggen had been a mistaken one. All had gone save the head which lay on the sand, and whose eyes actually seemed to wink at me as the flakes of the spume settled over the eyes, dissolving as the bubbles burst. The property was, I felt, safe enough. I put my hand into the pocket of my shooting coat but in an instant drew it out again with a scream of pain, for it had been severely nipped. I had forgotten the crabs.

Very carefully I took out one of these fish and held him legs upward, he making frantic efforts to seize me with his claws. He seemed a greedy one, indeed, for he was trying to eat the diamond ring which he had got half within that mysterious mouth which is covered with a flap like that over the lock of a portmanteau. Hence also projected part of the watch chain. I found that the brute had actually swallowed the watch, and it was with some difficulty that I relieved from his keeping both it and the ring. I took care to place the valuable property in the other pocket where the crabs were not.

Then I took up my head—or, rather old Hoggen's—and started on my way, carrying the final relic under my arm.

The storm began to decrease, and died away as quickly as it had arisen, so that, before I had traversed half the long stretch of sand that lay before me, instead of storm there was marked calm, and for blinding rain an almost insupportable heat.

I struggled on over the sand, and at length saw an opening in the cliff—which, on coming close, I found to be caused by a small stream which had worn a deep cleft in the blue-black earthy rock, and, falling and tumbling from above, became lost in the beach.

There was a look about the sand here that seemed to me to be somewhat peculiar. Its surface was smooth and shining, with a sort of odd dimple here and there. It looked so flat and inviting after my scramble over the rock and shingle and plodding through the deep sand, that with joy I hurried toward it—and at once began to sink.

By the odd shiver that traversed it I knew that I was being engulfed in quicksand.

It was a terrible position.

I had already sunk over my knees and knew that unless aid came I was utterly lost. I would at that moment have welcomed even Cousin Jemima.

It is the misfortune of such people as her that they never do make an appearance at a favorable time—such as this.

But there was no help—on one side lay the sea with never a sail in sight, and the waves still angry from the recent storm tumbling in sullenly upon the shore—on the other side was a wilderness of dark cliff; and along the shore on either way an endless waste of sand.

I tried to shout, but the misery and terror of the situation so overcame me that my voice clung to my jaws, and I could make no sound. I still kept old Hoggen's head under my arm. In moments of such danger the mind is quick to grasp an offered chance, and it suddenly occurred to me that, if I could get a foothold even for a moment, I might still manage to extricate myself. I was at yet but on the edge of the quicksand, and but a little help would suffice. With the thought came also the means—old Hoggen's head.

No sooner thought than done.

I laid the head on the sand before me, and pressing on it with my hands, felt that I was relieving my feet of part of their weight. With an effort I lifted one leg and placed the foot on the head now imbedded some inches in the treacherous sand. Then pressing all my weight on this foot made a great effort, and tearing up the imbedded foot leaped to the firm sand, where I slipped and fell and for a few minutes panted with exhaustion.

I was saved, but old Hoggen's head was gone forever.

Then I went toward the cliff, cautiously feeling my way, testing every spot on which my foot must rest, before trusting my weight to it. I gained the cliff, and resting on its firm base passed behind the fatal quicksand and went on my course to the stable strand beyond.

On I plodded till at last I came near a few houses built in a green cleft, whence through the cliffs a tiny stream, on whose banks stood the pretty village of Chidiock, fell into the sea.

There was a coastguard station here, with a little rope-railed plot, where before the row of trim houses the flagstaff rose.

As I drew near a coastguard and a policeman rushed toward me from behind a shed and grasped me on either side, holding me tight with a vigor which I felt to be quite disproportionate to the necessity of the occasion.

With the instinct of conscious innocence I struggled with them.

"Let me go!" I cried. "Let me go—what do you mean? Let me go I say!"

"Come now—none of this," said the policeman.

I still struggled.

"Better keep quiet," said the coastguard! "It's no use struggling."

"I will not keep quiet," I cried, struggling more frantically than ever.

The policeman looked at me right savagely and gave my neckcloth a twist which nearly strangled me. "Tell you what," he said sternly, "if you struggle any more, I'll whale you over the head with my baton."

I did not struggle anymore.

"Now," said he, "remember that I caution you that anything you say or do will be afterward used in evidence against you."

I thought a policy of conciliation was now best; so with what heartiness I could assume I said:

> "My good fellow, you really make a mistake. Why you seize me I do not know."
>
> "We know," he interrupted, with a hard laugh, "and if you say you don't know, why then you're a liar!"

I felt choking with anger. To be held is bad enough, but when the additional insult of calling one a liar is added, rage may surely be excused. My impulse on hearing the insult was to break free and strike the man, but he knew my intention and held me tighter.

"Take care!" he said, holding up his baton.

I took care.

"I ask you formally," I said, with all my dignity, "on what authority you treat me thus?"

"On this authority!" he answered, holding up his baton, and again laughing with his harsh, exasperating cachination. He playfully twirled his baton as if to impress on me a sense of his proficiency in its use.

He then produced a pair of handcuffs, which were put on me. I struggled very hard, but the two men were too much for me, and I had to succumb.

He then began to search me. First he put his hand into the pocket of my shooting coat and pulled out the watch and chain. He looked at it with exultation.

"That is old Hoggen's watch," I said.

"I know it is," he answered, at the same time pulling out a notebook and writing down my words. Next he produced the diamond ring, and the purse.

"That also," said I, "and that!" and again he wrote down my words—this time in silence. Then he put in his hand again and drew it out, saying:

"Only wet paper!"

He next put his hand into the other pocket, but drew it out again in an instant—not in silence this time.

"Curse the thing! What is it?"

I smiled as he lifted a crab out of the pocket with great carefulness and replaced it. When he had got thus far.

"Now, young fellow," said he, "what have you got to say for yourself?"

For the last few minutes a very unpleasant thought had in my mind been growing to colossal proportions. It was evident that I was being arrested for the murder of old Hoggen, and here I was arrested when in possession of his property, but with no witness to prove my innocence, and with no trace of the lost man himself to substantiate my story. I began to be a little frightened as to the result.

"What I have to tell you is very strange," said I. "I left Charmouth early this morning to walk to Bridport to get some crabs for my mother-in-law."

"Why, you have got crabs with you," said the policeman.

"I got them on the shore beyond," said I, pointing westward.

"Come! stow that!" said the policeman. "That won't wash here. There isn't a crab to be found on the shore between Bridport and Lyme."

"That's true, anyhow. Every fool knows that!" added the coastguard. I went on—

"I found the body of old Hoggen floating in the water. I tried to carry it on here, but the storm came, and it was as much as I could do to escape. Besides, the body all fell in pieces, and at last—"

"A nice story that!" said the policeman. "But if it fell to bits, why didn't you bring one on with you?"

"I tried some, but they fell to bits."

"The head didn't," said he "why did you not bring it? Eh?"

"I did bring it," said I, "but I got into the quicksand and it was lost."

The coastguard struck in.

"There is only one bit of quicksand on all this coast, they say, for I never see it myself. Why, man alive, it doesn't show once in 20 year."

"And the crabs?" asked the policeman.

"They were in old Hoggen's body!"

"And what were you doing with them?"

"I was bringing them to my mother-in-law."

"Oh, the filthy scoundrel!" ejaculated the coastguard.

"Did you carry them through the quicksand?" inquired the policeman.

"I did," said I, "and when I got out I found that the big fellow had eaten the watch and was trying to swallow the ring."

The policeman and the coastguard seized me roughly, the latter saying:

"Come, take him off. He's the plumpest liar I ever seen."

"Let us finish the search first," said the policeman, as he renewed his investigations.

The thought that I was in a really suspicious position now began to make me most uncomfortable. "My poor wife! My poor wife!" I kept saying to myself.

The policeman, in his zeal, again put his hand into the pocket with the crabs, and drew it out with a yell. Then he took out the biggest crab, which, by the way, as is sometimes the case, had one claw very much larger than the other. The left claw was the larger. He threw the crab on the shore, and was about to stamp on it, when the coast guard put him back, saying:

"Avast, there, mate. Crabs isn't so plenty here, that we walk on them. None here between Bridport and Lyme."

The policeman continued his search. He took the mass of wet papers and notes from the other pocket, and threw them on the ground, and went on diving into the recesses of the pockets. The coastguard was evidently struck with something, for he stooped and looked at the papers, turned them over, and fell down on his knees beside them with a loud cry. Then, in an excited whisper he called out:

"Look here! mate, look here! It's all money. It's thousands of pounds."

The constable also dropped beside the papers, and over the mass the two men stood gazing at each other with excited faces.

"Take care of it—take care!" said the policeman.

"You bet!" said the other shortly.

"What a fortune!"

The two men looked at each other, and then at me furtively, and somehow I felt that they had in common some vile instinct by which I was felt to be in the way. I remained, therefore, as passive as I could.

The two men eyed the papers. Said the coastguard:

"Where are the other things?"

"Here!" said the policeman, slapping his pocket.

"Better put them all together."

"Not at all. They are quite safe with me."

The men looked at each other and seemed mutually to understand, for, without a word, the policeman took the watch and ring and the purse from his pocket and laid them on the shore.

Both men eyed the lot greedily. Suddenly the policeman looked round and ran down the beach like a maniac shouting, "Stop thief! Stop thief!" At the very edge of the water he stopped and lifted the crab which had been making its escape. He brought it back and laid it on its back beside the other things. As he eyed the heap suspiciously as if to see that nothing had been removed, he said, shaking his fist at the crab:

"You infernal brute, *you* may have been stealing something." The accent with which he said the word "you" was evidently meant as a caution and suspicion of the coastguard. The latter took it as such, for he said angrily:

"Stow that!"

The two men then proceeded to search me further. They took from me everything which could by any torturing of greed have been construed into a valuable. They opened a seam of my coat and turned out the lining.

Then, drawing away, they whispered a little together, and, returning to me, tied my legs together, put a gag in my mouth and carried me round the point of a rock where we were out of sight of any chance comer. Then they brought hither the valuables, and, sitting down, began to reckon the worth of the lot.

One by one they opened the bank notes, and laid them flat. They were of all dates and numbers, and I felt as I looked at that, from this fact, if once lost, there could be no possibility of tracing them. They laid the gold in a heap with the watch and ring, and put the papers by themselves.

There was an immense amount of money—in gold only some £70, but in notes £57.300.

When the two men had figured it all out, they looked at me with a look that made my blood run cold—for it meant murder.

Again they looked at each other, and, with a whisper, withdrew to a little distance.

I turned partly on my side, so that I could watch them. There was no difficulty in this, and the fact of its being so added to my fear, for I knew that their being without fear of my taking notes of their movements meant that their minds were made up.

A short time sufficed them, and they turned again toward me. As they came, however, the bell of the old church at Chidiock began to ring. It was still but early morning and the bell was for matins.

The coastguard stopped—some memory stirred within him, and with it came a doubt. He paused a moment and spoke—"Mate."

The policeman realized the intention of mercy in the faltering tone, and answered as roughly and harshly as he could, turning quickly, almost threateningly, as he spoke.

"Well!"

"Mate, must we kill him? Wouldn't it do if he kept quiet, and let us get off with the money? No one knows of the thing—why need they ever know?"

"He won't keep quiet," said the other. "Better cut his throat, and bury him here in the sand."

The sailor looked at me, and, reading the inquiry in his eyes, I answered as well as I could with mine:

"I will be quiet!"

It was as plain as daylight that my life hung on the alternative, so I did not hesitate or falter.

I compounded a felony with a glance.

Notwithstanding my acquiescence, a violent discussion arose between the two men—the preserver of the peace being the more dangerous of the two.

The coastguard urged and argued that it were useless to commit a murder when the end they desired was insured. The policeman stuck persistently to his one point that it were safer to cut my throat.

To me the anguish was intense. All the misdeeds of my life rose before me, and also every reason why life should be dear. I implored the sailor with my eyes to let me speak, and after a little while he removed the gag, after cautioning me that if I spoke above a whisper, my first syllable should be my last.

I whispered but one argument.

"If you kill me, I shall be sought after. You are safer as you are with my promise not to inform on you."

The argument was cogent, and told, as sound logic usually does. So, after a terrible threatening in case of my breaking my pledge, they untied my legs and took off the handcuffs.

Then they brought me into a boathouse by the beach and there brushed me and removed any traces of travel or violence. Next they put me into a pony cart that stood ready by the side of the laneway leading to Chidiock, and drove me into Charmouth, depositing me at my own door. We did not meet a single person by the way.

The last words I heard were the whispered caution of the policeman—

"No one has seen you or us. Go back to your bed and pretend you were never out," and then they drove off again.

I took the advice, slipped off my boots and stole upstairs. My wife was still sleeping, so I undressed and got into bed. Lest I should wake her, I pretended to sleep, and soon, despite my mental agitation, slept, too.

I was awakened by my wife, who was up and dressed.

"Why, Augustus, you are desperately sleepy this morning, It is after 10, and breakfast is over long ago. Cousin Jemima would not wait. However, your breakfast is kept hot."

I awoke to broad consciousness, but thought it wiser to feign heaviness.

"Nevermind—I'll get up presently."

"But, my dear, you must get up now or you will miss the 'bus to Bridport. Remember, you promised to get some crabs for Cousin Jemima!"

"Oh, bother Cousin Jemima. There has been enough about crabs for one night." I said this with a sudden impulse and then stopped.

"Well, dear. I hope you have not had indigestion, too. Cousin Jemima says she has been very poorly and that it must have been from eating the new bread."

"Indeed!" said I, adding to myself, "I'm glad she suffered, too, for it was all through her that I had that terrible ordeal to go through."

I got up and went downstairs. All was usual; and presently I began to think I must have been dreaming. The idea grew; and the more I thought the matter over the more unreal and dreamlike it all seemed.

While, however, I was finishing my breakfast the servant came in and said that there were two men at the door who had crabs to sell.

"Send them away at once," I called out, angrily, "I want no crabs."

The servant went, and returned shortly, saying: "If you please, sir, the men say that they hope you will buy a crab; they have one which was got between Bridport and Lyme."

This statement rather staggered me, for I felt a kind of dread that my late assailants had come to look me up. I told the servant I would see to the matter, and went out myself to the door. There stood two men—but not the least like the others. The coastguard was a small man with a big beard, and the policeman was a large man, clean shaven. Of these two, one was large, and the other small, but the large man had a bushy beard, and the small one was clean shaven. I thought that both men looked at me very hard, so I pretended not to notice anything except the subject of barter, and said as unconcernedly as I could.

"Well, my men, so I hear you have crabs to sell; let me look at them."

The big man answered: "We have only one left. Here it is!" and, looking at me very searchingly, he produced from a basket a crab with a big left claw and a small right one. I could not help a start of surprise which did not pass unnoticed, so I thought it better to be more unconcerned still, and said: "No; that's not good enough. I think I do not care for it."

As I spoke, my wife approached the door, coming home, and with her were my mother-in-law and Cousin Jemima.

The men did not notice them, but the big man said to me, civilly enough: "All right, sir. It does not matter, but I thought it well to show it to you."

As he was putting the crab back in the basket, Cousin Jemima saw it, and came forward quickly.

"What is that, Augustus? Not a crab that you are sending away? You wretch!"—the last words sotto voce.

After a little haggling she purchased the crab, which, strangely enough, the men seemed unwilling to sell her, and for which I had the additional pleasure of paying.

Cousin Jemima took the crab in triumph to the kitchen, and the men went away toward Axmouth.

When I went back to the sitting room, I was assailed on all sides. Cousin Jemima, in tears, said that I had behaved like a brute—that I was sending away the only crab seen for days, just to vex and disappoint her.

My mother-in-law surmised that I did so because I wished to have to go over to Bridport, where, unnoticed I might play billiards and get tipsy, if not meet some "creature." Her daughter, to a small degree, shared in her feelings—particularly the latter.

I maintained a strictly negative position.

In the course of the day the wife of the parson, George Edward Ancey, came to tea—her husband was a justice of the peace, and, as a perpetual resident, was practically the magistrate of the place. In the course of conversation she remarked that George Edward had been very much upset and worried in the morning. That two cases of insubordination had been before him. One was a coastguard, who had affronted his chief boatman before the other men, and who, on being severely censured, resigned on the spot, and had already left the village. The other was a policeman, who had refused to go on duty, and who had been accordingly summarily dismissed. Mr. Ancey regretted his departure, for he had been looked upon as the most trustworthy and active officer in the place.

When these small facts came to my knowledge, I felt more than ever in a perplexity, for their combination and the accurate manner in which they fitted into the history of the morning seemed conclusive proof that the whole thing was not a dream.

Before supper time I went for a walk. As I was going out my wife said:

"Be sure to be home in time, Gus. There is a crab for supper and Cousin Jemima is going to dress it herself—"

A walk on the beach did me good, for it cooled my brain, and in the serener atmosphere of the evening I began to believe again that the whole episode of finding old Hoggen was a dream—a nightmare.

I returned home in a more cheerful humor, and, conscious of security and immunity from fear, felt kindly even to Cousin Jemima and tolerant of her foibles.

At the very threshold of my home my good resolution was tried.

On a chair in the hall sat Cousin Jemima awaiting my arrival, the very picture of grim, aggressive dissatisfaction. As I came in she sniffed—I saw that something was wrong and waited—she followed me into the dining room where, supper having been just served, my wife and her mother were seated.

"I said we would not wait a single moment for you, after your conduct," said the latter.

"What's up now?" said I.

"What's up, indeed!"—this with indignant sarcasm. "A nice gentlemanly trick to play upon two ladies whose appetites are not good."

"O-h-h," said I, with what I certainly intended to be utmost sarcasm spoken in the most polished way, "then you allude to something I have done by letter."

"By letter? certainly not! What are you talking of?"

"You said I had played a trick on two ladies whose appetites were not good, and I presume I must have done so by letter. Do you not see? The some one must be at a long distance from this, for I know no one here answering the description."

"You brute!" was the comment of Cousin Jemima, while my mother-in-law said nothing, but glared at her daughter, who smiled.

I sat down and tried to make matters a little pleasanter.

"Come, now, mother," I said, "tell me what I have done and what it is all about."

"The crab," said Cousin Jemima, in tones at once sepulchral and hysterical.

"Well, what about it?"

"You did it on purpose."

"What did I do? I am all in surprise."

Here my wife struck in.

"The fact is, dear, that the crab was a fraud, and mamma and Cousin Jemima, seeing that you were talking to the men, imagine that you got the whole thing up for a joke—that it was, in fact, what you call a 'plant.'"

"My dear, I am no nearer to the fact than I was. How was the crab a fraud?"

"Well, you see there was something very queer about it. It was quite fresh, you know, and all that, but it had been opened and was all cut to little bits with knives and then put back again, just as if some one had been searching it."

Here was a staggering proof that I had not dreamed. I almost gasped for breath and felt that I turned white.

The three women noticed the change.

"Are you ill, dear?" said my wife.

"He might well be," said her mother.

"Served him right!" said Cousin Jemima.

I recovered myself in a moment, and laughed as well as I could.

"You are a parcel of silliness, and I know nothing about it. Why, it was you, Cousin Jemima, who bought the crab."

After a while the conversation changed to other topics. I was now beset by a most extraordinary doubt. Was my whole adventure a dream, or was it not?

I cannot tell.

Some three months after our return to town we read in the *South Dorset News*, which some of our seaside friends sent us regularly, the following paragraph:

THE MYSTERY OF MR. HOGGEN.

"The strange mystery regarding the late Mr. Jabez Hoggen—the Charmouth millionaire—whose disappearance set Dorset and neighboring counties in a blaze, has at last been cleared up. Our readers will of course remember the disappearance early in August last of Mr. Hoggen, whose wealth and eccentricity were fruitful topics of conversation not only in the quiet village of Charmouth, his native place—but through all the neighboring country. Lyme, on the one hand, and Bridport on the other, and the inland town of Axminster and Chard, were well acquainted with the name of the wealthy eccentric. Mr. Hoggen was very retired and uncommunicative, and it so came to pass that when his disappearance became known, not a single person could even guess at any motive or cause for such a fact. No one was in his confidence. It was for a time generally supposed that he had been murdered for the sake of his reputed wealth, and suspicion was by the police baselessly attached to certain of the summer visitors to our pleasant Dorset coast. Our contemporary, the Bridport Banner, with that gross bad taste which, equally with its mendacity, characterizes its utterances, suggested—if we remember aright, the ribald shrieking forced on our ears by some drunken Conservative reeking with the scurrilous falsity of some paltry true blue (?) meeting—for we do not read the rag—that perhaps Mr. Hoggen had in his old age seen the error of his ways, and, overcome with the remorse for his adherence to the principles of liberalism, committed suicide. Time had given the lie, as it ever does, to such paltry attacks upon the noble dead. It has come to light that Mr. Hoggen took a passage in the name of Smith for Queensland in the Tamar Indien,[2] sailing from Southampton on the 26th of August. We are justified in supposing that the poor gentleman, oppressed with the decadent spirit which allows such vile rags as the conservative organs to flourish in this once pure soil, and longing for the purer atmosphere where the pollution of atmosphere conservatism is not left in sorrow his native shore. He was recognized on board by a native of Charmouth—one Miles Ruddy, a steward on the Tamar Indien. It appears that he was much upset by the recognition. The following evening, as the bell was sounding for the putting out of the ship's lights, a splash was heard, and the dread cry 'man overboard' was raised. Every effort was made to save the life of the human creature, whose head was seen for a few minutes bobbing up and down among the foam that marked the mighty vessel's track. But without avail. He never rose, and the ship was compelled to proceed on her course. A muster of the crew and passengers showed that the missing man was Jabez Smith, or, more properly, Jabez Hoggen. The depositions of the captain and officers of the ship and of several of the chief passengers regarding the event have been registered at Queensland, and we hasten to lay the facts just arrived by the mail before our readers."

A little time passed, and in some two months there appeared in the same print the following paragraph:

STRANGE HISTORY OF TWO CHARMOUTH MEN.

"The Australian mail just in brings from Victoria the details, as far as they are known, of a romance, unhappily tragic, concerning two late inhabitants of Charmouth. It appears that the two men, but a few months ago well known in our pleasant Dorset village, one having been a policeman and the other a coast guard, had but lately arrived in Melbourne. At first they did not seem of much account, but before long met with a lucky stroke of fortune—alas! fatal to them. After but a short absence, presumably in the northern gold fields, they had evidently made some wonderfully lucky discoveries of gold pockets, for on their return they made such purchases of land and houses as showed that they must have been at the time possessed of great wealth. Suddenly they had quarreled, for some unknown reason, sold again their property and together disappeared up country. A few days later their bodies, greatly mutilated, were discovered among the charred ruins of a deserted camp. They had either fought and killed each other, or they had been murdered. The fire of the camp had spread and partially consumed the bodies, so that nothing definite could be ascertained. In this romantic story we may read as we run of the vanity of wealth."

When I read the paragraph I felt my mind relieved, for here was assurance to me that I had not dreamed.

One evening long afterward I told my wife and her mother and Cousin Jemima the whole story.

My wife came and put her arms round me and whispered:

"Augustus, dear—you may have dreamed—I hope so, but, thank God! you are spared to us."

My mother-in-law said:

"I think you might have managed to keep some of the money, but you never do as you ought in such things. At any rate, you might have told us before this, but I suppose you have so much to conceal that things like this get lost among them."

Cousin Jemima, after frowning a while and pursing her lips as if thinking, said, sniffing:

"I believe it's all a lie!"

"My dear Cousin Jemima!" I remonstrated.

"Well! suppose it's not," she answered, sharply, "at any rate, you took the crabs from old Hoggen's body and brought them here—no you didn't bring them here, but you let me buy them—to eat! Ugh!! You brute!!!"

> *I am still in doubt about the whole affair.*
> *Was it a dream?*
> *I do not know!*

Chapter Four

WHEN THE SKY RAINS GOLD (1894)[1]

Bram Stoker

The earliest recollection of Victor Paterson was of a stern and unbending father to whom all around him paid almost extravagant homage, and who frowned when any of his children had the hardihood to appear in his presence. Indeed, he felt from the tears and kisses of his mother on such occasions that some kindly and protective power had been exercised on his behalf. While he was yet—as it seemed to him afterward—a very baby he had been conscious of a stern, loud voice raised in menace, and a soft, appealing one in reply from the mother to whose heart he was clasped; and he felt, rather than remembered, that to what had passed at that interview was due any kindness shown later on to him or to either of his younger brothers. This feeling was partly due to an interview several years later when he was a great, brawny boy. His father had sent for him to his library, and when he had entered and stood almost trembling before him, said:

> I have sent for you, sir, because you are now of an age to understand your position in life, and to realize what I have arranged concerning the future of yourself and your brothers.

Here Victor tried to mumble out some sort of thanks, but his father, holding up a warning hand, went on: "I want no thanks—no recognition of any kind. I have no desire whatever to have sons to make my own life worried to the extent that children can disarrange settled plans. Candidly I wish that none of you had ever been born, but since you are here, and as the law does not give me power of life and death over you, I have yielded to your mother's wishes that you should be in some way placed in an independent position. I have acquiesced in this the more freely since I shall thus be able to secure through your absence a larger measure of quiet for myself. I have, therefore, arranged that you are to have an estate of your own, and in order that you may not be closer to me than necessary I have chosen as your abode the island of Skye. You may be aware that my means are vast; let me add to your information this item that they are absolutely and entirely at my own disposal. What I do for you now is final, and you need never expect, during my life or at my death, any addition to your fortune from this source. As your mother has urged on me that you, as her eldest son, should have even better provision than your brothers, I have settled on you an estate which is of larger area, and which carries with it some territorial influence, for it makes you a laird. It will, under all ordinary circumstances, be adequate for your requirements, but be careful with it and husband your resources, for if anything should happen adversely you will find yourself in a very different position, and will never, under any circumstances whatever, get any help from me. Your brothers I have taken care of in a proportionate degree. As I daresay you have gathered from the peculiar bent of his education, Hobson will take his place at the royal navy. My influence can secure that for him, and also that he will be kept on the Australian station—certainly at first, and afterwards by his own wish, for the liberal provision which I make for him is contingent on his remaining in distant waters. Aide will be a mining engineer, and for his future is secured a large mining tract at the upper waters of the Amazon. Thus he, too, will remain far from me, and I shall thus be able to maintain my purposes unaltered, and my self-possession unimpaired. Today, therefore, you may all take farewell of your mother, as for me, I desire no farewells. I am creditably rid of you all, and shall henceforth forget that you have ever existed. You may, if you wish, look on yourself as the head of a new family and act accordingly. You will now please to make your brothers acquainted with my wishes and with the separate arrangements for their future made for them, as I have no wish to undergo a similar interview of this sort." So saying he touched the bell on his table and resumed his work. Victor, without a word, bowed, and withdrew. He straightaway called his brothers to him and told them exactly the messages which he had to deliver. Then, having taken an affectionate leave of his mother, he started that evening for Skye as the journey had been arranged for him.

At Skye he was all-powerful, and as he was of a nature at once masterful and kindly he soon became a sort of beneficent despot among his tenants. The estate which had been given him was of vast extent, and though much of the ground was poor and there were many mountains absolutely sterile, sufficient remained of more generous nature to make him rich even for a local territorial magnate. For nearly 10 years he had been in enjoyment of his fortune, and had grown almost to forget the loneliness and disappointments of his early years. The Island of Skye is not a place where life goes very rapidly, and the local pleasures are of a somewhat primitive kind, tempered with that spirit of obedience in all things to the chief which is common to feudalism and the semi-barbaric method of clanship.

He had but lately started on a sailing trip in his little yacht the Eagle, when one afternoon, leaving his yacht outside the rocks and island to the north he had pulled his punt in shoreward to enjoy the view of Quairang from the sea side. The day was hot, and all around him calm, and so coming as near shore as he could without losing, under the shadow of the cliffs, sight of the mountain top, he pulled in his oars and lay down lazily, letting the boat rock on the swell while the set of the tide drifted him along shore. The rocking motion and the heat made him drowsy, and for a while the whole scene around him faded away into the darkness of dreamless sleep.

He awoke with the sound of a distant cry ringing in his ears, and, instinctively sitting up and grasping the oars, listened for a repetition. It came quickly, and seeking with his eyes the direction of the sound, he saw on a cliff, near which the boat had drifted, a woman wildly waving a scarf with one hand, while with the other she pointed down the cliff, all the while screaming. Victor Paterson saw that there was some danger afoot, and being a man of action turned his boat's head to the scene, and, exerting his strength, drove her through the water with powerful strokes. A very short time brought him near enough to realize the cause of the screaming and the danger which it attracted. Another woman was struggling in the water at the foot of the cliff, which was here some 30 or 40 feet high. The air in her clothes had hitherto buoyed her up, but these were becoming saturated, and she was beginning to sink, when driving his boat alongside her he grasped her hand and drew her to the boat. The swell under the cliff was strong, and the little boat rocked about so much that he saw there was some difficulty in taking aboard the woman, who was of a large and heavy pattern. So stooping over the stern, he fastened the end of the painter round her waist and made it fast.

"Now," he said, "hold on to the boat and I will row ashore; it will be much safer than trying to get you into the boat with such a swell on."

The woman in the water gasped as she answered as pluckily as she could:

"Go on as quickly as you can! I'll do my best."

She was neither too young nor too well favored, and the tumble from the cliff into the sea had played sad havoc with her toilet; but Victor saw easily that she was a lady. Speech and thought and manner are above all accidents of flood and field. He pulled out a little way, so that he might see the coast and judge the nearest point where landing would be possible, and as he did so he opened to his vision the top of the cliff. The other woman who had been waving her scarf was still there, but had not realized the situation at a glance, and was running to and fro, and peering over the rocks in search of an opening where the boat might land.

She ran along the cliff to the most northerly point, where the land was highest, and at once turned and signalled the boat, shouting at the same time with a strong, clear voice to attract Victor's attention in case he had not kept eyes on her. As she pointed north, Victor turned the boat's head that way, and made to round the utmost point of rock. A few strokes took him to it, and just inside he saw a tiny strip of yellow beach at the bottom of a gully running down between the cliffs. Toward this he pulled, and within a couple of minutes succeeded in beaching the boat. He then jumped out, and, untying the rope from the lady's waist, carried her ashore. As he did so he felt her head fall over, and her weight to seemingly increase. She had fainted.

He laid her on the beach, and, as he did so caught sight of the other lady coming down the gully at breakneck speed, jumping from rock to rock, or plunging among the sedge and bog which marked the course of the tiny stream. As he carried the lady up the beach to where the tumbling stream had formed a tiny basin among the rocks, the new comer reached him, and helped to lift her from his shoulder; she gasped out, as she did so—

"She is not dead?"

"No! no! She has only fainted—and that only after we got to land. She will be all right in a few moments."

She threw herself on her knees beside her friend, and dipping her handkerchief in the bright water, bathed the face and smoothed the gray hair back, and generally adjusted the dishevelled clothing. It was evident that the invalid was recovering, so she simply waited. Victor waited, too, and during his wait was able to take stock of the new comer.

She was a young girl of not much more than 20 years, with well-made figure of the slim order, and radiantly beautiful. Her features were good, and her brown skin was so clear that the rosy hue of health, heightened by her mental disturbance, and the warmth of her charge down the hillside, seemed to shine through it from within. Brown hair, brown eyes full of a fire that took yellow color when the sunshine met them;

a mouth like pearl and ruby where the white teeth shone through the parted lips, looked in perfect keeping with the snowy frock of duck faced with a falling drapery of some sort of gauzy stuff of fairy green over the breast, and fastened with a brooch composed of a single flashing ruby. Victor Paterson felt a thrill go through him as he realized the feeling of Geraint of old.

"Here by God's grace is the one maid for me!"

It was a genuine case on his part of love at first sight, and the natural instinct of his race prompted him forthwith to so bear himself, that all things might be ordered to the accomplishment of his aim. Therefore, like a wise man, he simply waited.

When the elderly lady opened her eyes and saw the sweet young face bending over her she seemed at once to realize her position, and drawing down the face to hers kissed it and murmured:

Thank God, Riddy, it was not you who fell over the cliff—your father would never have forgiven me.

"Oh hush, Aunt Joe!" said the girl, "Hush, hush! you mustn't say things like that or I shall never forgive you. Ah, aunty dear; thank God you are safe. I have been in such dreadful fear. Thank you, sir! Oh! thank you for saving my dear aunt! And before he knew what she intended she seized his hand and kissed it, as women sometimes do under sudden, semi-hysterical emotion. Victor, though taken aback by the suddenness of the act, was equal to the occasion, and withdrew his hand gently, but with a firmness which acknowledged no resistance.

"No!" he said, and with a grave commanding dignity which went straight to the girl's heart, "No! you must not do that. I am not worthy of it!" Then seeing a certain embarrassment in both ladies he went on quickly:

"And now what is to be done? Have you a carriage here?" The young lady shook her head and the older answered:

"We walked over from Quairang, intending to spend the afternoon on the cliffs, and the carriage was to come out and wait for us on the road beyond at 8 o'clock, so that we might drive back to Portree by moonlight."

As she spoke Victor's mind was made up, and he said, so authoritatively that his words did not admit of any disputing:

"Then it is quite simple. You must not run the risk of remaining in your wet clothes. You must come on my yacht, and there you can make yourselves comfortably, and I shall sail you back to Portree!"

As he spoke he took from the boat's locker a revolver and fired one shot, and then three in rapid succession.

"The boat will soon be here," he added. He then ran to the top of the cliff, and a few minutes later they could see him waving his arms as he directed the approaching boat. It seemed to both ladies like magic, but in what seemed a few moments they were seated in a good-sized whale boat, which was driven through the water at great speed by four red-haired, big-bearded, brawny giants who spoke in Gaelic. Victor took the helm himself, the steersman having been left to find the carriage and bring it back to Portree.

Victor Paterson had hitherto been proud of his beautiful little yacht, but as he helped the ladies aboard he wished that she were more worthy of her visitors and that the accommodation were better. He ran down to his cabin and threw a bundle of flannels on the bunk, and then coming up, said to Aunt Joe:

"You must take off your wet clothes at once. You can either go to bed till they are dry or put on what you find. We have, of course, no women on board, so perhaps your niece will be your lady's maid. My men are capital hands at washing and drying, and all sorts of things, so you will not have to wait long."

The ladies retired below, and it seemed an incredibly short time till the clothes which the girl brought out of the cabin were brought back dry and actually ironed! Surely, there is no one so absolutely handy as a sailor. In the mean time an early dinner had been prepared, and when the ladies emerged in spick and span order they were greeted by the welcome sight of a most appetizing, if plain, meal. With her restored toilet Aunt Joe had on her best manner, and at once made the introductions:

"I am Mrs. Bates, and this is my niece, Miss Dana. And neither she nor I know adequately how to thank you for the vital help you gave me today, and for the courtesy and hospitality which you have shown us since." To which he replied with equal formality:

"I am Victor Paterson of Uiskorchie: they call me laird in my own parts. I am more proud and happy than I can say to be of any service to the ladies. There is too great a reward for any effort of mine in that you are any ladies whom I have been privileged to assist." To his surprise, the elder lady spoke out:

"Victor Paterson! why Riddy's great-grandfather had the same name. It would be strange if the accident of today should bring us a new relative or connection."

Riddy said in fun: " 'Us,' Aunt Joe? Mr. Paterson—the other Mr. Paterson—and you cannot be very near relatives."

"Nonsense, my dear Riddy. In great families all relationships are near enough and far enough, just as we like to make them. Old Mr. Paterson would be in close relationship with me in the highlands. Why any one can follow the connection; aye, and even understand it."

"What is the exact relationship, Aunt Joe?" she asked, demurely.

"He was my daughter's brother-in-law's father-in-law's father," came the ready answer.

They all laughed, and Mrs. Joe Bates remained mistress of the situation, while the badinage helped to put them all upon a familiar footing. They fell to upon the dinner, and enjoyed themselves immensely. They then went on deck and found that the sailors had rigged up an awning, under which they sat restfully and enjoyed the contrast of their own shady ease with the fierce glare of the sun. The waste of waters around them was like a sea of diamond and sapphire, whereon the distant islands seemed to rest airily as a bird hovers, while the shores were dim with the heat haze and the mountains stood out clear. As she looked, Riddy seemed to realize that Skye was well named, for it was, indeed, an aerial realm.

It was an ideal day for lazy sailing, and none of the party were anxious that the journey should come to an end. Victor was in a trance of delight. All the dreams of his young manhood seemed to have been realized at once, and the elements seemed to have lent themselves, as though obedient to his wishes. There was just sufficient breeze to fill the sails, and on even keel the pretty, swift-winged yacht drifted on to Portree. Presently tea was served on deck, and as they sipped it the evening fell, the sun sank lower and lower, till at length the great flaming disk was cleft along by the black, serrated line of the island. All three stood wrapt in speechless delight; for Victor the glory of earth and sea and sky had a new value in which was something of holiness, and with his eyes fixed on Miss Dana's face he waited in silence. In a few minutes the sun had sunk below the horizon's rim, and twilight was upon them. The red sky over the island still flared, but it was with a feeble light, which threw into indistinct poetical effect all the noble beauty of the scene. It was the true Scottish "gloamin'" in which is this strange effect; that looking upward there was nothing but light, while earthward there was nothing but darkness. It took the man-artist many a century to realize what the God-artist learned at a glance—that black is a color of exceeding value in art. With a sigh of delight, Miss Dana turned to her companion, and said:

"Oh, Aunt Joe, isn't it just noble? It is worth coming across the Atlantic to see. I wish we could have such twilight at home!"

Victor felt that his stock of knowledge was increased a little—his companions were Americans.

The sail by moonlight was like another sweet dream—the same, but different, as when children drink into their memories the glories of colored fireworks, and all the various charms which the same scene has when the shells and rockets spread their many colored fires. Following the red glare of the sunset and the misty poetry of the twilight came a sort of dawn, where the white, misty light of the moon sailed on after the departing day. Then the moon rose, full and broad, and threw a golden light over the world in such a way that all things denied its direct radiance became of inky hue. And then the twinkling lights of Portree, and the dim windows of the scattered houses around it began to shine through the night; and the old lady thought sweetly on things that had been, while the young people sat in silence and had strange imaginings.

But even such an idyllic journey must have an end, and although the shouting from the shore through the darkness—for even moonlight is dark by comparison, when a narrow harbor has to be won through a rushing tide—and the lanterns waving to and fro seemed all fraught with poetry and romance, the prosaic end of parting came. After another hurried thanks which seemed, and was, more formal—for not rugged, lonely nature, but the conventionality of civilization surrounded them— Victor took his way back to his yacht.

He slept but little that night, for he had a feeling that the morrow had something in store for him. At the dawn he arose and watched the shore which had now a new charm for him, for it was the casket that held his jewel. He knew that he dare not make a call so early, and sat and dreamed as the hour stole away. He heard the warning bell of the Glasgow steamer sound, and saw her cast off and cleave her way eastward to Oban. As he looked at her he mused and thought to himself: "There are some on that boat who go to meet those they love, and some who leave the better part of their lives behind them. As for me, either may be in store for me this day." From which one who could have read his thoughts would have known that he had resolved to put in the coming hours his fortune to the touch, "and win or lose it all."

At noon he took his way to the hotel, and there were few feminine eyes but turned on him admiringly, as with free, bold gait he strode up the little street.

But it was not long before he strode down the street again, not less free, but with his eager look turned to one of bitterness. The ladies had left by the Glasgow boat, without leaving a word for him, or even their address, or saying whither they were bound.

Victor went to his cabin, and with his soul filled with bitterness tried to fix some plan of action. He felt that Miss Dana was his fate, and there was for him no happiness, no rest, till he had won her. Back to his memory came, like the pictures in a diorama, every moment of the previous day since he had first seen her; and with each retrospect came a stronger conviction that all that had passed was sincere—that there was in those true eyes no deceit, no guile.

There must then be some other cause for the sudden departure.

There had not been time for them to have even had created a fear of him or of any advance of his. So he made up his mind to make for Oban, and try if he could see Miss Dana once more, and at least learn where or how he might meet her again. The order to sail given, the yacht flew over the water to Oban, and Victor had the melancholy satisfaction of seeing, as he drew near the port, that if he had started but a little earlier he might have got equal with the steamer, if not ahead of her. He did not neglect his chance, however, but tried round the hotels in case the American party arranged to stay the night. Then he tried the railway officials, but so many parties consisting of two ladies had left that it was hopeless to try to discover in which direction those he sought had gone.

Victor Paterson returned to his yacht, baffled and despairing, and forthwith sailed away for Portree again, for he felt that at least he might visit the enchanted spot where he had seen her who was henceforth to rule his thoughts. The next day he was sorry he had gone, for the place looked at felt so lonely that it made all his adventure seem only like a beautiful dream, from which this was the melancholy awakening.

More than two years passed, and during all that time Victor treasured in his heart the image of the lovely stranger. He did not know where or how to look, or he should have willingly begun a search through the world, so he did the only thing to be done, waited; possessing his soul in such patience as he might.

At last the goddess fortune brought him a clew. He was making a visit to Quairang in the late autumn, and was seated on the table rock, looking seaward to where the one sad, sweet adventure of his life had taken place, when he mechanically picked up a piece of old newspaper—a lunch wrapper left by some previous tourist. In Skye any kind of chance literature is not to be despised, and he threw his eye over it. It was not apparently of a very interesting nature; few trade journals are interesting to laymen of the craft, and this one, the Auctioneers' and Valuers' Gazette, was, seemingly, no exception to the rule. Mechanically, he read through lists of houses to let, and such similar advertisements, set forth in the most attractive auctioneer English; but at last he came across a paragraph which brought him sitting up all aglow:

> "We are glad to learn that the estate of Brassy Tower, near Westernford, on the Stanmore and Watford line, which has been so long in the market, has been at last disposed of through the instrumentality of Messrs. Topping, Son & Hickson of 32 Budge's corner, Watford. This noble estate, which is the last of the "ring fence" properties left on the north side of the metropolis, makes a departure from its historic traditions. In the walks which the feet of Burke and Steele rendered sacred to lovers of our national glories, the feet of a younger and an alien dynasty will henceforth tread. Where the gleams of sunlight falling through the leafy veils of summer, the brown mantle of autumn, on the "bare poles" under which the ship of winter sails toward the green islands of spring, traced the long hours in their succession as on nature's own sundial will now be recorded, we trust, happy memories of a childhood spent in the western world. The new owner of this delightful mansion, by whole sale Messrs. Topping, Son & Hickson have added another bay leaf to their career of commercial well doing, is Miss E. Dana, the millionaire American heiress, of whom the society papers have of late given certain mysterious hints."

A true lover is a person of limited ideas; while the epithet can apply to him his thoughts are limited to one. Thus it was only in accordance with the habit of things that Victor at once found his trouble at an end.

There might be more than one American Miss Dana, but of that supposition he took no heed. Here was Miss Dana with a local habitation
and a name, and of course it was his Miss Dana—he would be but a
poor-spirited lover, indeed, who would admit even to the secret recesses
of his soul a single doubt on such a subject. But complete assurance
makes its own doubts and as he turned the scrap of paper over in his
hands and sought vainly for further information Victor Paterson began
to have fears. What was the date of the paper? It certainly looked old,
but examine it how he would he could nowhere find the year. At last he
got a clew; in one advertisement allusion was made to Thursday, Oct. 1,
and looking at his pocket-book he found that in the current year Oct. 1
had fallen on Sunday; the newspaper was, therefore, of three years before
unless, indeed, it were very much older. It was characteristic of the man's
nature that as he carefully folded the precious scrap of paper and placed
it in his pocket-book, he rose and took his way toward the cave-like
entrance to the table rock of Quairang.

That night he slept at home. The next day he made preparations for
departure for an unlimited time; and on the day following he was on
the way to Glasgow on the bi-weekly steamer. While there was no clew
whatever to his departed object of affection, he was sadly content to wait:
but with the least hope his imagination filled the whole dark way before
him with a brilliant series of fortunate episodes.

When he got to London he put up at a quiet hotel, and, having
obtained an ordnance map of the county of Middlesex, he began to
study the topography of northern London. It cannot be imagined that
he expected to find the ordnance map in error, so it must have been a
tremor arising from some other cause that made his heart bound with
a new gladness when he found marked on the map, between Stanmore
and Watford, the name "Brassy Towers." Next morning he had taken
train to Watford, bringing with him only a small handbag with a sufficient change of toilet for all emergencies. At Waterford he had procured
a carriage and driven along the road to Stanmore. The driver certainly
must have thought him a very inquisitive person, for he insisted on being

informed as to the name and ownership of every house along the road; if he did not know, he had to stop the next pedestrian and make inquiry. After a drive of a couple of hours the ground began to rise, and presently the road ran under the shadow of a high red brick wall. Victor had a sort of presentiment that kept him silent; he felt that he would rather that the name of the house they were passing should be given to him than that he should have to ask it. He was not surprised when the driver said:

"That, sir, is Brassy Towers, where the Yankee ladies do shut themselves up." This gave Victor an opportunity of making inquiries, and within a few minutes he was given all that was known by the gossip of the neighborhood of the occupants of "the Towers," as the driver said the place was familiarly known. He was told that two ladies, one old and one young, lived there alone; that the young lady was very beautiful, and that they saw no company whatever; that sometimes they drove about the country side, in a fine carriage with fine horses—and that was all. When Victor asked if it was not about time to give the horses a rest the driver replied that there was a capital little inn at hand, and that he had hoped that they might rest there for awhile.

The inn at hand seemed to be a most capital little place for Victor Paterson liked it so well that he then and there determined to remain for at least the night; so he sent his bag up to his bedroom, which looked over the demesne of Brassy Towers, and sat down to lunch. When this was over he went up to his room and sat at the window studying the prospect before him, and trying to imagine what would be the end of his venture. Hope suggested some such glowing possibility, that all the air seemed charged with music at the very thought; but fear drew in front of his mind's eye a rugged veil of doubt, through whose rents a waste of dready darkness appeared. He could get no glimpse of the house, for a great grove of forest trees intervened, but now and then a mist of smoke rising above them showed its locality.

Victor remained as patient as he could until late in the afternoon, and then, having made his toilet with something of extra care, sallied out to pay his visit to the Towers, and to try to see Miss Dana.

And now he felt, for the first time in his life, Victor Paterson of secondary importance. Nevertheless, he held himself at his proudest; his type of man is at its best when fighting great odds—and what odds are so great as doubt to a lover. At that moment the whole fighting spirit of him—and it was an imperious one—was at its best, and any qualms which he might have of his ultimate success were relentlessly crushed down by an iron will.

The lodgekeeper would probably have denied him admission had he asked, but as he opened himself the wicket beside the great gate and passed on without hesitation, the man seemed to take it for granted that some right or business empowered him to enter, and stayed in his lodge, fully intending to deny any knowledge whatever of his entry, if questioned on the subject.

As he walked through the winding avenue, among, and at times under, the splendid trees, rich in all their summer beauty of foliage, which a dry autumn had aided in retaining till unusually late in the year, he marveled afresh at the rich beauty around him. Coming from the wild barenness of Skye such leafy splendor seemed almost tropical, and it was little wonder that, when a bend in the avenue opened it to his eyes, the beautiful old red brick house with its many angles and gables, its quaint little towers surmounted by miniature cupolas, on which the copper roofing was of a lovely soft green with age, seemed like an enchanted palace which held the fairy queen whom he had come so far to seek. There must be some natural law of compensation which make the boldest man the most timid under proper conditions, and vice versa, for this young laird, who had come the length of Britain to try to win a girl whom he had seen but once, and who had seemingly run away from him, felt more and more fainthearted as he approached the hall door. Here again, however, his inner qualm did not show itself in any outward demeanor, for he walked boldly to the door as though the house were his own, and, having rung the bell, at once entered the hall without waiting. It was quite evident, from the manner in which the butler came forward, that visitors at Brassy Towers were neither usual nor expected; for the man seemed at first surprised, and then in a deferential way indignant.

Before he had time to speak Victor said: "I want to see Miss Dana." The servant said as respectfully as he could: "Neither Miss Dana nor Mrs. Bates receive any visitors, sir."

This brought joy to Victor, for now he knew, what before he had only surmised, that the Miss Dana who lived at Brassy Towers was his Miss Dana. Without a word he placed a £10 note in the man's hand, and when the butler had swiftly and furtively conveyed it to his pocket, and he knew that the bribe was taken, he said:

"You will not get into any trouble. You, being in doubt, did not like to refuse admission to the visitors to your mistress without definite instructions. If you had known of course. * * * You placed the strange gentleman in the drawing room and came at once to inform your mistress herself; but forgot in the flurry of the moment to ask his name." The man bowed, and without a word showed him into the nearest drawing room and departed.

It needed all Victor Paterson's truculence of disposition to sustain him as he paced to and fro, for her could not but be aware that he was very much in the position of trespasser. But it is not only at the moment of death that the mind has retrospects and inspirations; the mauvais quart d'heure has a logic of its own in which there are comforting conclusions. At this painful time Victor felt the compensation of the hurried and ungracious departure of his friends from Skye. He had not been forbidden to call, and was therefore within his conventional rights.

Within five minutes Miss Dana made her appearance radiant in beauty, and with an added charm in a soft, shy blush; she came quickly into the room after the manner of one whose time is precious, and who must act on impulse. As Victor stepped swiftly to meet her and took her hand in his she raised her eyes to his, and said, frankly:

"I am very, very glad to see you." She pronounced the adverbs "vurry, vurry," but the quaintness seemed to Victor an added pleasure. She went on, "I feared we should never see you again!"

Victor's heart leaped. "Then you did not forget me!" was all he could say, but he still held her hand and she made no effort to withdraw it. And so they stood, seeming to both to stand soul to soul as hand to hand for a few flying moments, which had, however, in them the essence of an eternity.

His dream was broken by the hurried voice of Mrs. Bates in the hall.

"A what?"

"A gentleman, ma'am."

"And you showed in a stranger without permission? I shall see you later." The butler felt that he was earning his douceur.

As Mrs. Bates entered the room there was no semblance of haste about her, but there certainly was a reality of great haughtiness; even Miss Dana was surprised to see the metamorphosis in her aunt. When, however, Mrs. Bates recognized the visitor her face softened, and she was at once more like the lady whom he had known. Her salutation was hearty, but Victor could not but recognize that there was going on in her mind some duplicate process of thought. It was as though there were in the one person two different individualities, each with its own aims and objects, its own positive and restraining powers. At the sound of her voice the two young people had let go each other's hand, and stood a trifle further apart and in more conventional attitude. Victor still looked somewhat sheepish, as a man always does in moments of disturbed emotion; but, womanlike, Miss Dana retained entirely her ease and self-possession. Mrs. Bates looked from one to the other inquiringly, and seemed to make her mind up pretty quickly, for her face hardened somewhat, and she seemed to take a sort of formal possession of the young man. She sat down and made him sit beside her in the vis-a-vis, and plunged into conversation with a persistence which left no opportunity for her niece.

Victor felt somehow now quite content; his hand clasp with the young American with the look into each other's eyes which had accompanied it, together with the knowledge that these precious moments had become a secret which they shared made him self-confident. This bearing in itself helped to enlighten Mrs. Bates, for as the moments flew by she became more and more hard in her demeanor, and at last rising up suddenly she said:

"Mr. Paterson, may I have a few words with you in my boudoir? I have something of a business duty to do, and perhaps we had better do it alone. You will pardon us, Eurydice, will you not?"

"Certainly! Aunt Joe," replied Miss Dana, sweetly: and without a word further Victor followed her from the room. Mrs. Bates' side-long look was upon him, so he did not venture to turn his head toward Miss Dana; he had to content himself by looking in a mirror, in whose mysterious depths their glances met.

In the boudoir Mrs. Bates motioned to Victor to be seated, and she sat herself opposite to him, and without preface began her business.

Chapter II

"Mr. Paterson," said Mrs. Bates, "Do not think me ungrateful or wanting in any form of sympathy. There is every reason why I should, if I cannot please you, at least cause you as little pain as possible. You saved my life, and, indeed—indeed—I am not ungrateful; but I have a duty to do which I solemnly undertook to perform, and which I have, though not without some pain to myself and much self-denial, carried out heretofore. Now, I ask for no confidence from you. I simply want to lay a certain matter before you, and so the first part of my duty will be done. In a word, my niece must not marry! Her father's wishes forbid it imperatively, for the present, at all events, and she is herself under a very sacred promise which, until the conditions of it are fulfilled, she must abide by. Now I am old enough to know, and to have known by experience, that young girl's wishes and her day dreams are more or less dependent on her surroundings, and that what is forbidden is not of necessity a thing to be desired. It is for this reason that I have isolated her here—and condemned myself to share her very charming prison. I have been in hopes that as we lived a life of absolute seclusion, no disturbing element should come into her life in the shape of a man that she feels she could love—"

Here Victor broke in:

"Do you believe that such a hope can be realized?"

"You must not ask me that! It is not my belief, but the wishes of another, backed by a very solemn promise from myself and Riddy, that rules the present situation. I can but try—and try my best—to do what I think to be right!"

Victor thought a moment and then asked:

"Is there any valid reason—such a reason as average men of the world would accept as sufficient, why Miss Dana should not marry? I mean anything beyond and outside the will of the person to whom these mysterious promises were given? If there be then I trust that I am man enough to forget my own wishes and do what is best for the lady's—for any lady's—good!"

As he spoke he looked so manly and handsome that the old lady's heart warmed to him; but with a start she pulled herself together and went on:

"You must judge the matter for yourself. I shall do my best to give you materials for judgment. Riddy's father is a very remarkable man, of good extraction but entirely self-made, as the saying is. He left his home for reasons which we need not go into and went out to seek his fortune. After drifting about for awhile he became one of the adventurers to California when the gold fever broke out there. He was one of the 'Forty-niners,' as they were called, or "Argonauts," who crossed the Rockies amid incredible hardships and won fortune—those of them who survived. He was—is still—a man of iron will, and the most masterful man I ever met. I ought to know, for his brother was married to my daughter, and, of course, I saw much of them both. My son-in-law was a masterful man, too, and more than once the brothers almost came to blows: it was a constant dread to me lest one or the other should be killed. My own husband, poor Joe Bates, was a self-willed man himself, and glad I am that he and Riddy's father never met, for if they had, there not being the tie of blood between them to prevent actual murder, I fear one or other must have gone under. Well, Riddy's father soon became the leader of the party in which he had joined. He had a saying that 'any man could rule a crisis if he had sand in him,' and he certainly did come out when occasion called. Whether it was Indians, or starvation, or drought, or wolves, or bears, or snow storms, or burning prairies, he was in the front; and it was not long before they gave him a nick-name which sticks to him still."

"What is that?" asked Victor, who was getting thoroughly interested.

" 'Crisis!' If you were to mention that you knew Crisis Dana today anywhere in California where there is an old man present, it would be as good as a Washington introduction. Now and again, there were men who rebelled against his ruling, but they say that he was handier than any one with either gun or bowie, and, when the row was over, the rest of the party went on quite satisfied. I've heard tell that of all the parties that crossed the Rockies in '48 or '49 not one but lost more men all told than Dana's, so that there was sense in his ruling anyhow. Well, he kept his masterful spirit all the time, and the richer he got and the more powerful the less and less would he let any one interfere with him. But he is a good sort at heart, and once in my life, when I went to him in trouble and knelt to him, he took me up and swore to see me through it. I tell you I wasn't sorry then for his masterfulness, for, with his courage, it saved my poor girl's husband."

"Tell me about it," asked Victor. He spoke partly out of interest, and partly because he knew that there is no better way to win an old woman to your side than to listen to her and let her talk of the past. So Mrs. Bates, nothing loth, went on:

"Chris—that was Riddy's father—and my girl's husband had had an awful row, and I fear that Chris wasn't altogether wrong in the matter. Anyhow, they were not on speaking terms, and each had sworn before a host of their friends that they would never speak again. They said that they didn't fight it out and settle the matter there and then because they were brothers, but that henceforth they were strangers, and would treat each other as such. When things were this way, Spud—that was the name they gave my son-in-law—got into some trouble about a sluice that some one else owned. I never quite knew the rights of it, and I didn't want to know, for what I did hear didn't seem all right. The vigilantes took up the matter, and one night my girl came to me nearly dead with fright, and told me that there was a necktie party afoot; that they were after Spud, and that nothing could save him if Chris didn't take it up. I went off without my bonnet, and woke up Chris, and threw myself on my knees before him, and implored him not to let them string up his brother. He was kind to me—more than kind. He heeled himself right away, and swore that no harm should come to his brother, even if he had to waltz into the crowd himself and slice."

Victor could not but notice that as the old lady got on with her narrative, and as her memory began to realize past moments, she fell into ways of speech habitual to her in those days. Mrs. Bates went on:

"True it was that none but Chris could have reasoned with that crowd. But Chris was a good reasoner in such times, and he generally reasoned with a derringer. I followed him, though he had told me to run home and comfort Ante, and hung on the outskirts of the crowd. Christ got up and made them a speech like this:

'Boys, you know me! Well, I'm goin' to take a hand in this game!' Then some one called out:

'Go home, Chris. This ain't no place for you. We left ye out o' purpose!'

'Oh, indeed! So you left me out. Well, I don't generally get left, and I'm going to reason this out with you. But, perhaps, you don't know logic, so I'll give a lesson. There's a major premiss and a minor premiss, and there's a conclusion—you see I didn't go to college for nothing! Well, the major premiss is me and the minor premiss is this'—and he drew his gun and faced the crowd. 'And the conclusion is that the prisoner is going to be handed over to me, and I'll decide on him right here. And then if you're dissatisfied you are to let him go and tackle me. I'll hold up my hands for you, so help me God!' With that he stepped down from the box he stood on and went over and cut the rope that bound Spud. 'Now,' says he to him. 'this charge may be true or not—I'm not going into that—but the punishment is that you either go or stay here. If you go you must never show your face here again, for I undertake to these gentlemen that if you do I'll shoot you on sight. But if you stay I'll make good the harm done to Halligan's sluice and pay the owners what they ask themselves; and whilst you stay here I'll be responsible for you, whatever you may do. And if the vigilantes won't deal with me, then I'll put the rope on my own neck! So, pards,'—and he looked round him—'I think we've either got rid of a nuisance or else we've got one more good citizen amongst us; or if I'm wrong you'll be free before long from both the nuisance and the blasted fool that trusted his own flesh and blood. See!' "

"Well, with that the men all began to cheer and Spud came up to Chris and held out his hand, and the two walked away together; and they never had a hard word one for the other till poor Spud followed my girl to her grave 12 years ago."

"Then I say," said Victor, "that Mr. Dana was and is a splendid fellow, and no wonder he has such a daughter."

"Ah! And there I must go on," said the old lady sadly. "When Spud died—it was very shortly after Chris' own poor wife had gone. Eurydice was a good soul, and she asked Chris to ask me to come and take care of her baby girl—little Riddy. He made my home as happy as he could; and all that affection and thought could do he did to make us comfortable. Riddy was like a child to me, and I am sure no mother could love her better than I do." Here the old lady's eyes filled with tears—though she smiled through them as Victor muttered—"No wonder!" Then she went on:

> "Riddy and I have been together all her life since then, and if she were
> in reality my own child I could not be more fond of her. Her father

used to come and go, for he owns great mines in all parts of the West; in fact, his friends say he won't be contented till he has got the earth. But he never interfered with her education, or her bringing up in any way till she was quite a big girl. Then one day, when he came home after a long absence of nearly six months, he took Riddy by the elbows, and stood her up before him and said:

'Why, sister, the little girl is becoming a woman!' He said no more then, but I could see his brows knit, and I knew that he was thinking of something serious. When Riddy was gone to bed he took me into his study and made me sit down. He didn't sit himself, but walked about the room all the time—and you know how trying that is to a woman's nerves—or stood with his back to the fire while he spoke.

'That little girl is growing into a woman—she'll be up to high-water mark before we know where we are! Now, sister, I want you to make me a promise.' He stopped there and I felt my heart sink in my breast as I asked him: 'What is it Chris?'"

" 'I want you to promise me that you will not let Riddy marry any man without my leave!' I thought I'd try to keep that matter open, so I tried a little laugh, and said to him: 'Why, Chris, how am I to prevent her marrying? Maids like to choose for themselves—at least, they used to do so in my time—and I don't suppose they propose to change the system now.' If I had any sort of idea that I was going to put Chris Dana off his intention by any light word of mine, well, I might have known better. 'Look here, sister,' said he, 'I've got my own plans in life, and I intend to carry them out in my own way. What I want you to do is to promise me—aye, and take your oath on it—for though we men don't think much differ between the two, you women are afraid to break an oath, though ye'll lie all over the ranch. Swear to me, solemn and true, that you'll not let Riddy marry any man if you can keep her from it.'"

"No!" said I. "Chris Dana, you have no right to ask me to take such an oath!" Well, he looked at me full a minute; then I saw that dark look came up in his face that I heard tell of when he was about to shoot, and, says he, with quiet, cold words, that seemed to drop out one by one from a mouth of steel:

> "When you went down on your knees to me to take that precious Spud out of the hands of the necktie party you didn't stop to examine my rights. From that day to this I have never asked for a single favor: what I have had has been yours, and I didn't hear no complaint. Now I ask you to do one thing for me—mind you, a thing that any man has a right to ask about his own daughter—and yet you refuse!"

"Mr. Patterson, you men have your own rules of honor, and we women have ours, but there are certain matters which are common to us both. I ask you fairly, could I refuse when the duty was put to me in that way?"

"No! a thousand times no!" said Victor stoutly, so Mrs. Bates went on. "I took the oath, and then Chris rang the bell, and asked the help to ask Miss Riddy to be good enough to come down for a few minutes—not to mind coming in her dressing gown." So down ran Riddy in a few minutes. When she came in her father said to her:

> "Riddy, dear, I want you to make me a promise!"
>
> "What is it, father?"
>
> "I want you to promise, little girl, that you'll not marry any man without my consent."
>
> "But, father, I don't want to marry any one, consent or no consent!"

"All right, little girl; but promise me." Riddy is her father's daughter, and has a mind and a will of her own, so she thought the matter over a minute or two, and then said, suddenly:

> "Why do you want me to promise, father?" He admired her for speaking up to him, I could see it in his face as he said:
>
> "Little girl, isn't it enough that I want it?"

"Quite, father! But a promise is a very sacred thing, and may bind all one's life. Surely if I'm asked to do that I ought to know the reason!"

When Chris heard that he slapped his thigh, and burst out laughing. "Bully for you, little girl," said he, "you're a true chip of the old block. Well, come here, Sissy, and I'll tell you." So Riddy came and sat on his knee, and put her arms round his neck as she used to do when she was a baby, and she smiled at her father as he unfolded his reasons.

"You see, little girl, that this here is just about the hang of it. I've got my own plans, and I mean to work them out in my own way. It's all for you, my dear, in the end, but while I'm doin' it I don't want no board of inspection coming along an' interfering with me. You're the main shaft of my lode, little girl, and you and me understand each other: but I know well that when young people gets fond of each other, the woman's will goes into her husband's."

"But, dad, I've not got a husband, and I don't want one, and if I had one, I don't see why my will should leave me."

"That's all right, sis, but you're young yet, and mayhap some day you'll see some young man waltz along and his face will shut out all the rest of the sunshine of the world for you. What'll become of your will then? No! You're a good girl and an obedient daughter, and I know that if you promise me you'll keep your word. Then I'll know that I'm not to have any one coming messing about my property, and figuring up my profits, and wanting to boss the shebang generally! I tell you, little girl, that it needs all the nerve a man has got for big mining, and if I was to be thinking 'I'll have to give some explanation of this,' or 'maybe this won't pan out as well as Mr. Riddy expects,' why I'd feel as if I was handcuffed all the time—aye, and in leg irons and a straight jacket. You tumble, little girl?"

Riddy did tumble, for she held out her hand; and when the old man held out his she put it in and said, imitating his voice:

"Place it thar! Shake, pard! I promise!"

"Bully for you!" said the old man, as he held her from him at arm's length and looked at her admiringly. "And now, little girl, that's done so handsome that I'll tell you what I'll do. I'll try to take care that temptation don't come in your way. You'll go over to Europe and have a high old time. I'll buy you an estate, and you and Aunt Joe can shut yourselves up in it and have a picnic all to yourselves, without any disturbing young men about to sigh and sling poetry at you and make you feel generally how hard-hearted your old dad is. But just you wait! It won't be long before my pile is made; and then I'll come on! So if you look round then and care to pick out any young man for yourself, durn but I'll buy him for you, even it he's a royal prince!"

"I don't want any man that can be bought," said Riddy, hotly. "If I ever marry a man—with your consent dad, of course—it will be because he is worthy of all love and respect. Now, dad, I've been good, haven't I?"

"That you have, chick, as good as gold."

"And I deserve a reward?"

"Yes, little girl; what'll you have?" I could see that Riddy had been thinking, and I soon saw why.

"Dad," said she; "you've given me in one way a hard row to hoe. I'm not better than other girls or different from them, I suppose; and now that I'm tied up with a promise I may feel as you would have done— handcuffs, leg-bolts, straight-jacket and all—and may want to get free. Won't you slack the rope a bit so that it won't cut me every time?"

"How do you mean?" says the father, smiling, but with his brows set.

"Don't make it so hard and fast! Give some little element of chance: some condition that may or may not happen."

"But why should I? Hard and fast is just what I want."

"Yes, father; but the ropes may gall. Happiness may be at stake on my side; and your side is only to increase a store of gold." Right there Chris rose up smiling, and said he:

"All right, little girl, I'll give you something that may or may not happen: and when it does you may listen to a young man making love to you, and you may marry him without my consent."

"What is it, dear father?" asked Riddy, joyously but my own heart was heavy, for I knew Chris too well to think that he would take any chances on a point he valued. He kissed Riddy lovingly, and moving toward the door said, before he passed out:

"Well, little girl, I'm going to get gold and silver, so I'll give you, too, a chance on a specie basis! When the earth is silver and the sky rains gold you may marry whom you will, whether I like it or not!"

Riddy laughed, but she sang out after her father, imitating his voice: "Sold again, dad! You bluffed me this time; but mind, I'll take the chance to the letter and I'll keep my promise!"

"Well, Mr. Paterson," went on the old lady, "Chris was as good as his word, and he sent Riddy and me over on a trip, and told us to pick out the estate in all England that we liked best, and he would buy it. So we came to London, and by chance we heard of Brassy Towers, and Riddy took a fancy to it. Her father bought the place and made it over to her almost by return of post. Here have we remained all by ourselves; we have made no friends, for we thought that it would be easier for Riddy to know no one than to run any chance of—of—of being upset in keeping her promise to her father. A year after we came Riddy was feeling a little under the weather, and the doctor sent us on a trip to Scotland to brace up. All went well with us, and we kept ourselves to ourselves, so that we did not make a single friend, or even acquaintance, until that unlucky visit to Skye." Here Victor cut in:

"I can't indorse that!"

"Ah! my dear, that's all very well for you: but what of us?" Victor smiled. There was so much taken for granted by the old lady that he felt that his ground was in one way—and that not the least important to a lover—sure, and he could afford to laugh.

"I'm not so dangerous as I look, I assure you," was all that he said.

But the old lady was very resolute, and would not be put off. "You see how we are placed," she said: "what with Riddy's promise not to marry without her father's consent, and my promise not to let her do so, we are so tied up that we dare not entertain a proposal from any honorable gentleman, even if Riddy's heart was inclined to him."

Victor had had on his thinking cap all the time, and now it was evident that he wore it with some result, for suddenly he spoke out with the old masterful ring in his voice:

"Was not Riddy's promise that she would not marry without consent?"

"Yes."

"Well then there is no difficulty about her becoming engaged!" In his triumphant selfishness he had no thought except for his own happiness: but the old lady shook her head sadly. "And what of dear Riddy—is that a thing to start in life on?" she said—and, after a pause, added—"even if in all honor such a fine drawing of a promise were allowable." Victor answered from the noble side of his nature:

"And Riddy must do what is right, what is most honorable! God forbid that I should make her deflect by a hair's breadth!"

"Well spoken!" said Mrs. Bates, "well spoken! That makes me your friend!" And she held out her hand, which he took impulsively, and held in his. "And now that you know," she went on, "how affairs stand, you must try to help us. I believe that you care for Riddy, and you will not make the dear girl's life harder to bear than need be. She is only a young girl after all, and you are a man, and must help to shield her. Surely it is the duty of love to keep harm away!" As she spoke she looked at Victor appealingly, and the tears welled over in her eyes, and ran down her cheeks. Victor's noble nature arose to the appeal: he stood up, and taking her hand bent over and kissed it. "You are right," he said. "It is a hard duty, but I suppose all duty that is worth anything is hard! I promise to help you. I shall go away at once, and wait for a better time. I dare say Riddy will remember me if she thinks I am worth remembering."

"That's good: that's real good! And if I know Riddy Dana—and I think I do—nothing you could ever say or do would go deeper into her heart. And now, my dear boy, that you have done your duty like a man, I can perhaps make things easier for you. As you are to wait and hope, there is no reason why you should not see Riddy. Stay with us here today, and enjoy yourself. I will send to the hotel for your grip-sack, and I don't suppose that when you go away tomorrow—without a word of love to Riddy, or anything that can upset her—you and she will be less to each other, or be able to wait with less heart."

So Victor, stayed on, and that day never afterwards faded from his memory. Mrs. Bates trusted his honor, and, though she spoke no word of what had taken place to her niece, the two women understood each other completely by some of that subtle language of sympathy which belongs to their sex alone.

Victor and Riddy were together all day, sometimes alone and sometimes with Mrs. Bates. Together they wandered through the shady walks which the trees overhung heavily, being still in all their leafy splendor. The summer had run on unbroken, and the sapstill ran till the rich tints of autumn's livery were mellowed and deepened. The air was very still and something of an echo of the hum of summer insects came from the pastures. Under the great beeches and birches and elms, the ground, hardened by the drip and shelter of a century, was covered with dark green moss, which felt like velvet under foot. Though, truth to tell, this sensation was lost on the young people, or, rather, was lost in a less material experience, for they seemed to tread on air. In the gloom under the trees, from whence the tall branches rising in the light beyond seemed like a miniature forest, the two walked, oftener silent than not, and oftener, therefore, in more complete sympathy. Somewhere, far away, in the back of Victor's consciousness was the thought that this was the last, as it was the greatest, pleasure of his life. But he resolutely kept the thought in the background, and went on his way with full intent to enjoy. As for Riddy, the day seemed like the dawning of a new life. For long she had looked on the meeting in Skye as a beautiful dream, and was almost content to so think of it as not clashing with her father's wish or with her promise to him. And now the dream had come true: the "ideal he" had become materialized, and took Victor's shape. She began to realize how much more beautiful to the eyes of a maid is a real man than is the most perfect dream. Aunt Joe, strong in her sense of having done her duty, did not fear to leave the young people together. She had had his bag brought from the tavern, and had answered Victor's half-hearted protest, for he thought that she might be doing violence to her feelings in making him so welcome.

"Nonsense! my dear boy. Chris would never forgive me if I were not to show you hospitality. He wouldn't let you out of the house himself if he were here: even if he had to shoot you to keep you there, of if he intended to shoot you next day for being there!"

At sunset the air grew very chill, and as Victor and Riddy stood on the terrace and looked westward the scene was indescribably beautiful. As the red sun sunk the trees began to stand out blackly, till the whole mystery of evening was complete. More and more chill came up the misty breath of the valley, and Victor breathed a long sigh as he went indoors, having, as he thought, taken his last look at the beautiful scene which was now forever so deeply graven on his memory. In the dim light of the drawing room, where the lamps had not yet been lit, and where the leaping flames in the grate threw fitful shadows through the room, there seemed still to rise before him the wondrous color of the autumn.

Dinner that night was an ethereal function, and the music afterward was a dream of delight. Miss Dana had one of those pure, sweet voices, which, though seemingly having no special excellence, yet go straight to the heart. She sung without effort: and her songs were all simple, tender little things, like flowers of the garden of song. It was little wonder that Victor sat entranced. In his waking moments, when the stern reality of his situation came to him like discords in the melody, he did not know whether the brightness of the present or the darkness which must follow it were the stronger. Riddy ranged from Balfe to Schubert, and from Schubert to Mozart, and from Mozart to Dvorak, and from Dvorak to

Grieg; and at each new sweetness her lover's heart grew warmer and his fears more cold. After a simple good night whose after silence was more than speech, and where the gentle lingering pressure of hands, each to each, was an ecstacy, Victor went to his room. Pulling aside the heavy curtains, he looked again at the wide landscape now bathed in the light of a golden moon-mist.

Once again as he looked his heart grew bitter, for he felt that gold and gold alone—gold with its cursed power over a man's heart—stood between him and his hopes.

It may have been his fancy, but the whole universe seemed tonight strained with the tint of gold. The broad moon was burnished as a shield and the mist fell away from it in a golden halo and seemed to have wetted the yellow leaves, till they shone golden too. With a muttered curse he swept the heavy curtains back again and shut out the beautiful, sordid sight. For a long, long time he sat before the fire which he never heeded, for his thoughts were wandering toward Riddy, whom, in his mind's eye he saw wrapped in gentle sleep. He did not know that she too was sitting awake and dreaming of him where, too, the flickering fire gave a living reality. At last the fire of each died down into a simple glow: and this too faded into dull red and finally went out. Then the lovers shuddered in their sad, happy loneliness, and went to bed and lay awake thinking of each other.

In the morning Victor awoke early and, pulling the curtain aside, looked again on the scene which he now knew so well. The brightness and freshness of the morning was upon his soul and upon his eyes, just as it was on the flower and sward, and an exclamation of happy wonder broke from his lips as he drank in the beauty of the scene.

Before him lay a great open expanse of park, sloping away to the west, the sward dotted with great trees, towering singly, or massed in clumps till they faded in the distance in a vague line. Then, beyond still, lay a great sheet of water shining like a mirror in the morning light; and farther still away the hills that made the bounds of the valley of the Colne rose dimly blue with morning mist. But all the scene did not merely wear its habitual beauty of park and sward and grove. In the night had been one of those heavy still white frosts which usher in winter at the close of a late October. The whole ground, so far as the eye could reach, was one mighty sheet of silver, glistening in the light. The trees still wore their full panoply of leaves, but the autumn tints of these had been completed, and intensified by the frost of the night: they were now dead, for the sap in them had yielded to the frost which had burst their stems, and they only wanted to rigor of the ice itself to lessen in order to fall. The whole scene was a blaze of gold, and each tree was like a miracle of goldsmith's work. Chestnut and maple and elm and birch and beech, each with its own special glory of leaf, stood like a wonder of the gnomes in fairy land.

As he looked something of the old bitterness of last night against gold and all it wrought crept into Victor's heart. He could not entirely banish the idea that nature had put forth all her picturesque forms merely to cause him pain, and the feeling was intensified when his eyes, hanging over the landscape, lit here and there on the silver birch and the copper beeches which seemed to symbolize the baser forms of bullion. However, such thoughts were but fleeting, and were soon lost in the greater pain of the loss which he now felt to be coming close indeed to him. Victor Paterson was now at the crossing of the ways of his life: he felt that he had a stern duty before him, and one that demanded all the better qualities of his nature. With an effort he braced himself up and proceeded to dress himself. He felt the sting of his cold bath do him good, and it was with resolution manifest in his bearing and his springy stride that he opened the French window of the dining room and stepped out upon the terrace.

The sun was rising higher each moment, but as yet there was no potency in its beams, and the hoar frost sparkled as it crackled under his feet. He crossed the lawn and went under the spreading limes, where on last evening he had walked with Riddy, and where he had felt that their hearts spoke in communion through the mystic silence of the evening; and as he walked there fell upon his soul a great gush of tenderness until the tears rose in his eyes and trickled down his cheeks. It is a mistake to think men never cry; they do, but differently from women, and they hide it scrupulously. They even try to hide it from themselves. And then and there a noble resolution was completed in Victor's soul, that come what might he would spare Riddy all the pain he could; that he would so bear himself that no matter what he might suffer, she should rest free from any care that he might be able to avert from her.

So it was in a mood peaceful with the sweetness of self-sacrifice that he took his way again in front of the terrace, and sat in a rustic seat placed in the shelter of a birch tree, which was in its turn overhung by the spreading branches of a gigantic chestnut. The leaves of both trees were of most brilliant yellow, and they did not even quiver in the still air, so that the idea came once again with renewed force that the scene around him was of the kingdom of the gnomes. As he sat under the tree treading on the silver frost, and with the shadow of the golden leaves upon him he could see the terrace, and watched eagerly in case the morning beauty should tempt Riddy to come forth.

There is, perhaps, a sympathy so occult that even those who experience it are not conscious of its magnitude, and it may have been due to such a communion of souls that Riddy, waking early, had looked from her window, and beholding the wondrous beauty of the scene had hurried out to enjoy it to the full, or it may have been that two young people who really loved each other were imbued with an equal restlessness, which made them wake early, with an equal secret belief that there might be a meeting—by chance—and an equal hope that something might happen before Victor went away. However, be the occult causes what they might, Riddy appeared on the terrace in a dress of snowy white, and with a look in her eyes, happy and still yearning, that made Victor's heart leap to see. She did not see him, sheltered as he was by the thick foliage of the tree which drooped around him, but by some divine instinct she took her way toward him across the frosty grass, as though he were a magnet and she of iron. For the needles does not turn more truly to the pole than was the directness of her steps. Seeing her coming, he rose impulsively and stepped from under the tree, and that instant Riddy's eyes and his met. Neither knew if the usual salutation of the morning was uttered, for as their hands met there was as greeting which transcended speech. Without either suggesting it, they went back and sat together on the rustic seat.

For awhile they sat in silence and looked out on the beautiful expanse where the frost-clad sward rolled away below them into the distance of the spreading trees. Then Victor summoned up his courage to speak as conventionally as he could.

"What a beautiful scene, is it not? I do not think that I could ever forget it." Riddy tried to answer him, but something stuck in her throat and she was silent. The silence around them was so profound that the mooing of a cow in a distant pasture seemed close at hand, and the rolling of wheels which must have been on the high road sounded as if just behind the house. Victor came galloping up to the scratch again with another common-place:

"Is there anything which I can do in Skye or the Highlands for you or your aunt?" Riddy mastered herself this time, and answered him:

"Nothing, thanks—only sometimes to remember us!" There is a limit to the patience of the most self-sacrificing young man, and the fervor of Victor's speech as he answered thrilled through every fibre of Riddy's being and brought the hot blood mantling up in her cheeks.

"Ah! there won't be any trouble about executing that commission!" Then, seeing the perturbation of his companion, he added with a forced laugh: "Unless, of course, your command is a limitation!" Riddy made no answer, but the blush on her cheeks grew brighter. Then for awhile they sat in silence, and both were so wrought that neither could tell if the throbbing of the heart which seemed to come through the silence was that of self or companion.

All this while the sun was rising higher, and the potency of its beams was beginning to be felt: the silver of the sward was disappearing, and except in the shade the grass was cropping out emerald green after its dew-bath.

Crash! the lovers started, but smiled instantly as they saw that a chestnut had fallen through the leaves of its own high tree, and of the birch under which they sat. Then came another and another; the sun was doing its work in the high branches amongst the frozen stems. And then as the rays became more direct the stems of the leaves on the outside branches overhead became thawed from their icy rigidity, and, twisting and turning as they fell through the silent air, began to sprinkle the ground beneath. They did not notice these at first, for their thoughts were elsewhere; but as the sun grew stronger a perfect shower began falling on them, and making little shadows as they fluttered between them and the sun. The grass, still silver white around them in the shelter of the tree, began to be thickly strewn with the golden leaves.

Suddenly Riddy gave a cry and started up.

"Look, Victor! Oh, look! look!" she said. "It has come true: the earth is silver, and it is raining gold!" In the sincerity of great love, all such minor qualities as bashfulness disappeared, and, without a word, as though their souls had spoken to each other, Victor opened his arms. She sank into them, and their lips met in a long kiss. Then they sat together gazing into each other's eyes, and seeing nothing there except the perfect love, and that happiness which true love brings.

Their dream was broken by a dark shadow, and, looking up, they saw a big bronzed man with an iron-gray beard gazing at them and heard him say:

"Guess, little girl, you've got the bulge on me this time!"

With a glad cry of "Father, dear father!" Riddy threw herself into his arms, which he opened to receive her. The old man stroked her hair lovingly as he went on:

"And so it's all come true, Riddy, the silver earth and the sky raining gold! Darn! but these trees ought to grow out in the West, and we could have our specie ready coined. Gold! Silver! Copper! Its all here! Well, little girl, Aunt Joe has told me all—perhaps more than you know—and I'm glad you've chosen an honorable man. It doesn't matter, anyhow, for I've made my pile, and I came to tell you that you might choose for yourself."

Here he held out a great brown hand to Victor and went on:

"Anyhow, you've chosen your pard—and my little girl's pard is my pard! Shake!"

THE END

Chapter Five

BENGAL ROSES (1898)[1]

Bram Stoker

Chapter I

The mail had brought from Nice a cardboard box of flowers. The study
was hot and close despite the open windows, so when I opened it the
scent of the roses filled the air with a new fragrance. I took out the spray
on the top, a magnificent cluster of great pink Bengal roses; but the day
of glory of this kind is a short one, and the journey was long; the mere
motion of lifting the spray finished the work of destruction. I held in my
hand only a bare stock, whilst the moss green carpet was scattered with
the great petals of the flowers.

And then a flood of memory rushed over me, aided by that best of
mnemonics, a once-known perfume. I lit a cigar, and as I sat in my easy
chair with the roses beside me the light of the July evening paled and
paled till I sat alone in the darkness. Twenty years of hopes, struggles,
and success were obliterated and I lived again an old chapter of my boy's
life, which contained the fragments of a romance. All came back so viv-
idly that time and space were annihilated. I did not merely remember;

once more the things were! Ah, me! that chapter of boyish love and of jealousy, which has neither youth nor age! Once again I remember how these things worked into other lives, and then I lived the past again.

★   ★   ★

A sweet old garden of a country rectory, with the trellis covered with luxuriant Bengal roses. Hard by, and some prim old trees of yew and juniper, and arbor vitae. But the rose trellis was, of old, the most sweet, and is now most full of memories.

Beside it some former incumbent had placed an old Greek marble seat. This was always a favourite haunt of mine, and here I'm mainly learned my lessons and also studied such romances as were available. Being a delicate child I had been sent to live with rector, so that I might get plenty of exercise and fresh air and country living. Mr. Petersen was an old man, and, although never a brilliant scholar, was an excellent teacher for such a lad as I was. Mrs. Petersen was nearly as old as her husband, and as their circumstances were not good, I have no doubt that though the money that my parents paid was hardly earned, it was a welcome addition to the housekeeping. There was but one servant in the house; the gardener attended to the cows and pigs and my pony, these being the only animals kept. After a while I grew quite strong and hardy, and by myself took long walks and rides all around the country. It was my habit to study the county map which hung in the hall, and to so arrange my rambles and that by degrees I came to have a local topographical knowledge certainly not possessed by my tutor, whose age and circumstances, and whose habits of a quiet, retired life debarred him from such exercises. I had no companion of my own age, except when at home in London, for at Westoby Puerorum the children were few, and of such a kind that I had but little in common with them. We met at Sunday school, and as I did not care for their horseplay, and got disgusted with their perpetual lying, they voted me a muff, and left me alone—after I had proved in one or two pitched battles that at any rate I was not a coward.

I was about twelve years old when there came an addition to our circle in the shape of a granddaughter of Mrs. Petersen by her first marriage, an orphan, with neither home nor friends. Before she came there were anxious discussions between the old people as to the probable result of her coming. It was evident there was some old cause for anxiety, and once I heard a remark which puzzled me. It was made by Mrs. Petersen:—

"It is so good of you, Edward, and, my dear, I see through all your sweet forbearance; but it is not right that you should be troubled with folk that don't belong to you. Arabella always took her own way in spite of me—and of her poor father—and may be her daughter will want to do the same. We have lived too peacefully, you and I, dear, all these years to be willing to let any disturbance come through someone we never saw," and the old lady wiped away a quiet tear.

"Nay, my dear," said the rector, "I might well say, as Ruth said to Naomi, 'Thy people shall be my people.' And, my dear, your God and mine is hers also, and we are all children of His family. Let the little girl come. I doubt not that He will watch over and mould all things to good purpose." And so it was that Bella Devanti came to us.

I do not think that anyone was so pleased at the idea of her coming as I was. The old people at concern for the future, and the maid, who saw in prospect more waiting and more cooking and washing and another bed to make, grumbled to the gardener, who, though he had no prospect of added work, grumbled sympathetically. For me there was no concern. In those days I suppose I took it for granted, as other boys do, then beds are made and victuals cooked and clothes washed by some dispensation of providence specially arranged for the benefit of boys. The young bird when it opens its mouth where the provender abided by the parents' instinct takes little thought of whence or how it comes. The thinking belongs to a later period, when there are other little beaks open and other tiny voices that clamor at need.

When Arabella Devanti arrived I proceeded with the simple, selfish directness of a schoolboy to fall in love with her, despite the great gulf of five years fixed between us. In this I was not alone, for the feeling was shared in common but the whole household. Even the maid and the gardener gave in, and, as is the wont of such, changed the form or cause of their grumbling, for of course of grumbling was perennial. When

Maria, that was the maid, found that Miss Devanti insistent on making her own bed and looking after herself, as she alleged that she had always done, and began straightway to take apart in the labor of the household, she grew almost rebellious. Finally a compromise was arranged, to the effect that Bella was to be allowed to help in the cooking if she left the rougher domestic work to Maria. Her pretty little foreign ways became a new pleasure in the household, and there was, I am bound to say, a marked improvement in the cuisine. She used to do things with eggs that I dream of yet.

Bella and I became at once great friends. She helped me with my lessons, and taught me music and drawing; and I taught her to ride my pony, and to play cricket, and le-gras, and other games of an old-fashioned kind, which were a tradition in the rectory. We used to sit every day, when the weather was fine on the old marble seat; and the Bengal roses, all summer long, used to keep shedding their great petals over the green moss beneath. There I learned my lessons; Bella was a good mistress, for she would not allow any trifling or inattention. I began to feel, after a while, that her sway was a strong one, and that if I wanted her to do anything I must begin by being master of my work.

Quite three years passed in this way, and I was now a good sized lump of a boy, and began to fancy myself a man. In school this feeling generally finds an outlet in a plentitude of hats, and a choice of neckties; but in our rustic life there was no such outlet, and even the increase of my passion for Bella did not move me to try to add to my attractions in her eyes. She was always most kind to me, and there was between us a genuine affection. She used to tell me all her little secrets, and I to tell her mine. Still, I never felt quite satisfied. There was not that complete abandonment or effacement of herself—that losing her own individuality in that of the other—which the masculine lover, even from his cradle, seems to demand. There always was for her, even in those day dreams which she shared with me, to be some order of things other than present, something to come yet of quite a different kind to that which existed. Indeed, some unknown individual was to make his appearance was to charm us both by his worth and beauty and the gallantry of his bearing. With a seeming generosity she always insisted on giving me a portion of the pleasure of his society, and on my angry remonstrance and disclaimer to share at all in his hateful presence she would laugh softly through her blushes, and then, after a while, tried to soothe me by some added deference to my wishes—my wishes regarding something else. As a matter fact I grew intensely jealous, and the keen eyes of jealousy found food everywhere and in everything. Although I loved Bella more than ever, I began to have moments of what I believed to be hate for her also.

It was at this time that we had a break in the monotony of our lives at Westoby Puerorum. Our squire had in his youth been a pupil of Mr. Petersen. Indeed, it was after the young squire went to college that the old squire presented him to the living; and whenever the young squire— now the squire himself, and no longer young—came to Westoby Grange he always managed to pay a visit to his old tutor. This necessitated something of a drive, for the Grange was in Westoby Magnus, and was distant some eight miles. He had been away for a long time, for his winters were spent abroad, and he had several other estates, so that his summers were divided. He chiefly lived at a place nearly two-hundred miles away, where the ground was high and the air more bracing. This time he had only a small party at the Grange, and when he rode over to see Mr. Petersen he took with him a young gentleman to whom at first I took a liking. It was only when I found that Bella had taken a liking to him also that I began to recognise in him certain evil qualities. He seemed as frank as a boy for all that he was a captain in a crack cavalry regiment. He was sitting on the marble seat between Bella and me before either of us seemed to realise the fact that he was only a stranger after all. Even after I had begun to realise his bad qualities—and perhaps to invent some for him also—I could not but like him. He was such a handsome fellow, so bright and cheery, and with such a winning manner, that I could not help it; but I could not forgive Bella for liking him also, and the more jealous I grew up him the more unreasonably angry I became with her. He did not remain very long, for the squire's visit was but a flying one;

but before he went he promised to ride over from Cotterham, where he was quartered, and to bring me some flies of his own tying, which he had found most effective in the waters of our county. When he had gone, Bella and I sat under the Bengal roses and talked of him in the shade from the afternoon sun. It angered me whenever Bella found new points to admire in him, and so after a while I began to turn the conversation. It was now getting on for sunset, and it was our habit to take the clouds round the setting sun as a garden wherein to found our romances. This evening, with some instinct or intention, I grew more definite than ever in my description of the hero who was to come, making him in every essential the exact opposite to Captain Chudleigh, even to the extent of making him a great noble instead of a "honourable" and a younger son, which the captain was. Bella would not give her own views as to what the hero should be like, but she differed with me point by point as we went along. This made me very angry, and in my boyish petulance I stood up and said to her passionately:

"I believe you're in love with him, Bella! Take him if you want to! I don't care!" I was striding off when she rose up and ordered me so imperiously to come back that, without thinking of any opposition to her wishes, I returned to the seat. She had sat down again; her face was very pale and her dark eyes were blazing. She held her hands for a moment clasped over her heart, and then after a pause said to me:—

"Robert"—this was cutting, for hitherto she had never called me anything but "Bobby"—"Robert, you have no right to say such a thing to me—to anybody. You are born a gentleman, and nothing could justify such an affront. I take it now that you do not know better, and that you were angry, though what cause of anger there is I fail to see. But such a thing must never occur again! You are getting old enough to think for yourself." I was crushed. "Getting old enough!"—"getting!" I who had for years been nurturing a passion for grown-up woman! It left me speechless.

I sat silent a while, and felt myself grow red and white by turns; and then a gush of some feeling came over me, and despite all I could do the tears came to my eyes and ran through the fingers which I held before my face. In an instant Bella changed, and spoke to me lovingly, entreating pardon, and trying, as she spoke, to take away my hands. I repulsed her, and would have risen and run away, but that she held me tight. I suppose the difference in our ages became then more marked than it had ever been, for, with sudden impulse, I threw myself on my knees on the grass beside her, and, hiding my head in her lap, had my cry out, whilst she tenderly stroked my hair, silent all the time, with the instinct of a true woman.

We seemed better friends than ever after that night. I could not but feel that there had come some sort of chasm between us: but the recognition of such a thing was the first step to its bridging, and although I said no more of any feeling which might be between her and Captain Chudleigh I tacitly recognised such a thing as possible and respected it.

Less than a week elapsed before Captain Chudleigh paid his promised visit, and when he came Bella was the one who seemed to avoid him, whilst he and I grew great friends. We all three sat under the roses after luncheon—we called it lunch to strangers, but it was in reality our dinner—and were together all the time except for half an hour when I was rummaging in the attic for an old book of etchings by Piranesi which Bella thought she had seen there some months before. I did not find it, however, and when I came back they were both silent, and he was just about taking his leave. They had quite forgotten about the book. I offered to ride a part of the way with Captain Chudleigh, and he acquiesced heartily, although I thought I saw him make a queer kind of face to Bella when he thought I was not looking. He was silent for a while after we had started, but presently he grew quite gay and laughed and sang and made jokes to me as we rode along. When it was time for me to return he promised that he would ride over again some day soon. When I got back I found Bella still sitting under the roses, and so abstracted that she started when I spoke to her.

Some days afterwards I got a line from Cotterham, saying that Captain Chudleigh would on the following day ride over to lunch with the squire; and that he would, if he might, look into the rectory on his way back, when perhaps Miss Devanti and I would give him a cup of tea under the roses. He came, and we had tea on the marble seat. Mrs. Petersen not being very well had lain down, and the rector was writing his sermon for the next day. It was a very pleasant afternoon, and we all enjoyed ourselves. When the sun was setting Bella sent me to look if Captain Chudleigh's horse had been cared for, and I went willingly, for he rode beautiful horses. When I came back Bella and the captain sat silent at either end of the seat, he with a rose in his buttonhole which had not been there before. This gave me a new pang jealousy, and I did not offer to ride part of his way, although I had been looking forward for the last twenty-four hours to the pleasure of so doing. Bella and I said but little to each other that evening.

The next day I went out for a long walk, taking my lunch with me, as I usually did on such occasions. This expedition had been planned nearly a week before, for I was to explore an old ruin which I had never visited, and Bella had taken much interest in it. When I got so far as I could on the high road I went to strike across country; but in leaping my first ditch I turned my ankle, and had to abandon my expedition, for that day at all events. However, I ate my lunch, and when I felt sufficiently recovered began my journey home. It was very tiring and my ankle pained me much, so that when I got into our own grounds I was thoroughly fagged out. The afternoon sun was beating strongly down, and the shade of the trellised roses, with the cool, green moss, looked so inviting that I lay down and forthwith fell asleep.

I waked to hear voices on the other side of the thick trellis—Bella's voice and Captain Chudleigh's! They were whispering; but, low as their voices were, I could hear distinctly, and what I heard made my heart beat and my ears tingle. He was telling Bella of his love for her, and she murmured an answer that satisfied him, and then I heard their kiss. Boy as I was I knew that I had no right to be there, and so I crawled away out of earshot, being careful to keep the trellis between us, and reached my own room without anyone seeing me. I lay down on my bed, with my heart and my temples throbbing, and felt anew all the pangs of jealousy with despair added. I waited there till the evening fell, and then, when I knew I would meet no one, left the house and came round to the front door, making what noise I reasonably could, and limped in to where the family were at supper. They were all concerned when they heard my accident, which I took care not to say had taken place early in the day. Fortunately the pain and fatigue accounted for my pale face and nervous manner. Bella wanted herself to bathe my ankle, but I insisted that Maria should do it. She was looking so radiantly happy that I could not bear the sight of her.

All the next day Bella was very sweet, and we sat on the marble seat, I with my ankle bandaged on a chair in front of me. As the day wore on I expected that Bella would make some confidence, and I was by that time prepared—after some upbraiding—to give her my sympathy and approval. Self-love demanded that the occasion should not pass unnoticed. But the confidence never came, and I grew resolved that if she chose to keep her secret she might, and that I also would keep mine. The only satisfaction I had—and when I look back on it I think it was a pretty mean one—was that I would not let her do the smallest service for my lame ankle. On this point I was as doggedly resolved as I could be about anything.

Bella's secrecy seemed to me not a negative but positive thing. I almost began to think that she had told me a falsehood, and to imagine all sorts of things. Being ever on the watch I did detect now and then some small acts of secretiveness rendered necessary by her possession of so big a secret. For instance towards the end of the week there came a letter which made her blush and her breast heave, but she never said a word of it. Of course, I pretended not to notice. That night I lay awake thinking of it, and as I lay awake I heard a very low whistle. I rose softly and looked out of the window. I heard a stir in Bella's room, which was next to mine, and in a few minutes I saw her step out of the porch—the door was never locked or bolted at the rectory—and steal softly in the direction of the rose trellis. This struck me as so strange that, in spite of the sense of the meanness of the act, I determined to see what it all meant. My jealousy had already told me, but I wanted to be sure. I stole softly to the back of the trellis. There was a yellow moon, and the shadows were black so I came close unnoticed. There I heard the voice I expected and feared to hear, and which if I had not heard what have disappointed me.

Captain Chudleigh's voice was resonant and resolute, and there was in it something of a triumph, but Bella's voice was faint and tremulous, nevertheless it was sweet, sweeter than ever, with a thrill in it which I had never heard before, and which made me as I listened grow cold with despair, although my heart flamed anew with jealousy. I heard Captain Chudleigh say:—

"I have got it—the bishop's secretary got it for me—and now we can be married where and when we will!" There was no answer; but she evidently drew close to him, for I heard the sound of a kiss—a long one. Then she said:—

"Oh! Reggy, is it necessary that we keep it a secret? It will pain my grandfather and my grandmother so much, and they have been so good to me!" His answer was given with decision.

"My dear Bella, it is necessary. My father would not allow our marriage if he knew of it in time. You see, neither of my two brothers has any family, and the governor says that as I have no fortune I must marry money, and as I might succeed I must marry rank." Bella said, shyly:

"Then, Reggy, we had better say goodbye. Here! Now! If all our parents are against us, where can our happiness lie?" Reggy evidently drew her to him as he whispered, tenderly:

"But we love each other, Bella: and the governor will forgive us when we are married," and there was much more to the same effect. Then Captain Chudleigh took out a paper and read it to her in the moonlight. I can see that his arm was round her as they stood in the moonlight, hidden from the house by the yew tree behind the marble seat. When they showed signs of going I lay down close, close behind the trellis, for I was afraid to stir lest they should see me. After some efforts and many good-byes Bella tore herself away, but not before Reginald Chudleigh had secured her promise that she would meet him at Mirkenfield church at seven in the morning on the second day following.

When Bella had stolen back to her room her lover stood looking after her, and I heard him mutter a low curse—an angry, dissatisfied curse on himself—and then as he turned away I heard him say it:—

"Poor little girl! Poor little girl! It is too devilish bad! So sweet and trustful! If I didn't love her so; or if I had more money!" And then I lost sight of him as he passed into the shadowy darkness of the trees.

After a while I, too, stole back to my bed. My mind was in a turmoil, but through all its murkiness I remember a fixed resolution in my heart—that I, too, would be at Mirkenfield, for I felt that some wrong wasn't intended to Bella. I knew the place, for I had two or three times been over there. It was a tiny village, which time and desertion from economic causes had made tinier still. The church was an old one almost in ruins, which was left always open since no one ever went into it between Sunday and Sunday.

★　★　★

A box of flowers, with a rich and fragrant cluster of Bengal roses, called up memories of a chapter of boyish love and jealousy. In a sweet old garden of a country rectory the lad became enamored of the seventeen-year-old heroine, charming Bella Devanti. When the squire, Captain Chudleigh, came on the scene other feelings were aroused, for Bella pushed aside the boy's admiration to listen to the man's professions of love. With jealousy, tinged by hate, Bobby listened behind a trellis of roses: and on overhearing a plan for a secret marriage at early morn in the village church, resolved to be present.

Chapter II

The next day when we sat together on the old marble seat Bella was very tender with me. I was full of emotion myself, for, now that I was sure that she loved another—vanity is so great in boys that I still held myself to be a rival—I could find it in my heart to be very tender to her. Once or twice I mentioned the name of Mirkenfield's, but when I saw that she held her peace, though the quick blush betrayed her somewhat, I said no more, but waited.

As she said good-night that evening Bella's voice and manner were full of tenderness, and as she lay in her room I heard her more than once sob. That night was like a never-ending nightmare to me, and I sometimes wondered whether it was not all a dream.

It was nearly ten miles to Mirkenfield, so at the earliest glint of dawn I rose, under the impression that I had not slept, and stole downstairs. I heard the clock strike four as I stepped out of the porch, keeping out of sight of Bella's window. As I had not heard Bella stir I took it that she was still asleep. I went into the fields, for I did not want anyone to see me, and at length struck the road beyond the nine clump. There, before me on the road, I saw hurrying along none other than Bella! I slipped into the wood again, and ran and walked as quickly as I could so that I might get well ahead without her seeing me. As I knew the shortcuts I easily effected this object, and within some two and a half hours arrived within sight of Mirkenfield. Then I slipped into the fields and woods again, and came round to the back of the church. Keeping round the corner I saw two men waiting, carefully hidden behind a great clump of yew trees from the sight of any casual stranger passing on the road. One of them was Captain Chudleigh, and the other was the groom whom I had seen with him when he wrote over to Westoby Grange.

Captain Chudleigh had only just arrived, and was making inquiries from the groom. From their secretive manner, however, and the mysterious way they looked round them, I came to the conclusion that there was some mischief on foot, and so I stole softly behind the yew trees and listened. I heard the master say:—

"Is he here?"

"Yes, sir: in the vestry. I was afraid he might be seen and it would not do as he is a stranger."

"Has he all the properties which he requires?"

"Yes, sir; his surplice and bands and the bogus registry book, and all. He is fly one, sir, up to every move on the board. But beg pardon, sir. He says he must have the cash beforehand. He didn't want no credit but the spondoolicks down. Them was his very words."

"Here it is. You share it, I suppose?" and he threw disdainfully to the groom a bag which chinked as the latter caught it.

"There," he said, "take it and be sure you clear out as quick as you can. Remember it is a penal servitude for the pair of you if it should come out afterwards."

"All right, sir. No chance of anything going wrong. No one ever goes into the old church, and it being a church—she—the lady won't have no suspicion. My eye, sir, but he's a clever one at fixing things."

"Take care it is all right. Be here to witness as the clock strikes. In the meantime look after the horses while I go up the road to meet her." Then he murmured again as he had done that night:

"All right! indeed. All wrong! And a nice pack scoundrels we are, with me the biggest of them!"

I began to realize to the full the cruel wrong that was intended, and my mind was made up what I should do. I stole away from the yews, and when I was out of earshot ran up to the parson's house, which was across the graveyard from the church. I rang the bell softly and waited with my heart in my mouth. The door was opened by the parson's *locum tenens*, a tall, powerful, fresh-coloured young man, with a frank eye and a strong, resolute jaw.

I gasped out, "May I see you at once, and privately?" He eyed me for a moment and with a look which began with a smile and ended with a frown, and said, quickly:

"Come in here, my boy!" and threw open the study door, which he shut carefully behind him. "Now," he said, "tell me frankly what it is, and without fear."

I told him who I was and then what I knew and suspected. He interrupted me but once, when he said, angrily:

"The scoundrels, and in the very church, too. Well, we shall see!"
When I had finished he said:

"You have done very wisely in coming to me, and at once. Come with me now, and do not say anything unless I ask you. This is a case when we must both be silent and discrete—for the present at all events." He hurried across the churchyard, walking on the grass so that his footsteps would not sound. I followed him. He opened the vestry door quickly and we went in. As the door opened a man turned round to us, a clean-shaven man, who had on a surplice and bands, and whose face had an evil, crafty look. He grew very pale when he came in, and glanced around hurriedly as for a way of escape. The parson strode forward, and with a wrestler's grip caught him by the throat, and motioning me to open the door took him and pushed him before him right across the churchyard and into his own study. At first the man tried to struggle; but he very soon gave up the idea as he felt how powerless he was in the grasp of the athletic young parson, and he was evidently afraid to cry out. When we were in the study his captor made him sit down, and then said:—

"Now tell me all about it." The fellow threw himself upon his knees and began a confession of how he had been employed to take part in a mock marriage. As he was speaking, the clock on the mantel chimed the quarter to seven, so the parson stopped him:—

"There is no time to lose. I shall tie you up and leave you here for a while. If you try to struggle or cry out I shall at once take you myself to the nearest police-station, and give you in charge. In the meantime I shall see how matters go, and then decide how I shall deal with you." He then got some cord and tied up the fellow most scientifically, gaging him with a gag extemporized from a handkerchief. He then put on his surplice; and, coming out, locked the study door behind him. He called to his housekeeper, and told her to come quietly into the church as the clock struck the hour, and to bring the gardener with her. Then, telling me to come with him, he went back across the churchyard. He told me to remain in the vestry, but to look at the service through the door held partially open, and to remain unseen as long as I could.

Presently I saw Bella and Captain Chudleigh come into the church, followed a little after by the groom, who sat in a corner behind a pillar. Then, but a minute later, there came, unobserved by Bella or Captain Chudleigh, an old man and woman, who I surmised to be the housekeepr and the gardener. When the groom saw them he sheared off a little, so as to keep the pillar between them and himself. The parson stepped out from the vestry. When the groom saw him he started and grew very pale. He half rose as if to move off, but the parson, who had to pass close to him, said:—

"You are a witness, I suppose. Come up close!" And thenceforward he kept an eye on him to see that he did not run away. When the bridal pair stood before the Communion rails the parson said:—

"You have a license from the Bishop, I understand; show it to me." Captain Chudleigh took it from his pocket and handed it to him. He read it through carefully and then asked him:—

"Are you the Hon. Captain Reginald Chudleigh, bachelor, mentioned in this document?"

"I am." Then turning to Bella he asked:

"Are you the Arabella Devanti, spinster, mentioned herein?"
"I am."

Then he proceeded with the marriage service. As there was no one to give away the bride he performed that function himself. As Chudleigh answered "I will" his voice faltered and he grew very, very pale, but Bella's voice was low and clear and fraught with love as she made her acceptance.

When the service was over the parson said a few brief words, hoping that the marriage performed that day might lead to peace here and hereafter, and exhorted the married pair that they should trust each other and be ever true. He finished with a solemn warning that they had that day undertaken a new life, and that whatever wrongs and faults had been should be now forgotten, except to afford them a light and a warning against evils to come. Whilst this short homily was being delivered

Captain Chudleigh looked ill at ease and impatient, and now and again bit his lips; but he controlled himself, and was silent.

Then they came into the vestry, and I hid behind a surplice hanging on the wall. On the table were the great volumes of the registry which the parson had taken from the chest, and in the one of marriages the young parson proceeded to write the new marriage. He had beckoned the two old people to come along with the groom, and said, as he asked them to sign:

"Witnesses are necessary by law, so I have asked these two who were present to add their names." So they both signed, Captain Chudleigh again repressing his impatience. Then the groom and the old people went out, and Captain Chudleigh, who had begun to have an anxious look on his face, turning to Bella, said:

"Will you wait a moment in the church, my dear, whilst I say a word to the clergyman?" Bella smiled at him lovingly, and saying as she shook her finger at him archly, "Don't be long," went out and waited in the church. So soon as she was gone Captain Chudleigh closed the vestry door, and, coming close to the clergyman, said to him in a low voice:—

"Is it all right?"

"Yes; it is all right!" answered the other, with an exceedingly firm, not to say aggressive, manner.

"All is as arranged?"

"All as it should be."

"Then my man will pay you the sum agreed on. He has the money. The books, are they all right?"

"Quite right!" Captain Chudleigh began to move to the door, but he looked ill at ease, and his manner was a hanging dog manner. As he put his hand on the latch to open it the parson spoke:

"Captain Chudleigh!" He turned and raised his eyebrows interrogatively.

"Captain Chudleigh, are you satisfied that you are duly and solemnly married?"

Chudleigh let go the latch and came close as he asked, angrily, in a low voice:

"What the devil do you mean?"

"I mean this," said the other, unconsciously throwing himself into a fighting attitude, for his college days were too recent to be easily forgotten, "that you came here with the intention of committing a foul and dastard wrong to a sweet and innocent woman, and of committing it by the help of the machinery of the Church and the law, and in the very shadow of God's own House. But God be praised! Your wickedness was known in time, and you are now as surely and securely married as can be by the Church's law and the law of the land. Oh, man, have you no shame—no remorse? You are young! You cannot be all hard and bad! It is not too late! You have a sweet and good wife, though in not confiding in her relatives she has run a fearful risk, and for her sake I shall be silent so far as I can. But go down on your knees and thank the Almighty that He has vouchsafed in His mercy to save you from the actual commission of such a grievous sin—though the moral guilt be heavy on you all the same."

For half a minute Captain Chudleigh hung his head, and a dark scowl spread over his face; but then the man in him asserted itself, and with a fierce stamp of his foot, as if he was crushing something evil, he said:

"You are right! I am a black-hearted scoundrel, and unfit to tie the shoe of that sweet woman. But, thank God! it has not been too late. Let me tell you—though I can't expect you to believe me—that I was as miserable over this dastard act as a man could be, and to the last day of my life I shall thank you for having saved her—and me!"

"Do not thank me," said the young clergyman, moved. "Thank Almighty God, and hereafter in your life show by your deeds that you are grateful for so great a mercy. And thank also one other, only for whose quick thought and energy this evil would have been wrought." Chudleigh turned quickly.

"Tell me who it is, so that I may give him thanks."

"You can thank him when he's a man. He is only a boy now."

"Bobby? God bless him!"

"And now, Captain Chudleigh, join your wife; and take my advice—go straight with her to her uncle, and tell him of the marriage. I shall deal with those scoundrels of yours so that they may not try to blackmail you. Your conduct—your later conduct—has made one willing to help you. Send the groom to me presently; and, let me advise you, get rid of him as soon as you can. He is a dangerous man." But Chudleigh would not go at once.

"No!" said he, "I have a duty to my wife; and it had better begin now. I shall have no secrets from her! Let me tell her all, and then, if she will forgive me, we can begin life afresh."

So the parson took me into the graveyard, and we stayed there nearly half an hour, till Bella came and called me in. Her eyes were swollen with crying; but despite it, she looked happy, and Chudleigh's face was also not without its traces of deep emotion. Bella thanked the parson, and held his hand whilst she did so; and then she took me in her arms and kissed me, but said never a word: she knew what I understood. Then the Captain came and held out his hand, and said with a tremor in his voice:

"Won't you shake hands, Bobby? Bella has forgiven me, or I would not dare to ask!" So we shook hands.

Then Bella and her husband drove back to Westoby Puerorum and I walked back as quickly as I could; but they had gone before I arrived, and Mr. and Mrs. Petersen were beginning to realise what had happened.

I suppose the young parson took strong measures with the rascals and frightened them effectually, for they went away and were never troublesome.

And now Bella is a countess, and her husband and children adore her. And on the anniversary of her wedding day she and her husband always send me a bunch of roses from wherever they may be. If there are no roses then they send some other flower that has memories—perhaps lest any of us should forget.

"I lectured him on the danger of coasting down steep hills."

Figure 6.1 Illustration appearing with Bram Stoker's "A Young Widow." (From *The Boston Sunday Herald* [March 26, 1899])

Chapter Six

A YOUNG WIDOW (1899)[1]

BRAM STOKER

When I had dusted the little boy down and he had grown calm after his fright, I lectured him on the dangers of coasting down steep hills, until at all events he had acquired some mastery of the bicycle. He seemed duly penitent, and acknowledged in his boyish way that if I had not ridden after him and steered him he might have been killed. He was still tearful when he stammered out:

"I wish my mother could have thanked you!"

"Never mind, my boy!" I said; "you don't say anything; unless you tell your father."

"Can't," he said, as his tears burst out afresh: "Father's dead years ago."

I said no more, but left him at the house which he pointed out as that in which he lived. He told me that his name was Robbie Harcourt, and he hoped he would see me again. "Why don't you call?" he added, as he ran up the steps.

As I rode home I thought to myself that the mother of such a pretty boy must be a sweet creature. A widow, too. I noted mentally. Young widowhood is always more or less a pleasing thought to a bachelor, especially when, like myself, he is beginning to notice his hair thinning on the top. I told Robbie where I lived, so I was not altogether surprised when next day I got a letter in a lady's hand signed "Ada Harcourt," thanking me for what she deemed the great service I had rendered her and all her family. That letter, even after I had answered it, somehow impressed me, and every morning for a week, as I shaved myself and noticed the thin place "on top," my thoughts reverted to it. I always ended by taking it from my pocket and spreading it on the dressing table in front of me.

Then I took my courage in both hands and called at Woodbine Villa. The short time which elapsed between my knock, which began boldly and ended timidly, and the opening of the door was such as I am told drowning men experience—filled with a countless multitude of embarrassing memories. The trim maid who opened the door looked a little surprised when I asked if Mrs. Harcourt was at home; but with an apologetic "Pardon me a moment, sir," darted away, leaving the door open. She came down stairs again more slowly, and, in a somewhat embarrassed, giggling way, asked me to please come in. "My mistress, sir," she said, "will be down in a few minutes, if you will kindly wait!"

I entered the pleasant drawing room and tried, in the helpless way of embarrassed visitors, to gain some knowledge of my hosts by their surroundings.

Everything was pretty; but the faces of all the pictures and photographs were strange, so that it was as with recognition of an old friend that I came across a photograph of Robbie, evidently done some two or three years before.

I was ill at ease, for manifestly my coming had in some way disturbed the household. Overhead there was rushing about to and fro, and the sound of drawers opening and shutting, and of doors banging. I thought I could hear somewhere afar off the voice of my friend Robbie, but in a

different and lighter vein than when I had listened to his tearful promises of amendment. Then I became gravely anxious; a full sense of my
impropriety in calling pressed upon me, for light steps drew near the
door. Then there entered the room the most beautiful young woman I
thought I had ever seen. Her youth, her dancing eyes, her pink cheeks
suffused with blushes, and the full lips showing scarlet against her white
teeth, seemed to shine through the deep widow's weeds which she wore
as a ray of sunshine gleams through a fog. Indeed, the simile was multiplied as the gleam of golden hair seemed to make the "weeded" cap a
solemn mockery. She advanced impulsively and shook me warmly by
the hand, as with very genuine feeling she thanked me for my heroic
rescue of her "dear Bobbie." At first she seemed somewhat surprised at
my appearance, and, seeing with a woman's instinct that I noticed it,
said frankly:

"How young you are! Why, from what Bobbie told me, I thought you
were an old—a much older man!" The thin space seemed to become
conscious, as though a wave of either heat or cold had passed over it,
and as I somehow seemed to recognize in the fair widow an "understanding" soul, I bent my head so that she could see the telltale place
as I remarked:
"To children we grown-ups seem often older than even we are!"

In a demure way, and in a veiled, not to say smothered, voice she
answered: "Ah, yes, that is so. To us who have known sorrow time passes
more quickly than to their light-hearted innocence! Alas! alas!" She stopped
suddenly, and, putting her deeply edged handkerchief to her face, gasped
out: "Pardon me, I shall return in a moment," and left the room hurriedly.
I felt more than uncomfortable. I had evidently touched on some tender
chord of memory, though what I could not guess. All I could do was to
wait till she returned and then take myself off as soon as possible.

There was some talking and whispering on the stairs outside. I could
not hear the words spoken, for the door was shut, but suddenly it opened,
and Bobbie, red-faced and awkward, shot into the room. He was a very
different boy now. There were no tears, no sadness, no contrition. He

was a veritable mass of fun, full of laughter and schoolboy mirth. As he shook hands with me he said:

"I hope mother has thanked you properly!" and turned away and stamped with some kind of suppressed feeling. The ways of boys are hard to understand.

When Mrs. Harcourt returned, which she did very shortly, now quite composed, and looking more beautiful and more charming than ever, Bobbie slipped away. There was somehow a greater constraint about his mother. Some impalpable veil seemed to be between us; she was as if more distant from me. I recognized its import, and shortly made my adieux. As she bade me good-by she said that we might perhaps never meet again, as she was shortly going to take the boy abroad; but that she rejoiced that it had been her privilege to meet face to face his brave preserver. She used more of such phrases, which for days after seemed to hang in my memory like sweet music. The maid, when she let me out, seemed sympathetic and deferential, but there was in her manner a concealed levity which somehow grated on me.

For the next fortnight I tried to keep Mrs. Harcourt out of my thoughts, with the usual result. You can't serve ejectments on thoughts! They are tenants at will, their own will, and the only effect of struggling with them is that they banish everything else, and keep the whole field to themselves. Working or playing, waking or sleeping, walking, riding or sitting still, the sweet, beautiful eyes of Mrs. Harcourt were ever upon me, and her voice seemed to sound in my ears.

I found that my bicycle carried me, seemingly of its own will, past her door on every occasion when I had to use a lamp. Seeing at last that her intention of foreign travel had not been carried out, I ventured one day, in an agony of perturbation, to call again.

When I was opposite the house I thought I saw in the window the back of Ada's head— I had come to think of her as "Ada" now. I was, therefore, somewhat surprised when, after some delay, the maid, with a demure face, told me that Mrs. Harcourt was not at home. I felt almost inclined to argue the matter with the maid, who was now giggling as on the former occasion, when suddenly Bobbie came running out of the back hall and called to me:

"Oh, Mr. Denison, won't you come in? Ma is here and will be delighted to see you!" He threw open the door of the drawingroom, which was the first room on the ground floor, and ushered me in, turning round and grinning at me as he said:

"Ma, here is Mr. Denison come to see you. Excuse me coming in!" With that he went out, shutting the door behind him.

I think she was as much startled and amazed as I was, as she stood facing me with her cheeeks [*sic*] a flaming red. She had discarded her widows' weeds, and was now in a simple gray frock, with pink bows at neck and waist, which made her look years younger than even she had done before; her beautiful golden hair was uncovered. As I advanced, which I did with warmth, for it seemed to me somehow that the discarding of the widow's dress opened up new possibilities to herself, she bowed somewhat coldly. She did not, however, refuse to shake hands, though she did so timidly. I felt awkward and ill at ease; things were not somehow going as smoothly as I wished, and the very passion that filled me made its repression a difficulty. I couldn't remember a single thing which either of us said at that interview; I only recollect taking up my hat and moving off with mingled chagrin and diffidence. When I was near the door she came impulsively after me, and taking me by the hand, said:

"This is goodby, indeed, as I shall not be able to see you again. You will understand, will you not?" Her words puzzled me; but she had made me a request, and such, though it entailed denial of my own wishes, could only be answered in one way. I put my hand to my heart and bowed.

As I walked away, all the world seemed a blank space, and myself a helpless atom whirling in it alone.

That night I thought of nothing but Mrs. Harcourt, and with the gray of the dawn my mind was made up. I would see her again, for I feared she would leave without even knowing my feelings toward her. I got up and wrote her a letter, saying that I would do myself the honor of calling that afternoon, and that I trusted she would see me, as I had something very important to say. When I retired to bed after posting the letter I fell asleep and went on dreaming of her, and my dreams were heavenly.

When I knocked at the door in the afternoon the maid looked all demure, and showed me, without a word, into the drawing room. Almost immediately following her exit Mrs. Harcourt came in. My heart rejoiced when I saw that she was dressed as on the previous day. She shook hands with me and gravely sat down. When I had sat also, she said:

"You wanted to say something to me?"

"Yes," I answered quickly, for the fervor in me was beginning to speak. "I want to tell you that—" With a gesture she stopped me:

"One moment! Before you say anything, let me tell you something. I have a shameful confession to make. In a foolish moment I thought to play a joke, never thinking that it might reflect on my dear dead mother. Bobbie is not my son; he is my only brother, who has been my care since my mother died, years ago. When he told me of the brave way you saved him, and when the kind letter you sent in answer to mine showed me you had mistaken our relationship, Bobbie and I laughed over it together, and I said what a lark it would be to pretend, if occasion served, to be his mother. Then you called, and the spirit of mischief moved me to a most unseemly joke. I dressed up in mother's clothes, and tried to pass myself off as Bobbie's mother. When I had seen you and recognized your kindness, I seemed in all ways a brute; but all I could do was to try that it might go on no more. Oh, if you only knew!" She put her pretty hands before her face, and I saw the tears drop through them. That pained me, but it gave me heart. Coming close to her, I took her hands and pulled them away, and looked in her brave eyes as I said:

"Oh, let me speak! I must! I must! I came here today to ask you to—. Won't you let Bobbie be my brother, too?"

And he is.

"Won't you let Bobbie be my brother, too?"

Figure 6.2 Illustration appearing with Bram Stoker's "A Young Widow."
(From *The Boston Sunday Herald* [March 26, 1899])

WHERE'S IT'S MOTHER, ANYHOW?

Figure 7.1 Illustration appearing with the American editions of Bram Stoker's "A Baby Passenger."

(From *Daily Iowa State Press* 1, no. 175 [April 26, 1899])

Chapter Seven

A BABY PASSENGER (1899)[1]

BRAM STOKER

One night we were journeying in the west of the Rockies over a road
bed which threatened to jerk out our teeth with every loosely-laid
sleeper on the line.

Traveling in that part of the world, certainly in the days I speak of,
was pretty hard. The travelers were mostly men, all overworked, all over-
anxious, and intolerant of anything which hindered their work or interfered with the measure of their repose. In night journeys the berths in the
sleeping cars were made up early, and as all the night trains were sleeping
cars, the only thing to be done was to turn in at once and try and sleep
away the time. As most of the men were usually tired out with the day's
work, the arrangement suited everybody. You can understand that on
such journeys women and children were disturbing elements. Fortunately
they were, as night travelers, rare, and the women, with that consideration
for the needs of their men folk which I have always noticed in American
female workers, used to devote themselves to keeping little ones quiet.

The weather was harsh, and sneezing and coughing was the order of the day. This made the people in the sleeper, all men, irritable: all the more that as most of them were contributing to the general chorus of sounds coming muffled through quilts and curtains, it was impossible to single out any special offender for general execration. After awhile, however, the change of posture from standing or sitting to lying down began to have some kind of soothing effect, and new sounds of occasional snoring began to vary the monotony of irritation. Presently the train stopped at a way station: then ensued a prolonged spell of shunting backward and forward with the uncertainty of jerkiness which is so peculiarly disturbing to imperfect sleep; and then two newcomers entered the sleeper, a man and a baby. The baby was young, quite young enough to be defiantly ignorant and intolerant of all rules and regulations regarding the common good. It played for its own hand alone, and as it was extremely angry and gifted with exceptionally powerful lungs, the fact of its presence and its emotional condition, even though the latter afforded a mystery as to its cause, were immediately apparent. The snoring ceased, and its place was taken by muttered grunts and growls; the coughing seemed to increase with the renewed irritation, and everywhere was the rustling of ill-at-ease and impotent humanity. Curtains were pulled angrily aside, the rings shrieking viciously on the brass rods and gleaming eyes and hardening mouths glared savagely at the intruder on our quiet, for so we now had tardily come to consider by comparison him and it. The newcomer did not seem to take the least notice of anything, and went on in a stolid way trying to quiet the child, shifting it from one arm to the other, dandling it up and down, and rocking it sideways.

All babies are malignant; the natural wickedness of man, as elaborated at the primeval curse, seems to find an unadulterated effect in their expressions of feeling.

The baby was a peculiarly fine specimen of its class. It seemed to have no compunction whatever, no parental respect, no natural affection, no mitigation in the natural virulence of its rancor. It screamed, it roared, it squalled, it bellowed. The root ideas of profanity, of obscenity, of blasphemy were mingled in its tone. It beat with clenched fist its father's face, it clawed at his eyes with twitching fingers, it used its head as an engine with which to buffet him. It kicked, it struggled, it wriggled, it writhed, it twisted itself into serpentine convolutions, till every now and then, what with its vocal and muscular exertions, it threatened to get black in the face. All the time the stolid father simply tried to keep it quiet with eternal changes of posture and with whispered words, "There, now, pet!" "Hush; lie still, little one." "Rest, dear one, rest!" He was a big, lanky, patient-looking, angular man with great rough hands and enormous feet, which he shifted about as he spoke; so that man and child together seemed eternally restless.

The thing appeared to have a sort of fascination for most of the men in the car. The curtains of a lot of berths were opened, and a lot of heads appeared, all scowling. I chuckled softly to myself, and tried to conceal my merriment, lest I should spoil the fun. No one said anything for a long time, till at last one wild-eyed, swarthy, long-bearded individual, who somehow looked like a Mormon Elder, said:

"Say, master, what kind of howling piece is it you've got there? Have none of you boys got a gun?"

There came from the bunks a regular chorus of acquiescence: "The durned thing had ought to be killed!"

"Beats prairie dogs in full moon!"

"When I woke up with it howlin' thought I had got 'em again."

"Never mind, boys, it may be a blessin' in disguise. Somethin' bad is comin' to us on this trip, an' arter this 'twill be easy work to die!"

The man spoke up:

"I'm sorry, gentlemen, if she incommodes you!" The words were so manifestly inadequate that there was a roar of laughter which seemed to shake the car. West of the Mississippi things are, or at any rate they used to be, a bit rough, and ideas followed suit. Laughter, when it came, was rough and coarse; and on this occasion even the lanky man seemed to feel it. He only tried to hold the child closer to him, as if to shield it from the hail of ironical chaff which followed.

"Incommode us! Oh, not at all. It's the most soothing concourse of sweet sounds I ever heard."

"Bully for baby syrups!"

"Pray, don't let us disturb the concert with our sleeping."

"Jerk us out a little more chin-music!"

"There is no place like home with a baby in it."

"Just opposite where the man moved restlessly with the child was the bunk of a young giant whom I had noticed turning in earlier in the evening. He had not seemed to have noticed the disturbance, but now his curtains were thrust aside fiercely and he appeared lifted on one elbow as he asked in an angry tone:

"Say you, where's its mother, anyhow?" The man replied in a low, weary tone, without looking round:

"She's in the baggage car, sir—in her coffin!"

Well, you could have heard the silence that came over all the men. The baby's screaming and the rush, and roar, and rattle of the train seemed unnatural breakers of the profound stillness. In an instant the young man, clad only in his under-flannels, was out on the floor and close to the man.

"Say, stranger," he said, "if I'd knowed that, I'd a bit my tongue out afore I'd a spoke! An' now I look at you, my poor fellow, I see you're most wore out! Here, give me the child, and you turn into my bunk an' rest. No! you needn't be afeered"—for he saw the father shrink away a little and hold the child closer. "I'm one of a big family an' I've nursed the baby often. Give her over; I'll take care of her, an' I'll talk to the conductor, and we'll see that you're called when the time comes." He put out his great hands and lifted the little one, the father resigning her to his care without a word. He held her in one arm whilst with the other he helped the newcomer into his empty berth.

Strange to say, the child made no more struggle. It may have been that the young blood or the young flesh gave something of the warmth and softness of the mother's breast which it missed, or that the fresh, young nerves soothed where the worn nerves of the sorrowing man had only irritated; but, with a peaceful sigh, the little one leaned over, let its head fall on the young man's shoulder, and seemingly in an instant was fast asleep.

And all night long, up and down, up and down, in his stocking feet, softly marched the flannel-clad young giant, with the baby asleep on his breast, whilst in his bunk the tired, sorrow-stricken father slept—and forgot. And somehow I thought that, though the mother's body may have been in the baggage car at the other end of the train, her soul was not far away.

Figure 8.1 Photograph of "Mr. Bram Stoker" (*ca.* 1905)

(From *The Bystander* 8, no. 96 [October 1905]: 37)

Chapter Eight

LUCKY ESCAPES OF
SIR HENRY IRVING
(1900)[1]

BRAM STOKER

"People have asked me whether anything happened to the play or players during Sir Henry Irving's present tour of this country. To such inquiries I have been obliged to reply in the negative. When I am asked whether anything could have happened there is a different story to tell. Many things might have happened and the possible results might have been fatal," said Manager Bram Stoker yesterday, as thus:

In Kansas City we all stood in the mammoth convention hall speculating upon the proceedings of the party scheduled to meet there. We wondered how their business would be transacted, as we have nothing analogous to it on the other side, you know. As we were walking about admiring the huge structure we were startled by the cry of fire. We rushed toward the entrance way. The smoke blinded us and blocked us in our flight. A voice called: "This way. This way." We hurried in the direction from which it sounded. There was a knocking on a side door, which was shortly opened, but not until we were nearly suffocated with the fierce heat and smoke. As we crowded our way from the building we were followed by a volume of flame and the smoke rolled about us in great clouds. Within the next few minutes the massive iron beams and braces at which we had been looking began to come down with a mighty crash as they fell section by section, curling and twisting like corkscrews. The walls fell, and the building was a wreck.

Had we been there at the time of the fire and had we been delayed in getting out something even worse than I have described might have happened, you see.

★   ★   ★

"We were crossing the Missouri river one night. It was during flood time. The structure shook as does a tram car as it passes over a rough crossing. You have doubtless experienced that jarring feeling which occurs at such a time.

"We went ahead. The bridge began to sway and sink toward the river. The engineer threw on all steam. Ours was the last carriage. We feil [*sic*] the rear portion of it drop and dip into the water. One more pull and a tug by the locomotive ahead of us and we were finally landed on terra firma.

"Now, really something serious might have happened had we crossed the river under such circumstances and had our carriage broken away from the balance of the train and been precipitated into the river.

"At another point on our journey we crossed a low trestle work over a stream much swollen by recent storms. The water was pouring over it four feet above the rails. Nobody knew if all the bridgework was standing or not. The engineer went ahead, however, slowly and cautiously at first and then at greater speed. Suddenly we felt a strain and then a shock. The engine had dropped into the river, dragging with it the first carriage, which was a baggage wagon. The engineer and firemen were drowned. The peculiar predicament in which we were placed was rapidly becoming fraught with new dangers when a scow came along down the river. We boarded it and were saved. We had just left the carriages when the trestlework collapsed and the train disappeared in the river.

"We might have all been lost if things had happened just that way and the scow had not happened by just in time.

★ ★ ★

"While we were in Indianapolis the soldiers' monument was visited. Two members thought they could get a better view of the surroundings by climbing out on a horizontal flagstaff. This they did. A sudden puff of wind, aided by the added weight of the pole, caused it to break with a snapping sound. They were carted away in wheelbarrows—what was left of them.

"Now, if things had been just that way when we visited the soldiers' monument you see something of the kind really might have happened to us.

"In the Washington monument we went up in the lift to a height of almost 500 feet. We gained a charming view of the beautiful capital city and the green fields of Virginia, not so very far away. In leaving we all got into the lift together. The car man started us on our downward trip. We descended slowly at first for a distance of about forty feet, when the great rope broke and down we went in a flash, to strike upon the hard concrete floor at the bottom of the shaft. When we were taken out there was not a whole bone left in any of our bodies.

"That might have happened on our trip to the top of Washington monument, had the elevator collapsed, and it might have done so, you know.

"When we landed in New York our company of seventy people was obliged to walk up town, because all the vehicles usually available were in service in the Dewey parade. Each member was obliged to carry his or her gripsack and hat cases. We had proceeded but a short distance when we were met by a seething crowd running to view the parade from a point not yet passed. We were caught in the mad crush, and twenty-two of our number were trampled to death. Their open and dismantled gripsacks, with the contents strewn about, presented a unique and interesting study in economy.

"All this might possibly have happened had we not landed some days before the parade and had we been caught in such a crowd. You might say, you know, that the members of the company, bearing this quasi episode in mind, are exceedingly pleased they are leaving Chicago before the Dewey day parade.

★   ★   ★

"In one of the Western states, the name of which for obvious reasons I will not mention, some of the dispersed members of disrupted gangs of train robbers gathered together. In a lonely spot the train slackened. A few shots were fired at the forward end, when suddenly a masked man, wearing a rakish black slouch hat and armed with a Winchester, appeared at each door of our carriage. It was hands up right away. They took all our valuables away from us. From the women they took such trinkets and articles of value as they could find. Two men resisted and were instantly killed.

"In some way or other it had become rumors about that millions of dollars we had collected in this country were carried with us, all in gold coin. This was what prompted the robbery. The only safe aboard was the regular traveling box in the express wagon. The express messenger was shot and killed, as were the engineer and fireman. Jesse James and his companions drew the strong box from its place and burst it open with a charge of dynamite. They found only a small sum of money. Jumping on their horses, they rode away into the darkness.

"This didn't happen at all, but it might have if Jesse James was not dead and the bands of train robbers broken up and scattered about the country, no longer following their old-time calling.

"One evening at a most important part of the play and on the last night of the stand one of the players fell on stage, stricken with heart disease. He died immediately, without recovering consciousness. The affair was so dramatic and depressing the curtain was rung down and the audience dismissed. We could not repeat the performance in that city, and it was altogether a sad and serious event.

"None of our players were suffering from heart disease, but if one had been how easy it would be for such a thing to occur.

★   ★   ★

"In a certain city one of the players stopped at a cheap hotel. Part of the food furnished consisted of canned stuff. It was unwholesome, and he was poisoned by ptomaines and died. However, none of our players stopped at cheap hotels, and none were poisoned.

★   ★   ★

"One day a member of the company was sitting in a hotel window smoking. An old man, quite shabbily dressed, passed him by several times, scrutinizing him closely. He came into the hotel office and asked if the man's name was this or that, repeating his real cognomen. He received an affirmative answer and insisted upon seeing the player. The latter claimed that the old man, who bore every evidence of being a tramp, was not known to him. The old fellow grew so persistent that the proprietor called a porter to eject him. In the scuffle which ensued the porter was a little rougher than he anticipated and the old fellow fell to the floor. His injuries were of such serious nature that he was carried away to a hospital. The next day, just before he died, he said the player was a long lost son for whom he had searched for years, and he left him a fortune of $2,000,000. When this news was circulated in the profession he received within a month over a hundred offers of marriage from ladies.

"Such a thing might have happened had some old duffer thought he recognized in one of the players his heir from who he had been so long separated. Why, there are no end of romances possible.

"The progress of the war in South Africa is bringing about so many changes in the nobility that the death of a British general, as announced by the papers one morning, permitted one of the players to awake and find himself in possession of a dukedom and an enormous fortune.

"Had there been a ducal general killed with an heir in our company we might have had a duke numbered among our galaxy of stars. However, fortunately or unfortunately, Dame Fortune thus far has not permitted us to carry a duke with the company."

Chapter Nine

WHAT THEY CONFESSED: A LOW COMEDIAN'S STORY (1908)[1]

BRAM STOKER

Chapter I: A "Wash Out"

Just about Christmas time of a year in the "nineties" a British theatrical company was traveling in a special train between New Orleans and Memphis. As sometimes happens in the Southern States of America, and especially in the region of the Mississippi, one branch of the Northern line had met with what the railway engineers call a "wash-out," and the train had to go on the western section of the line, by Vicksburg.

A score or so of miles below the latter town the line had to cross a broad valley through which a river passed westward to flow into the Mississippi. A great flood was out, and the Bayou—the local name for such a valley—was flooded. Here the line is carried across on a trestle bridge of perhaps a couple of miles in length. The flood was so great that the water had risen some three or four feet over the top of the low-lying bridge. It was undoubtedly a ticklish passage, for no one could say whether or no the structure of the bridge was intact.

Little wonder, then, that many members of the "troupe" were frightened, and that as the train forged out farther and farther into the wide expanse of flowing water, and as the southern shore became more and more dim, the last dregs of their courage became merged in the growing feeling of panic. Some of them so lost their heads that they began to openly make confession of the sins of their lifetime—a strange experience to their listening companions.

A few years afterwards one of the latter—then the Second Low Comedian of another theatrical company—related the incident to his new companions during the course of another journey under far different conditions.

"It was only when we were actually in the water that any of them began to concern themselves. Indeed, at first no one seemed to mind, for we had often before made a dash over a flooded stream. But when the speed slackened and the rush of the wheels in the water made a new sort of sound they all ran to the windows and looked out. Some of the festive spirits thought it a good opportunity to frighten the girls, and put up a joke on the more timid of the men. It didn't seem a difficult job so far as some of them were concerned, for the surprise was rapidly becoming terror.

"Everything seemed to lend itself to the presiding influence; the yellow water seeming to go two ways at once as it flowed past us and as we crossed its course; the horrible churning of our wheels which seemed to come up from under us through the now opened windows; the snorting and panting of the engine; the looks of fear and horror growing on the blanching faces around; all seemed to culminate towards hysteria.

"The most larky of the men was young Gatacre, who was the understudy for Huntley Vavassour, then our leading juvenile. He pretended to be terribly afraid and cowered down and hid his face and groaned, all the time winking at some of us. But presently, as the waste of water

grew wider and wider, his glances out of the window became more anxious, and I could see his lips grow white. All at once he became ghastly
pale, and, throwing up his hands, broke out into a positive wail of terror
and began to pray in a most groveling manner—there is no other way to
describe it. To some of us it was revolting, and we should have liked to
kick him: but its effect on the girls was dreadful. All the hysteria of panic,
which had been coming on, broke out at once, and within half a minute
the place was like the Stool-of-Repentance corner at a Revival meeting.

"With this exception I am glad to say that there was a goodly per-
centage of sensible people who kept their own heads and tried, for very
shame's sake, to make their friends keep theirs.

"It seems to me that really good women are never finer than when they
are helping a weak sister. I mean really helping, when it isn't altogether
pleasant work; I don't count it help to a woman lashing out wastefully
with other people's Eau de Cologne and ostentatiously loosening her
stays, and then turning to the menkind, who are looking on helplessly,
with a "phew!" as if they knew what was wrong with her all the time. We
all know how *our* women help each other, for we are all comrades, and
the girls are the best of us.

"But on this occasion the womenkind were a bit panicky, and even
those who kept their heads and tried to shield the others from the effects
of their hysterical abandon were pale and rocky themselves, and kept one
eye on the yellow flood running away under us.

"I certainly never did hear such a giving away as in the confessions of
some of them, and I tell you that it wasn't pleasant to listen to. It made
some of us men angry and humiliated to think that we could be so helpless. We took some of the girls and tried to actually shake them back into
reason; but, Lord bless you! it wasn't the least use. The more we shook
the more we shook out of them things which were better left unsaid. It
almost seemed as if confession was a pebbly sort of thing that could be
jerked out of one like corn out of a nosebag.

"The whole thing was so infernally sudden that one had no time
to think. One moment we were all composed and jolly, and the next
there were these poor women babbling out the most distressing and

heartrending things, and we quite unable to stop them. The funny thing, as it seems to me now, was that it never occurred to any of us to shove off and leave them alone! Anyhow we didn't go—at all events, till the fat was in the fire. Fortunately the poor girls didn't have much to confess that seemed very wrong to most of us."

"Did none of the men confess anything?" asked the Singing Chambermaid. There was in the tone of her voice that underlying tone of militant defiance which is always evident when the subject of woman in the abstract is mentioned in mixed company. The Second Low Comedian smiled as he replied:

Certainly, my dear! I thought you understood that I was speaking of the young ladies of both sexes. You remember that the first—in fact, the one to set them off—was an alleged man.

"Well, these things, you see, made the painful side of the incident, for it is not pleasant to hear anyone say things which you know they will grieve for bitterly afterwards. But there was another side which was both interesting and amusing—the way in which the varieties of character came out in the confessions, and the manner of their coming. If we hadn't known already—I speak for myself—we should have been able to differentiate the weaknesses of the various parties, and to have got a knowledge of the class of things which they fondly hoped they had kept hidden. I suppose it is such times that reveal us to ourselves; or would do so if we had grace to avail ourselves of our opportunities. Anyhow, the dominant note of each personality was struck in so marked a way that the scene became a sort of character garden with living flowers!"

When the applause which followed his poetic "tag" had ceased there was a chorus of indignant disappointment:

"Is that all?"

"Why stop, just as it was getting interesting?"

"Just fancy, with material like that, to fade out in vague generalities."

"Can't you tell us some of the things they said?"

"What's the use of telling us of confessions when you keep it dark what they were?"

"Was there anything so very compromising, to you or to anybody else, that you should hesitate?"

"'That's just it,' said the Second Low Comedian, with a grin. "If there were anything compromising I would tell it with pleasure, especially, I need not say, if it concerned myself. But of all the confessions that were ever written or spoken, I suppose there never were any as little compromising as on this occasion. There was hardly anything which would injure the character of a sergeant in the Archangelic police force. Of course, I except the young man who began the racket. There was not one of those who 'confessed' who did not compromise himself or herself. But the subjects were so odd! I didn't know there were so many sinless, wickednesses in the whole range of evil!"

"What on earth do you mean?" said the Leading Lady, with wide-open eyes of stage amazement. "Do give us some examples, so that we may be able to follow you!"

"Ah! I thought that was what you wanted!" he answered with a wink. "You would like to hear the confessions, good or bad, or rather bad or worse, and judge for yourself as to their barometric wickedness. All right! I will tell you all I remember.

Chapter II: The Leading Lady and the Juvenile

"There was our Leading Lady, I mention no names, who had been on the stage to my own knowledge twenty-eight years, and she was in the second lead when I met her first at Halifax in 'Wibster's Folly,' which was a popular stock piece on the Yorkshire circuit."

"She confessed to having deceived, not only the public but her friends, even her dear friends, of the company and would like to put herself right with them all, and have their forgiveness ere she died.

"Her sin was one of vanity, for she had deceived them as to her age. She had acknowledged to twenty-nine; but now in her last hour, with the death drops on her brow, and the chill of the raging flood already striking into her very soul, she would confess. They knew how hard it was for a woman to be true when dealing with her age; women at least would understand her; she would confess that she was really thirty-three.

"Then she sank down on her knees in a picturesque position, which she had often told her friends she made famous in 'East Lynne,' and held up her hands and implored their forgiveness.

"Do you know that nearly all those present were so touched by her extraordinary self-sacrifice in that trying moment that they turned away and hid their faces in their hands. I could myself see the shoulders of some of them shake with emotion.

"Well, her example was infectious, she was hardly on her knees when our Juvenile Lead took up the running. With a heart-breaking, bitter sob, such as adorned his performance in 'Azrael, the Prodigal,' he held his hands aloft with the fingers interlaced, and looking up to the gallery—I mean the roof, or the sky, or whatever he saw above him with either his outer or his inner eye—he mourned his malingering in the way of pride.

"He had been filled with ungodly pride, when during his very first engagement, having been promoted through sheer merit—having swept, if he might say so, upward like a rocket through the minor ranks of the profession—he had emerged in sober splendor amongst the local altitudes.

"Oh! even that fact had not bounded his excesses of pride. That evil quality, which like jealousy 'mocked the meat it feeds on,' had grown with the enlarging successes which seemed to whirl upon him like giant snowflakes from the empyrean. When the 'Mid-Mudland Anti-Baptist Scrutinizer' had spoken of him as 'the rising histrionic genius, who was destined to lift from the shrouded face of Melpomene the seemingly ineradicable shadow which the artistic incompetence of a re-puritanised age had thrown upon it,' he had felt elated with the thought that on his shoulder rested the weight of the Banner of Art, which it would be his duty as well as his pride to carry amongst the nations, and unfurl even before the eyes of their kings.

"Ah! but that was not his worst sin; for with the years that had carried the greatness of his stormy youth into the splendor of his prime young manhood had grown an ever-increasing pride in what he knew from the adoring looks of women and their passionate expressions of endearment, both written and verbal, was the divine gift of physical beauty and perfection. In which gift was included the voice at once sweet and powerful, which evoked that enthusiastic tribute from the 'Bootie Local Government Questioner,' wherein occurred the remarkable passage: 'It is rare, if not unique, to find in the tones of a human voice, centred in no matter how perfect a physical entourage, at once the subtlety of the lyre, the great epigrammatic precision of the ophleclide and the resonant drum-sounding thunder of the clarion and the bassoon.'"

"So, too, were included a bearing of grace and nobility which 'recalled,' as the Midland, humoristic organ, 'The Pushful Joe,' remarked. 'The worth of the youthful Emperor Gluteus Maximus.'

"Oh! these things were indeed sources of a pride which was at best a weakness of poor humanity. Still, it should be held in check; and this in proportion to its natural strength.

"'Mea culpa! Mea culpa' he said in that tone with which he used to thrill the house in 'Don Alzavar, the Penitent; or, the Monk of Madrid.' He went on further, for pride seemed to have no limit, but essayed when fixed in daring and lofty natures to scale the very bastions of Olympus.

"He was proud—oh, so proud!—that in this dread moment when he stood hand in hand with his fell brother Death, he could see its earthly littleness. It was when depicting the roles in which he had won his greatest fame, he had, with the best and purest intention, he assured us, dared the blue ribbon of histrionic achievement in essaying the part of 'Hamlet' in the Ladbroke Hall. He had found his justification of Metropolitan endeavour in the striking words of the 'Westbourne-grove and Neighbouring Parishes' Chronicle of Striking Events,' 'The triumph of our youngest "Hamlet" is as marked as the many successes in less ambitious walks of histrionic renown!' "

"He was interrupted by our First Low Comedy Merchant, who said:

" 'Time, old man! There are others who want a chance of public confession whilst death still stares us in the face.' He was followed by our Heavy Man, who added:

" 'It's a good idea, as well as a new one, to confess your notices. Anyhow, it makes a variety from having to pretend to read them every time you strike a man for a drink.' The Leading Juvenile glared at his interrupters, in the manner which he was used to assume as Geoffrey Plantagenet in 'The Baffled Usurper.' He was about to loose the vials of his wrath upon them when our First Singing Chambermaid, who had been furtively preparing for her effort by letting down her back hair, flung herself upon her knees with a piercing shriek, and, holding up her hands invocatively after the manner of 'The Maiden's Prayer,' cried out, interrupting herself all the while with muttered sobs of choking anguish:

" 'Oh, ye Powers, to whom is given the priceless guardianship of maiden life, look down in forgiving pity upon the delinquencies of one who, though without evil purpose but in the guilelessness of her innocent youth and with the surpassing cruelty of the young and thoughtless, hath borne hard upon the passionate but honourable love of dukes and marquises! Peccavi! Peccavi!! Peccavi!!!' with which final utterance she fell fainting upon her face and struggled convulsively; till, seeing that no one flew to her assistance, she lay still a moment and then ignominiously rose to her feet and retired, outwardly sobbing and inwardly scowling, to her section.

Chapter III: A Dual Effort

"Hardly, however, had she spoken her tag when two aspirants for Confessional honours sought to 'catch the Speaker's eye.'

"One of them was the Understudy of the last confessor; the other the First Old Woman.

"They were something of an age and appearance, being on the shady side of something and stout in proportion. They both had deep voices, and as neither would at first give way their confessions were decidedly clamourous and tangled, but full of divine possibilities of remorse. They both had flung themselves on their knees, right and left, like the kneeling figures beside an Elizabethan tomb. We all stood by, with admiring sympathy manifested in our choking inspirations and on our broadening smiles.

"It was a pretty fair struggle.

"The First Old Woman was fighting for her position, and that is a strong stimulus to effort; the other was endeavouring to win a new height in her Olympian ambition, and that is also a strong stimulus to endeavour. They both talked so loud and so fast that none of us could follow a word that either of them said. But neither would give way, till our Tragedian, beginning to despair of an opening for his confession, drew a deep breath and let us have it after the manner of his celebrated impersonation of the title-role of 'Manfred' in the alpine storm. In which you will remember that he has to speak against the thunder, the bassoon, the wind, and the rain, not to mention the avalanches, though he generally makes a break for them to pass.

"The women held out as long as they could, and finally, feeling worsted by the Tragedian's thunder, they joined against the common enemy and shrieked hysterically in unison as long as their breath held out.

"Our Tragedian's confession was immense. I wish I could remember it word for word as he gave it, with long dwelling on his pet words and crashing out his own particular consonants. We were all silent, for we wanted to remember for after use what he said. Being a tragedian he began, of course, with Jove:

"'Thou Mighty One, who sittest on the cloud-capped heights of Olympus and regardeth the spectral figure of the mighty Hyster seated in his shadowy cart, deign to hear the murmurings of a heart whose mightiest utterances have embodied the noblest language of the chiefest bards. Listen, Oh Son of Saturn; Oh, Husband of Juno; Oh, Father of

Thalia and Melpomene; Oh, Brother of Neptune and Pluto; Oh, Lover of Leda and Semele and Dance, and of all the galaxy of celestial beauties who crowned with love the many-sided proclivities of thou most multitudinous-hearted God! Hear the sad wail of one who has devoted himself to the Art of Roscius! Listen to the voice that has been wont to speak in thunderous tones to the ears of a wondering world, now stilled to the plaintive utterance of deepening regret. Hear me mourn the lost opportunities of a not-unsuccessful life! When I think that I have had at my foot the ball of success, and in my sublime indifference spurned it from me as a thing of little worth, well-knowing that in all the years, genius such as mine must ever command the plaudits of an enraptured world, what can *I* say, or how announce the magnitude, or even the name, of my sin? Hear me, then, oh, mighty Jove—'

"Just then the dull threshing and swishing of the submerged wheels changed to the normal roar and resonance, as we left the trestle bridge and swept into the cutting beyond. The first one to speak was the prompter, who said:

Your attack was a little slow, Mr. Mirabel. It's a bit hard that the curtain has to drop before the invocation is properly begun!

"All the same I can tell you it was a pretty nasty experience, and I'm not looking for any more of it. We were all mighty glad to find solid ground under our feet once more, and to know that we could—as we did—look on the whole thing that had passed as a sort of hideous dream.

"I need not tell you that we all kept such secrets as could be in any way embarrassing to the poor, panic-stricken creatures who in the agony of their fear confessed them."

PART III

UNKNOWN JOURNALISTIC
WRITINGS BY BRAM STOKER
(1891–1908)

Chapter Ten

RECOLLECTIONS OF THE LATE W. G. WILLS (1891)[1]

BRAM STOKER

W. G. Wills was essentially a man of artistic temperament. The habit of a Bohemian life, during which he had manifested several different gifts, and had made his mark in several quite different ways, had rendered him almost a child of circumstance. His nature was a most affectionate one. I suppose that in the whole multitude of his friends and acquaintances—and they were many—there was not one who did not love him. He was, perhaps, as little of a self-seeker as any man of his time; and it is a rare thing to find any one who has arrived at anything approaching his eminence who has retained so much simplicity as he had. This very simplicity, although it stood as a rock in the way of his material prosperity, and prevented him from accumulating any fair proportion of his earnings, was to him a sort of armour, and protected him from dangers which would have destroyed a perhaps stronger man. It enabled him to hold his place everywhere with the utmost good nature, and tended to the strictest preservation of his native independence. His bearing even before Royalty, was the bearing of his daily life; and he was one of the few who knew how to put down, with a well-bred self-possession and an easy toleration, the arrogant pseudo-patronage of a certain Court functionary. He chuckled over the remembrance of the incident, as one day, during a summer stay at Etretât, he told me of his encounter with that functionary. Etretât is that pleasant watering place on the Norman coast, which Wills was one of the first to appreciate, and whither he turned the footsteps of many of his friends. It was on this holiday, where we spent the days idly together, that I saw most of poor Wills; and it was then that I learned to see the true sweetness and depth of his character through that veil of weakness which was all his own. He had an indecision which became a positive quality. Many a morning, when we had started for a ramble together, he would change his mind twenty times as to what form our excursion would take, or whither it would tend, whilst we were crossing the terrace of the Casino. But there was always one end which suited us both, and when in doubt I would play this trump. Then a short while would find us swimming out in the blue waters of the little bay, he wearing a battered old straw hat which seemed to have a special charm for him. He would stay for a long time in the water, lazily floating whilst he enjoyed the picturesque outlines of the flanking cliffs and the views of the distant headlands caught through the bold caverns in the storm-pierced rocks. He was a man full of bright and sweet imaginings, and on some of our Etretât days, as we strolled through the leafy woods or along the summits of the cliffs, he would reveal perfect glimpses of a fairyland of a mind full of tender thoughts and delicate fancy. In his method of work he was open to, and appreciative of, advice. He had, however, at times an almost unconquerable aversion to finish or even to proceed with his work. He would linger over it as long as he possibly could; but then when time, and those for whom time would not stand still, became inexorable, he would start into full swing, and would in a short time accomplish wonders. Sometimes the delays thus caused were embarrassing. I was present, some fifteen years ago, at a rehearsal of one of his plays, *Sappho*, produced

in Dublin. The rehearsal was on Saturday, and the play was to be produced—and was produced—on Monday; but up to the time its close the
manuscript of the last act had not arrived. The company, though, they
may have guessed it, were officially ignorant of the cause of the postpone-
ment of the rehearsal of the last act, and despite their anxiety accepted the
assurance of the management that on Monday all would be well. All did
go well at the rehearsal on the Monday forenoon and at the performance
on the Monday night. His beautiful play of *Olivia*, though taken from
Goldsmith's charming story, has all the qualities of an original work.
Indeed, it is one of the finest plays of the century, and is likely to hold the
stage for many a year to come. It had, of course, its perfect opportunity,
inasmuch as it had the good fortune to have Miss Ellen Terry to play the
heroine; but the play is a truly fine one, and will surely last. Wills was a
master of diction, and some of his poetry is of the finest quality, though
the general merit is now and again marred by carelessness. There are lines
of his writing which might have been Shakespeare's, so perfect are they
in lofty measure and in compactness of thought. As, for instance, that
splendid line in *Charles I*:

Time Is the Tardy Advocate of Kings

I think that all of his plays he had the most affection for *Charles I*.
Between him and Henry Irving an abiding friendship existed, and he
loved to talk of Irving to his friends. It was a shock to all his friends—for
there were but few who knew at all of his illness—to hear that he died in
a hospital; but it is a comfort to them to know that he was there simply
by his own wish, and with the consent of those immediately around
him. His circumstances were never better then at the time of his death.
Though he had made his fame chiefly as a dramatist, he himself considered that his forte lay in painting. In his early days he loved subjects with
a story, and specially those of a sad or tragic character—as, for instance, a
dead woman floating in the river by night, or some such somber subject,
which would tell its own story. For years he lived in Paris, and he kept
on his atelier there, even after the other work on which he was engaged

had practically necessitated his living in London. In his artistic life he appeared to have picked up most easily and retained most tenaciously those traits of Bohemianism of all countries which were most to his own financial detriment, and most to the benefit of his friends. He earned a considerable amount of money, and as his own life was of the simplest, and his own needs were of the fewest, his friends were compelled to spend for him the major part of his earnings. He was a good and loving son and brother—affectionate in all his domestic relations, and a friend beloved by all who knew him. Light lie the earth over his honest loving heart.

SIR HENRY IRVING: AN APPRECIATION BY BRAM STOKER, HIS LONGTIME FRIEND (1904)[1]

Figure 11.1 Photogravure of Sir Henry Irving (1904), by William Brooke, Edinburgh.

(From Austin Brereton, *The Life of Henry Irving*, vol. 2 [London: Longmans, Green, and Co., 1908], frontispiece)

In "The Manchester Guardian" for October 28 there appeared the following appreciation of Sir Henry Irving by Bram Stoker, long associated with him:

To-day Sir Henry Irving will be presented with an address by the citizens of Sunderland, to which place he has returned to play an engagement after an interval of nearly half a century. Forty-eight years ago, when a youth of eighteen, Henry Irving made his first appearance as an actor on the boards of the old Sunderland Theatre. His second and last visit is made this week, and his coming is treated as a civic event. Not merely as a player does he come, but as one who has won distinction, not only for himself, but for his chosen art, and, in its own way, for his nation.

In his time of choice the stage was a very different matter from what it is now, and "going on" it was not unaccompanied by grave rigors. Macready, the towering stage figure of the immediate past—he had retired but a few years before—brought up his own children without having seen the interior of a playhouse. A little longer than a generation had elapsed since the name of "player" had been omitted, rather than erased, from the vagrancy statute. There were few of the inducements or rewards which are now offered to stage aspirants. Salaries were small, and all the usual discomforts of life followed an almost inadequate living wage. Social life, as the young actor of today knows it, was unknown.

If ever an actor was born to the stage Henry Irving was an instance. The stage was then, as it has ever been and is now, his world. Not only did he become a distinguished actor, but he founded a new school of acting. He it was who did away with the stilted styles of the setting forth of character and incident then in vogue, who threw the light of nature into the darkest corners of both tragedy and comedy and in doing so increased the mordant powers of each. Those only who remember the storm of opinions that waged round his characterization of Macbeth and

Hamlet can understand to the full the extraordinary change he wrought. He believed that the highest phase of the art of acting was impersonation, and to this end he used all his powers. He went back to fact and history, and followed the author's meaning from his survey of the natural materials whence he drew his characters. The long gallery of the portraits which he set forth in an actor's medium are more than six hundred. Many of these were, of course, small parts played in his early days, but some are sufficiently great to mark not only an enormous energy but a seemingly endless resource. Quarrel how we will with Irving's work, find what fault we may with conception or representation—and, for my own part, I do not admit such cause of quarrel—we shall always find his characters interesting, self-centred and consistent. And if opportunity be granted to us we shall find that he has thought over more deeply than we have every point which allows of discussion, and can defend his view.

So long as he was an individual player he could not show whole plays as he thought they should be shown—with all parts complete and in harmony and proportion each with and to the other. It was for this reason, rather than from ambition or desire of gain, that he took the cares of management. No one who is without the circle of the playhouse can have any conception of what the proper management of a theatre entails. The ceaseless labor; the multitude of petty cares and worries, the never ending struggle after completeness. It is not sufficient to do the day's work, no matter what its bulk may be. To-morrow has to be thought of, and the day after, and the year after. And if the work undertaken is on grave lines, then difficulties are multiplied many times over. Periods of history have to be studied: at times literature and the records of art ransacked for guiding hints. Experts must be found who can undertake various branches of the work. Painters and musicians, costumers, peruquiers, armorers and the producers of that comprehensive list of items, otherwise unclassified, called "properties"—all these people have to be found and arranged with. Add to these troubles the cares of the exchequer and it can be imagined how great is the strain on one man. For over twenty years Irving did at the Lyceum Theatre what in many other countries is done by the nation, the municipality or the court. And his single-handed venture made his theatre as well as himself illustrious and known all over the civilized world. To the services of the stage he first sought for and gained the aid of great artists in the production of his plays. A quarter of a century since such men as now are glad and even proud to join in stage collaboration did not have such views. The opportunities which he gave and to which he invited them, the experience in a certain phase of their own craft, the bringing home of their ideas to a new circle of admirers—always grateful to artists—even the substantial rewards which followed their labors have assured the continuance of such effort. Up to the 80's the artists who devoted themselves to the stage could alone be counted on by ambitious managements. But then came, at Irving's call, men who had already won great fame. Such men as Sir Laurence Alma-Tadema, Sir Edward Burne-Jones, Seymour Lucas, Keeley Halswelle, and Charles Cattermole were willing to give their art, their lore, their experience and their imagination to aid in great stage work.

In the matter of stage lighting every scenic artist of his time and of the future owed, and still owes, a debt of gratitude to Henry Irving. He first taught them how to produce soft effects with various colored lights thrown one through the other; to use together gaslight and limelight, both "open" and concentrated lights; to produce silhouette effects by turning down or up certain portions of the footlights, and so leaving the edges of the stage in comparatively dimmer light. All these things are nowadays matters of general knowledge and general use. But in the survey of an artistic lifetime it is but just to call to remembrance to whom they are due. Such musicians as Sir Arthur Sullivan, Sir Charles Villiers Stanford, Sir Alexander Mackenzie, Sir Julius Benedict, and Edward German were willing to subordinate their own art to assist in the completion of magnificent stage ideals. It is not too much to say that for twenty years the "productions"—to use the name applied to the ensemble plays—at the Lyceum were everywhere, in other countries as well as our own, regarded as exemplars of artistic excellence, completeness and taste. Certainly the public showed their appreciation of it. The records of

Sir Henry Irving's management show a result of public patronage which has no parallel. The money test may be a low one, but at least it is found to be accurate, and it is thus valuable. Since 1878, when Henry Irving began management on his own account, the public of Great Britain and America had paid more than £2,125,000 to see him play. I can vouch for the figures, for the money has passed through my own hands.

Other instances of public appreciation of what he has done are not lacking. In many ways has come the recognition of the great position which he made and won for himself. Queen Victoria conferred on him the honor of knighthood. This was the first time that such an honor had been conferred on an actor—the first time that, in any country, state honor had been given to a player as such. When the French government gave M. Got the Legion of Honor it was expressly stated that it was conferred on him as a professor. It remained for Britain to lead the way. Three great universities, representing England, Scotland, and Ireland, have given him degrees—Dublin and Cambridge as Doctor of Literature, Glasgow as Doctor of Laws. He has received addresses from cities and universities, caskets and scrolls without number. He has been asked to give and has given lectures at the universities of Oxford, Cambridge (where he gave the Reid lecture), Dublin, Manchester, Columbia (New-York), Harvard, Chicago and Princeton, at the Royal Institution and at many less celebrated places. He was the first actor asked to speak at the Royal Academy banquet. On the occasion of his knighthood he was presented with a golden box containing an address signed by every member of the profession to which he belongs and to which he has brought so much honor—an event unique in the history of the stage. He originated, organized and mainly supported in its earlier years the Actors' Benevolent Fund, which has been of inestimable benefit to many poor players.

Even his social life, he who is so personally retiring, has had an important place in the life of London. For over twenty years there had hardly been an illustrious visitor who was not his guest at the Old Beefsteak room of the Lyceum Theatre. "First nights" at the Lyceum were occasions of prime social importance, and the informal supper parties on the stage which followed these performances were really gatherings representing all that was best in the life of the nation. At the diamond jubilee of Queen Victoria, and again at the time arranged for the coronation of the King, it was Sir Henry Irving's privilege to entertain, by royal sanction the nation's guests. On both those occasions the Indian princes and colonial notabilities attended in state, and the theatre, prepared for the reception after the nightly performance by a sort of Aladdin's lamp process, was a scene of magnificent splendor. The last was indeed the final glory of the old Lyceum. For within a month its doors were closed forever.

This is the bare outline of the record of the young actor who began his artistic life in Sunderland, and whose return thither is celebrated to-day. The detail can be filled in by any whose lives and memories are long enough—of good work, great work, done; in his art as an actor; in his productions as a manager; in his charity; in his helpfulness to others; in his loyalty to King and country; and in his noble example of self-suppression and righteous dealing as a man. Alone and unaided from first to last by State or private help, he made his theatre a veritable temple of art and an example to all the world of how a theatre should be and can be conducted. In the doing of it he won the admiration and respect of all the world. And beyond even this he has been given, what no man can of set purpose win, a personal devotion unparalleled in artistic history, from countless numbers of persons whom he has never seen except in cheering masses. And he has so blessed the lives of a multitude of others less fortunate than himself, so strewn his way with good deeds of which I, perhaps, as his almoner for more than a quarter of a century, alone know, that, if gratitude and love and justified hopes and good wishes can effect it, the closing nights of his artistic life which are yet to come will be starred with new successes and new honors.

Let us hope that many long years of well earned rest to follow them will be crowned with happiness.

Chapter Twelve

12,000 MILES OF IRVING'S AUDIENCES (1906)[1]

BRAM STOKER

Figure 12.1   Illustration, "Irving between England and America," from a drawing by Fred Barnard (1883), after the picture by Sir Joshua Reynolds, "Garrick between Tragedy and Comedy."

(From Charles Hiatt, *Henry Irving: A Record and Review* [London: George Bell and Sons, 1899], 201)

The late Sir Henry Irving was much more than a great actor; he was a great educator.

When he began his own management he resolved that a theater could be a place of education, and he made it so. The committee appointed for the revision of the Bible, when they had finished their labors, went in a body to the Lyceum and placed it on record that "this theater is a place for good."

Wherever he went he became a recognized educational force. He was asked to lecture at Harrow school, at Oxford, by Dr. Jowett, at Cambridge and most of the other great universities in all parts of the world.

If all the people who went to see Irving were placed in a long line, allowing each a yard of space and the sun shone at the head of the procession, when it set nearly 12 hours later a thousand miles of people would still be waiting to see Irving. They would stretch 12,000 miles, allowing the low average of $2,000 for each performance. And of all the millions of people who saw him there was not one who did not take away some noble thought.

Chapter Thirteen

WHERE HALL CAINE DREAMS OUT HIS ROMANCES (1908)[1]

BRAM STOKER

Figure 13.1   Photograph of Bram Stoker (*ca.* 1906) by W. & D. Downey, London.

(From *McClure's Magazine* 30, no. 3 [January 1908]: 366)

There is a distinct truth in the statement often made that in the Isle of Man Hall Caine is a sort of uncrowned king. Any one who has ever walked or driven with him in Summertime on any of the main roads of the island can have had ocular proof. Ordinarily the population of Man is not a very great one. The occupations of farming and fishing, which are the main industries of the island, are neither of them extragregarious.

But for some two months in the year the place absolutely changes its character. It becomes the pleasure ground par excellence of Great Britain. Between the middle of July and the middle of September something like half a million of visitors pour into it—not at once, of course, but in sequence. The great bulk of them are of the working and middle classes from the great industrial centres and mining regions of England, Scotland, and Wales. These good people work hard for fifty or fifty-one weeks in the year, during which strenuous time they put by thrifty a little fund for the holiday of a week or a fortnight. Splendid steamboats, some of them carrying as many as two thousand persons, make quick passages daily from and to the mainland in times varying between two and six hours, according to distance.

Famous Pleasure Resorts

A glance at the map will show the peculiarly favorable position of the island for purposes of short spells of pleasure. It lies midway between England and Ireland, between Scotland and Wales. It is exceedingly beautiful, full of hills and mountains, deep-lying glens, and trickling streams. The coast is rock bound and exceedingly picturesque, with steep cliffs and rugged headlands, between which nestle charming bays suitable for boating and bathing. The air is sweet and mild, as Man lies in an arm of the Gulf Stream which runs up from the Atlantic between England and Ireland. From the top of the Shaefell, the highest mountain on the island, and which lies in its heart, one can see on a clear day the mountains of Mourne in Ireland, Snowdon in Wales, Galloway in Scotland, and of Cumberland in England.

There is a legend thus accounting for the creation of the Isle of Man. The Devil was walking in Ireland, and got angry about something. In his rage he kicked a piece out of the ground into the sea. The hold became Lough Neagh, the clod the Isle of Man. It is said that in size and shape the positive and negative agree. There is certainly an approximate resemblance. For the truth of the rest of the story I am unable to vouch.

The enormous migratory population may be fairly taken to represent working and middle class Britain, so that their verdict on most things may be accepted as a consensus of opinion of the great bulk of the inhabitants of the country. It cannot be doubted that their verdict on the literary work of Hall Caine is a unanimous one. It bears out the telling of commerce, for the published copies of the author's writings already run into millions. An author, of course, is known in and by his work, and naturally his personality becomes the rallying point of an affection which would otherwise have to remain quite impersonal. Not since the time of Charles Dickens has the public made such a hero of any man of letters. Their feeling has become one of actual devotion.

The first expedition made by visitors on their short and well-earned holiday is to Greeba Castle, his island residence. He, being a good-hearted man, gives them full opportunity for their wishes, and his whole estate is free to his many friends. Greeba is not a mediaeval castle, but a house built perhaps a hundred years ago in picturesque castellated form. Time has covered it with the "sweet oblivion of flowers," to use De Quincey's exquisite phrase; but the flowers are represented here by clustering masses of different varieties of ivy, which have crept their way up the rugged stone walls till the whole edifice is a brilliant tower of green rising above a clustering wood under the steep hill forming the northern side of the Valley of St. John's, through which runs the high road between Douglas and Peel.

Here the gate is open by day and night, and from early morning, when the legions of the "trippers" go out on their aesthetic pilgrimage, groups and bands of them climb the steep path up to the castle and whisper or shout, according to their individual tastes, their greetings to the ears of the walls of the great novelist. It would be manifestly impossible for so hard-working a man to hold personal communion with all of so many friends; but he gives no inconsiderable time to them. This is in itself a trying ordeal to a man so nervously sensitive. Indeed, a walk along the adjacent road is to him a little exhausting, for it resembles a royal progress. All day long there is a stream of traffic which is simply endless. Great breaks containing twenty or more persons, carriages of single or double harness for the more exclusive, bicyclists in droves, mortor [*sic*] cycles enjoying both speed and isolation. They come in hundreds, thousands. And one and all the men raise their hats, and the women smile and call out friendly greetings. At times when there are groupings round "half-way" houses for the purpose of baiting cattle—and humans—there are salvos of applause. Courtesy demands acknowledgment of these courtesies, and during a stroll Hall Caine's hat has to be less on his head than off it.

Making a Royal Progress

It is the same when he travels in his motorcar. Breaks and carriages and cycles are drawn up to see him pass; indeed, teh [*sic*] drivers earn much pourboire by blocking the road so that their patrons may get a good view of him. The Manx drivers, by the way, are rather a poor lot, and seem to be congenitally afflicted in the way of driving on the wrong side of the road. Hall Caine uses his motor a good deal. It is his way of taking the air, and after lunch every day he rides some fifty or a hundred miles. He always sits beside the driver, so that he can get the draught and scour of the air. The Manx rule of speed is a nominal fourteen miles—but there are some motorists who are said occasionally to exceed it. Hall Caine is a law-abiding man as becomes a member of the House of Keys—as the Manx Parliament is called—and a Justice of the Peace. But he does not court special privileges being as democratic as it is possible for a loyal subject of King Edward VII to be. He pays income tax, though, as an inhabitant of the Isle of Man, where there is no income tax, he is exempt. He does not knowingly exceed the speed limit, though every policeman in the island when he sees him coming stands well out that he may have the pleasure of saluting. He drives a Delaunay-Belleville car of 28–40 horse power speed—the same car which the French manufacturing company exhibited at the British Motor Exhibition a year ago.

The novelist's daily routine, when he is working, is as follows: He wakes early and gets to work at once, though without leaving his bedroom, or at times even rising from bed. He makes his first appearance to his household before lunch, which is at 1 o'clock. This was, by the way, a custom also of the first Lord Lytton. After lunch a cigar in the conservatory.

A Novelist's Estate

Hall Caine's possessions in the Isle of Man are many and various and extensive. And, best of all, he has won them for himself by his own genius, power, and work. He is of Manx stock, and although born at Runcorm [sic] in Lanscashire, through the accident of his mother's travel, was reared in Man.

Years ago, when I first visited him in the Isle of Man—he was then living in Peel—he drove me in a carriage to the house wherein he spent much of his time as a boy, a two-storied thatched cottage at Ballavolley near Ramsey on the Peel Road. It was a poor enough place, the upper story being in the nature of an attic! Here he lived as a child with his paternal grandmother and his uncle, a farmer who supplemented his income by butchering. When lately I saw the place again it was all changed. The old house had been pulled down and a new and somewhat more pretentious one had been built. The rude walls of former times had given place to brick, and the old picturesque thatch had been changed for unromantic slate.

This is the only place associated with his youth which has been changed in so marked a way. The other place, where he lived for a time, at a much later period, still remains in somewhat the same circumstances as formerly. This is the schoolhouse at Kirk Maughold, lying high on a bleak headland on the other side (the eastern) of the island. The place is bleak and so windswept that one can well imagine, even in the height of Summer, when the island seems to bask in the sun, how in Wintertime

Hall Caine who was a schoolmaster there for a time, had to have a rope stretched from living house to school by clinging to which he could make a safe passage when a gale was blowing.

During my latest visit to Hall Caine he drove me around to Ramsey by Snaefell and came back to Greeba by the Curragh. Before debouching again on the high road we stopped at a picturesque and very ancient church at Ballaugh. This name again is a good example of Manx as distinguished from Irish pronunciation of words spelled alike. Ballaugh in Manx is "Bal" spoken softly, followed by a quicker giving of "laugh," (the synonym for cachinnation,) pronounced in English. Ballaugh is in Irish pronounced as if spelled "Ballah," with the accent on the first syllable. In the graveyard of this old church lie many bygone ancestors and relatives of the Caine family.

When Hall Caine, having won success and secured fortune, made up his mind to settle in Man, he did it wholeheartedly. His whole interests in life became centered in the place, and he began, after Shakespeare's fashion, to establish himself as an owner of real estate. He purchased Greeba Castle, which was then in a dilapidated condition and had but a small of acreage of land attached to it. This estate he has enlarged until all up the mountain behind the house, except the portion which, being public property, is unpurchasable, he has acquired; while the whole face of the hill across the valley is now his own property. From the window of his bedroom at Greeba, he can look out on a wide vista—all his estate.

Hall Caine in Politics

He began to take a part in the public life, and became a member of the House of Keys. In nearly every beneficent project, every enlargement of national life, every strenuous claim for ancient rights and protection of public privileges, won of old and preserved through a thousand years of custom, but now assailed at times in the whirl of changing conditions of British life and development, he has been either an originator or a participant, and often both. He is now in such a position with reference to the island of his ancestry and adoption that a very exalted person has been heard to speak of Man as "Hall Caine's Island." To many hundreds of thousands of visitors he is the island—that part of it which lives in their thoughts and hangs in their memory.

His home is very delightful and a very happy one. His wife is as well as wife a good and helpful and sympathetic comrade. She answers to the ideal qualifications expressed in the old sea song, Tom Bowling: "His Poll was kind and true." In a large circle of friends she is a great favorite and highly honored. To the guests within her gates she is an ideal hostess; by her husband and children she is looked up to and beloved. The Hall Caines have two sons, both young, and both clever. The eldest, Ralph, is a publisher, whose firm is in the name of Collier & Co. He has not been long in business, but has already published many successful books, among them being "Brewster's Millions" and many other American books. He was publisher for the Queen of her "Christmas Carol," two or three years ago. He has been chosen by the Chief Liberal Whip of the present British Government as a candidate for Parliamentary honors at an early date. The younger son, Derwen, has chosen the stage as his walk in life. Although still very young he is already an actor and manager, and is shortly to produce and take out on a tour a play dramatized from one of his father's works. Thus the coming generation share among them the roles in life in which their father has become famous—with the one exception that he did not become a professional actor. But all the same he is an actor of a kind, and one of no mean rank. His gifts as a story-teller have been enthusiastically praised by all who have ever had the pleasurable experience of hearing him. His "actor's qualities" have done him yeoman's service in the writing of his plays.

In two different ways he has manipulated this phase of art. In public by reading, as it is called, but in reality reciting, a story of his own. Several times he has done this, and in some of the largest halls of Great Britain has carried great audiences to wild enthusiasm. In another way, too, quieter, more domestic, more intimate, he can thrill with voice and eye, expression and gesture. When a new novel of his has reached a point in its preliminary development—that stage when the incubation of the main plot and supporting ideas are complete—he will perhaps tell the story to an intimate friend. This is indeed a treat to hear. The man seems to be all afire. He grows more earnest as the story goes on—voice and expression and gesture all work together till the effect is panoramic. You seem to see and realize the whole at once—characters, situation, plot, milieu. You are almost as breathless at the close as the narrator himself, as with pale face, pallor following hard on the flush of earnestness, and with glowing eyes, he sinks back in silence. It has been my own good fortune to be the listener on many such occasions. The story of many, of most of his novels, has been told to me in this way, both at first conception where intention is vague and nebulous and only general principles and hazy individualities with a living heart somewhere are in evidence; or later when the period of thought is over and the work to be carried out by writing is in, what he calls the "back of his head." This latter stage is, of course, compared with the first conception, very much what the completed picture is to the sketch. It has more of the vital quality than is possible to mere words, howsoever potent of suggestion these may be. Such a brief story can convey the intention of the author in perfection and can teach something of the whole scope of the subject.

To a writer of this nature his surroundings can be very helpful. When in his pretty dining room at Greeba, a visitor can admire the quaint old furniture of oak collected there—can understand certain effects of Cumbrian and Manx home life. This old oak press and dresser which covers one side of the inner half of the room between the pilaster and the service door, brings back at a glance the whole atmosphere of the salesman's home wherein it had rested for two hundred years. The two great fireplaces with overmantels of carved oak, black with age, bring back legends if not memories of the stirring times of the English revolution— one of them was for a time in the house of George Eliot and afterward in that of the late Wilson Barrett. The very dining room chairs, of oak, of comfortable girth and heavy of weight, being fortified by cross bars and cross pieces above and below the seat, tell mutely of huge men of such weight and stature as to be able to combat the storms on and among the hills and fells. In the hall the old oak press, carven in high relief with scriptural subjects, which was given to him by Dante Gabriel Rossetti, is not only a memorial of a loving friendship of the two men—one sinking in the vale of years, the other rising to the top of the hill when he had descended—but also a record of a time when in remote places among whirling snow and obliterating fog the farm kitchen was the studio, the aspiring genius made its essay in art with what materials were available.

Some Literary Mementos

The more modern relics have a personal value of memory to their owner: to others are of passing interest. Here is a water color of Ruskin's study at the time, now long gone by, when the novelist visited him in Brantwood. Here is a study of one of the feminine creations of the author of "Lorna Doone," with a graceful inscription to Mrs. Hall Caine written at considerable length in the holograph of R. D. Blackmore. Here is a print of "The Blessed Damozel," with an affectionate letter of D. G. Rossetti. All over the house are interesting memorials and trophies of the kind, mostly with a personal interest. Gifts to the author from friends, souvenirs of travel and adventure in foreign lands, portraits of literary, political, and artistic friends, historic curios of his chosen home—the Manx Island.

In his method of working Hall Caine exhibits extraordinary care. He first of all familiarizes himself with the subject chosen for the novel or play. If it be fixed in a place not already familiar to him, he goes to the place and studies on the spot all that pertains to its history, life, and special conditions. He thus gains a true insight into the details which will later on come into the structure of his story. For instance, he has for the last two Winters made his residence in Egypt, and has with all the instinct of an experienced journalist got on the "inside track" with regard to the politics, hopes, fears, aims, ambitions, and difficulties of that more than interesting and important country. This will enable him to show such a survey of Egyptian affairs in the novel on which he is at present at work as will at once lift it into more than the importance of a novel. The book, however, will not want such aid. It will, I can promise—if the effect of the telling of the story can be relied on, and by experience I know it can—prove to be a great novel.

P A R T   I V

UNKNOWN INTERVIEWS WITH BRAM STOKER (1886–1890)

Figure 14.1 Illustration of "Mr. T. Hall Caine," Bram Stoker's dear friend, from a photograph by Messrs. Elliott & Frye.

(From Raymond Blathwayt, *Interviews* [London: A. W. Hall, 1893], 144)

Chapter Fourteen

IRVING AND HUDSON: BRAM STOKER TELLS WHAT HE THINKS ABOUT THE CONTROVERSY (1886)[1]

(Special Dispatch to *The Boston Herald*)

NEW YORK. Oct. 31, 1886. Mr. Bram Stoker, the confidential business manager of Mr. Henry Irving, arrived today on the Etruria of the Cunard line. When Mr. Irving's cablegram of last Friday to your correspondent concerning Mr. Wilson Barrett's letter of Oct. 18 was shown to Mr. Stoker, he became intensely interested, and read the dispatch and Mr. Hudson's subsequent explanations of it eagerly.

"This is all very strange and unexpected to me," he said. "When I left London, nothing of the kind had turned up. I don't know what to make of it, and I scarcely know what to say."

"But you knew Mr. Hudson while he was a member of Mr. Irving's Lyceum company?"

"Well, yes; that is, he was one of the young men who did small parts. I don't suppose his parts necessitated the speaking of a dozen lines."

"Were Mr. Hudson and Mr. Irving on terms of close intimacy or friendship?"

"No."

—"But Mr. Hudson, in support of the position he has assumed in the controversy with Mr. Irving, shows a letter which he says Mr. Irving wrote him, assuring him of his personal regard and friendship, and the letter is signed Irving."

"Such a letter really does not mean anything out of the ordinary, and Mr. Irving writes hundreds of letters to people—his secretary does— and even I come in for a share of them. Mr. Hudson's father may have asked Mr. Irving to send his son a line to encourage him, which Mr. Irving would readily do. It is strange this letter should be signed simply 'Irving.' It is really very queer, for I am positive Mr. Irving never signed a letter that way in his life. You know in England only noblemen use the surname alone as a signature, and for Mr. Irving to so sign would imply Lord Irving. His signature is always Henry Irving, with the given name abbreviated, but never omitted."

Chapter Fifteen

A CHAT WITH
MR. STOKER ABOUT
IRVING (1886)[1]

Figure 15.1   Illustration of "Mr. Bram Stoker" (1885) at "Mr. William Creswick's farewell benefit at Drury Lane Theatre."

A familiar figure to many New-Yorkers was seen among the passengers on the Etruria, which arrived here yesterday, a tall broadshouldered man, with auburn beard clipped in Van Dyke fashion. It was Bram Stoker, well-known as Henry Irving's business manager. Soon after his arrival he was seen at the Brunswick Hotel and chatted pleasantly and directly about Mr. Irving, Miss Terry and "Faust."

"Both Mr. Irving and Miss Terry," said he, "derived an immense amount of benefit from their holiday among you good Americans. In Miss Terry's case the absolute rest she enjoyed at the seaside made a new woman of her, and Mr. Irving, too, though he travelled about a good deal, returned feeling better than he had for months before. I need hardly tell you that 'Faust' is doing an enormous business at the Lyceum. The houses to-day show absolutely no diminution as compared with those we had in the first weeks of production. The spectacular effects are remarkably striking, and the Brocken scene, particularly, seems to set the people wild. By the time I got back to London I expect that a new scene which has been in preparation for some time will have been introduced. This is the 'Witches' Kitchen,' which will be a fit pendant in wild supernaturalism to the Brocken scene."

When asked as to the object of his visit here Mr. Stoker was becomingly diplomatic.

"I have come on business connected with the Lyceum," said he, "but for a few days I am hardly at liberty to state the precise nature of it."

"Is the report sent over here by cable and published here this morning to the effect that Mr. Irving will open here next September true?"

"Well," said Mr. Stoker with a smile, "there are so many rumors nowadays that one cannot believe all one hears. If any such thing is definitely settled, however, it is news to me."

Regarding the controversy between Messrs. Irving and Wilson Barrett regarding the acting of Mr. Hudson, Mr. Stoker had nothing to say.

"Since my arrival," he said, "I have heard of Mr. Irving's cable dispatch and Mr. Barrett's letter, but I have seen neither of them. I know nothing of the circumstances, and naturally cannot tell you anything you do not already know."

When Mr. Stoker was told that it had been seriously reported that his presence here was due to the controversy referred to, his amusement was frank to the point of vociferousness.

"It's too absurd to deny seriously," was his only comment.

Mr. Stoker will probably remain in New-York only a short time, but the date of his return to England is not definitely fixed.

Chapter Sixteen

THE GANGWAY SEATS AT THE LYCEUM (1890)[1]

M r. Bram Stoker was recently interviewed by a *County Council
Times* man, who asked of the genial acting-manager:
"What do you think of the decision of the London County Council
regarding the Lyceum?"—"What am I to think? What can anyone
think?" replied Mr. Stoker with a shrug of the shoulders which was
meant to express, "The thing is too absurd for anything." "It is not business; it is a most improper way to go about business. Mr. Irving will treat
the Council with the utmost respect, but the proceeding of Tuesday is
so unbusiness-like that it is absolutely unarguable. We have had inspec-
tions here over and over again, and the arrangements have always given
satisfaction."

"What part of the theatre will be affected by the change demanded?"—"I
cannot say. I don't know what the Council want us to do."

"Well, if their resolution is indefinite it is certainly comprehensive. It
says that the gangway seats must be abolished."—"We have had no com-
munication from the Council up to the present, and all I know about the
matter I have seen in the press. We have no gangway seats as the term is
ordinarily used. We have the flap seats, and the same kind of arrangement

exists at the Middlesex Music Hall and Drury-lane Theatre, and there has been no attempt to interfere with them. These arrangements have been in existence at the Lyceum for fifty years, and all manner of persons have inspected the place, the London County Council, the Metropolitan Board of Works, the Lord Chamberlain, and many others, and not only have they been satisfied , but they have generally been very complimentary. We have always done our best to meet the views of the authorities, and made every endeavour to avoid friction. The County Council requested us not to allow standing, and we said 'Certainly,' though they had no power to enforce such an order. It would be much better if people understood what they were talking about, for then they would not make such reckless and utterly untrue statements as did Mr. Ford, or give other people unnecessary trouble. Who is this Mr. Ford?"

PART V

RARE AND UNCOLLECTED WORKS
BY BRAM STOKER (1896–1906)

RIVAL "FIRST-NIGHT" SHOWS.

Figure 17.1   Illustration of Henry Irving and Bram Stoker (1890)

(From *Judy: or the London Serio-Comic Journal* [April 16, 1890]: 184. Image reproduced with permission of ProQuest. Further reproduction is prohibited without permission.)

Figure 17.2   Illustration of "Miss Ellen Terry" (1891) from a photo by Window & Grove.

(From *The Strand Magazine: An Illustrated Monthly* 1 [January–June 1891]: 44)

Chapter Seventeen

SIR HENRY IRVING AND MISS ELLEN TERRY IN *ROBESPIERRE, MERCHANT OF VENICE, THE BELLS, NANCE OLDFIELD, THE AMBER HEART, WATERLOO,* ETC. (1896)[1]

Bram Stoker

The practical cause of Henry Irving's success has, after his gifts as an actor, been his constant, unwearied and single-minded devotion to his chosen work. When in 1856, then a boy of eighteen, he took the final plunge from clerkship, which he began at thirteen years of age, into art, he had already behind him several years of steady toil rigourously given in the leisure hours of his daily working life. In those days, as now, the working hours of a London clerk were as long as the work was poorly paid, and it needed a very fixed resolution to keep a young man constant to the self-imposed task of studying and exacting an endless art. Early and late he was at work, studying plays and parts, and half starving himself to pay for the few lessons kindly given to him at an hour in the morning so early as to be inconvenient to himself by an old actor who believed in his future and who predicted for him great things. This devotion to his aim, however, bore good fruit; and in the earlier years of his stage work at Sunderland and Edinburgh, when the bill was changed so often that it was necessary for a young actor to learn sometimes three or four new parts in a week, he was always able to keep ahead of his work by means of the reserve of some hundred stock parts in which he was in stage language "letter-perfect." This was not only a saving of exhausting labour and a spurning of the prompter's assistance—always a thing to be feared—but it enabled him to give to each part which he undertook something of the necessary care of elaboration. To act a part it is not sufficient to know the words. Dress has to be considered, as well as bearing, manner, intonation, the time suitable to the true setting forth of the phases of the character—in short, all those aids and accessories which go to the convincing of the spectator as to the *vraisemblance* of the character. The artistic exactness, added to his undoubted genius, at once told in his favour, and he began very soon to creep up the ladder of success. Material prosperity is not the measure of a young actor's success. Such, no doubt, follows in due course, but in early days the standard of advancement is in the growing importance of the parts entrusted to him. Young Irving found his possibilities of ultimate success multiplying fast. To-day when the work of the stage is more highly elaborated, when the length of runs makes a sufficiently lengthy preparation possible and even advisable, when the life of a single drama runs at times into years of continuous existence, when actors are well paid, hold a worthy position in society and have fair prospect of sharing in the good fortune of their time, it is hard to realize the difficulties of a young actor forty years ago. There were then comparatively few theatres in the great cities of Great Britain; none at all in the small ones. In the middle-sized communities the demand for the drama had its only satisfaction in the visits of "Circuit" companies, that moved from place to place in sequence at regular periods of the year. There were few, if any, plays which went touring as the great metropolitan successes do nowadays, with First, Second, Third, or even Fourth Provincial Companies. Though the great actors were received and made much of wherever they went, the small fry had few friends beyond their own circle, and few chances of making any except the chance meetings in lodging-houses and places of refreshment. The meagre salaries of those days were insufficient to allow the recipients to indulge much in the graces of life; and the long vacations, during which they had no opportunity of earning anything at all, made it almost impossible to save against a rainy day. There is a general impression in the great world outside the circle of theatrical life that actors are improvident folk. This is entirely erroneous; in no other degree of life are earners of weekly wage more thrifty. Beyond this, in no other degree of life are wage earners so good and helpful toward friends and relatives outside their immediate families.

The class of life in which young Irving found himself was not full of seductive luxuriousness, but it was full of endless and laborious work, of exasperating monotony of daily routine, of anxieties—material and artistic. In such a life it is easy to give way in purpose, to lose ambition, to seek and often to find some duodecimo Capua in which to sink into comparatively luxurious ease. But genius always, if it be true to itself, finds some expression for itself and some way for its manifestation. Irving never faltered, never despaired, never lost hope. Through good times and bad he kept true to his own instinct, always studying. His studies were not merely in the daily routine of the parts he had to learn or which he wished ultimately to play; he took much wider ground than this. As he studied new characters he made himself thoroughly acquainted with all that surrounded them, historically and artistically; so that he came in time to have an instinctive knowledge of the atmosphere and surroundings in which each of his histrionic creations moved. In these days the student who aims high lives in easy places; for everywhere he finds works of reference in every branch of human thought and endeavour ready to his hand. Forty years ago, however, there were no public libraries in the modern sense. Only in a few of the great cities were there libraries at all; and learning had to be achieved in an uphill manner. Sometimes we hear sneers at self-educated men. Of all baseless scoffing, this is the very worst, for self-education implies not only success already achieved, but an indomitable character exhibited steadfastly in the winning of it. Men who are really learned, who know the value and the difficulty and the rarity of self-culture, are ever the warmest admirers of those who have won such distinction for and by themselves. To-day the very highest of Henry Irving's distinctions is that he has been granted degrees *honoris causa* by three of the greatest universities in the world. In fact, there are few men who hold Doctorships given in such a way by England, Ireland, and Scotland.

Is it any wonder that a man who all his life has exhibited so unfailing a belief in, and a devotion to, his chosen art, who has so wide an experience of its difficulties and its trials, and so thorough an understanding of its possibilities, finds so keen a pleasure in the vast and growing importance of the drama as a factor in national and social life? Whenever he lays the foundation stone of a new theatre—and this is a function which he is often called on to fulfill—he says that he feels it an added joy to life. Life to him, if it has been full of work, has also been, for now very many years, full of honours and rewards. His portion has indeed been "love and honour and troops of friends," and he has the satisfaction of knowing that all he has been honestly and honourably won. Two continents have shown him in continuous and in unmistakable manner their full appreciation of his work as an artist, a scholar and a man; and have recognised to the full that he has in his own chosen work upheld the name and fame of his native land. Any man would be proud to carry the honours bestowed on him, all worthily won by hard and earnest work—genius directed skillfully and consistently toward a goodly aim. He is not only a Knight in England, but is a member of the illustrious House Order of Combined Saxe-Coburg Gotha and Saxe Meiningen—for learned and cultured Germany loves to honour genius and great work. He is Doctor of Letters of Dublin University, Doctor of Letters of Cambridge University, and Doctor of Laws of the University of Glasgow. This is truly the recognition by scholars of a scholar's work and a tribute to the advancement of his chosen art which he has so nobly furthered. It may truly be said of him with regard to the art of the stage that he "found it brick and made it marble."

For more than twenty years his artistic home at the Lyceum Theatre in London became one of the great centres of thought and art. His work there was recognised as a standard by which other players and other managers in his own and other countries were to measure their achievements. Every stranger coming to London could not consider his survey of British life and effort complete without a visit to the Lyceum Theatre. When he was given by Her Majesty the honour of Knighthood, thus winning for the first time in his own or any other country a place for his art in the Court and Governmental purview, the whole of the members of his own craft united in presenting him with a magnificent casket of gold and crystal, in which was a great volume containing an address and all their signatures. Such a thing was alone unique in the history of the stage.

The latest of the many plays which Henry Irving produced at the Lyceum broke in a certain way new ground. For the first time a great French author wrote a play manifestly and ostensibly for an Englishman to act. Irving had for a long time had a wish to portray the character of Robespierre. Victorien Sardou also had a wish that Irving should render some piece of his. The ideas of the two men were exchanged through

friends and by letter—for Sardou has never crossed the English chan-
nel—and in due time the play was written.

It was a difficult task which the great dramatist had set himself, for
the life of Robespierre is so well known that there were endless limi-
tations to dramatic possibility. The knowledge of the master of stage-
craft, however, is very vast on all subjects connected with the French
Revolution; and from hints and inferences regarding Robespierre's life
and motives he built up a great drama which, when put upon the stage
by Irving, has proved to create an extraordinary interest in two great
nations. Of course, as is necessary in all historical plays, certain changes
had to be effected. It is not possible to give in the "two hours traffic
of the stage" all the series of events and changes which have led up to
great achievements or catastrophes. It is sufficient if the myriad motives
of many people are crystallised or concentrated into the motives and
purposes and actions of a few. This is the keynote of dramatic excellence, and the master-hand of Sardou has struck it in this great drama
which shows in little the mighty upheaval which marked the end of the
eighteenth century. In this stormy time there were great men who were
heard for only a passing hour and little men who seemed great in their
momentary poise amidst the whirling throng. There were great motives
which led to terrible results, and little motives which eventually led to
magnificent endings. The possibilities for the exhibition of heroic and
mean motives are admirably shown in the prison scene which serves as
a background to individual action of the dramatic characters. Here are
grouped many moving incidents, every one of which, from the grue-
some "game of the guillotine" to the self-sacrifice of friend for friend and
stranger for stranger, are recorded in history, though not all taking place
at once within the narrow bounds of a single prison within the space of
half an hour. The reality or the realism of such scenes shows how great
and manifold were the opportunities of one steadfast purpose, though
such had not its origin in the loftiest aims, and enables the spectator to
realize how it was that such a man as Robespierre could have done so
much for good or ill. Through it all—through ambition, pride, vanity,

the remorseless logic and action of a pedant—shines the softening touch of nature, which, when it warms the father's heart, brings in irresistible pathos to draw the hearts of the spectators closer to his own. There is a note of pity through all the overwhelming clamour which marks the struggle and downfall of Robespierre in the Convention.

Figure 18.1 Photographs of some of the late Sir Henry Irving's characters.

(From *The Bystander* 8, no. 98 [October 18, 1905]: 113)

Chapter Eighteen

HENRY IRVING'S FIGHT FOR FAME (1906)[1]

Bram Stoker

In the endowment of Henry Irving for this life-work was one supremely dominant quality which, in any age, at any place, is absolutely necessary to worthy success—tenacity of purpose. That he had great gifts in the way of histrionic ability, of thoughtfulness, of reasoning powers and all those forces which naturally lead from causes to effects—of literary grace, of sympathy, and of understanding of character—has been well proved by his work of forty-nine years upon the stage; and, inferentially, by the labor of those antecedent years which helped to fit him for his later work—for, be it always remembered, it is in youth that the real battle of success is fought, when many roads seem to lie open; when the blood is red and pleasure woos with claimant voice — howsoever sweet it may be. But all those later-mentioned personal gifts fix only the direction of force; they do not and can not supply it. It is dogged tenacity of purpose which, in the end, prevails; which urges and forces into action the various powers and gifts which go to make up one's individual equipment. It is this quality which sustains the shrinking heart, which forces the trembling nerves, which restores the wearied brain and muscle, which conquers sleep, and which makes halcyon pleasure seem rather the sport of the butterfly than the worthy pursuit of manhood.

He Showed a Wonderful Talent for Impersonation when a Very Young Boy

Even in his boyhood Irving showed a taste for acting which gave him preëminence amongst the young cousins with whom he was brought up in Cornwall. When, as a boy of thirteen, he began the life of a London city clerk, his taste had ripened and his mind became fixed upon the stage as his objective. He did not neglect the business which he had undertaken—through all his life no one ever knew Henry Irving to do that; but all his leisure was given to the study and practice of his chosen art. He was not content with imagining; he was always on the search for character impersonation. An old school friend of his, Charles Dyall, afterwards director of the Walker Art Gallery, Liverpool, writing of him thirty years afterwards, told a story of how, when, in his early days in Manchester, he had been given a part in one of John Brougham's comedies—that of a youth who wished to appear a man, but was unable to repress his boyish ways and habits—he invited a young son of an actor comrade to his rooms and later on "took him off" to the life in his part. I have seen him, myself, on a voyage to Calais, "study" and eccentric individual all the rough journey—and it was rough—from Dover. Any one who saw him play *Digby Grant*, in Albery's comedy, "Two Roses," could never forget the perfection of his bearing, appearance, and manner of dress in the part of a man, schooled in poverty and poverty's littlenesses, who had suddenly come into the possession of wealth. Years afterwards I met the prototype—the late Chevalier Wikoff, originally from Philadelphia and a close companion of Edwin Forrest in his early days. Every detail of the original, from his tasseled smoking cap and faded dressing gown up to his magnificent self-assertion and the cunning with which he disguised his weaknesses and the imperfections of old age, was there. And yet Wikoff had not been so old a man when Irving had studied him. His knowledge of the character was basic and elementary; the man grew old in reality as he had grown old in the actor's mind.

In his young days Irving at least paved the way for his later triumphs. He studied earnestly, and whatever he undertook to do he tried with all his might to do well. No one ever knew him sloppy or indeterminate in any part he took in amateur theatricals, in any piece he recited. Thus it was that, whilst the energies of others, during the moments of supreme endeavor, were given to recalling the words of the text, he was putting all his strength into the expression of them. It was little wonder that, when, amidst a fairly typical gathering of young men and hobbledehoys who formed what was shortly afterwards called "the City Elocution Class," the boy of fifteen was allowed, in a tolerant way, to make his effort. He won instant success. He fairly electrified all by his force and passion in his declaiming of "The Uncle." At this period he was described as rather tall for his age; his face was very handsome and was set in amass of black hair, and his eyes were bright and flashing. It was the same youth grown to the prime of manhood when, at the Lyceum, thirty-one years afterwards, the commanding force of his passion in the play scene of "Hamlet" swept the audience like a storm.

In His Earliest Acting Days He Began to Study the Philosophy of His Art

But not only in those early years did Henry Irving develop his own powers. The work which he did then—the slow laborious toil of early mornings and late nights—aided much in his work when he became an actor in reality. Before he took an engagement he had made himself letter-perfect in a vast number of characters. He knew all the small parts in those plays of Shakespeare which were commonly acted, and in many that were acted but rarely, if at all. But he did not content himself with letter-perfection. He knew almost instinctively—with that instinct which is the result of conscious thought running freely—that acting is not merely the delivery of words, but that situations have to be studied, as also the relations of any one actor to all the others on the stage. Thus he had in his own mind some concrete idea not only of the bearing of the character of the expression of the acts and moods set down for him by the dramatist, but also of his special purpose in the general scheme of the play. Doubtless he altered an infinity of detail in these matters when he came to gain experience and to understand the rules of his craft.

> *Those rules of old, discovered, not devised,*
> *Are nature still—but nature modernized.*

Still later, when he became a producer of plays—when he had to understand for himself so that he might teach others all that belonged to the play and to every character, situation, development, and dominant idea in it—he began to realize more fully the philosophy of his chosen art. With this philosophy it is impossible to deal within the scope of an article, but I have in hand a book of my "Reminiscences of Henry Irving," and in it I hope to be privileged to say something of this subject gained from a rare intimacy of twenty-seven years. Be it sufficient to remember here that, when he entered on the active life of a player, he felt the full value of his previous thought and study. In the "fifties" stage matters were much cruder than they are now. The old "stock" system was based on an almost nightly change of the bill, and this required from young actors the perpetual study of new parts. Sometimes as many as six or seven had to be studied in a single week, and with the added difficulty that the "parts" were few and often imperfect. In stage parlance a "part" is that portion of the text which contains the lines allotted to the character, together with the necessary cues—the last words of each preceding speech. It is not hard to see what a vast help to a young player it must have been to know already and to *understand* the lines he had to speak. In such cases he could spend the time, necessarily given to the text by those not equally well prepared, on dress and concomitant matters. At this stage of theatrical evolution dress was an important element in the perplexities of the young actor. The "wardrobe" was usually limited, and priority of claim was a rigid rule. The "Tragedian," the "First Old Man," the "Heavy Father," the "Jeune Premier"—or "Juvenile Lead"—and the seconds and thirds of all these cults had choice in sequence of their importance—an importance fairly well expressed by the place toward the head of the salary list. Thus, when the "young men" came to be clothed, they had to be content with the leavings of the others. It was not a bad symbol of his having his "marshal's baton in his knapsack," that Irving had prepared himself for his task by other ways than by skill in the use of his sword. He had also attended to what might be called the commissariat department. He had spent with infinite pains and endless thought somewhere about a hundred pounds sterling on dress, wigs, and property—all those little means of giving finishing touches to appearance which belong to the equipment of an actor's craft. It is not too much to say that the consciousness of being properly, if not well, dressed is an assistance to any artist. It was not merely for self-pleasure that Rubens donned his best clothes when he took in hand his brush and palette and maul-stick.

The same care and foresight marked Irving's work on the stage, and for the stage, all through his long and strenuous life. He never left anything to chance. He never grudged or shirked work in any possible way. As an actor he always came to rehearsal—even to the first, whereat custom allows certain laxity—admirably prepared; letter-perfect in words, and with distinct ideas as to how every word should be spoken and every movement and action carried out consistently. His dress had been carefully thought out, made, and fitted not only to look well, but also to move in with ease. As a manager he had literally thought of everything. When he came to discuss scenery with the scene painters, he could tell them offhand not only about entrances and exits, not only of the picturesque effects which he wished to produce so as to heighten and aid the imagination of the spectators, but even of the suggested *sentiment* of the scene. This he would himself heighten later on by his lighting, for no one else could light a scene like Irving. I do not believe that any one before his time tried properly to do so. Since he showed the way, others, of course, have followed, but when he began there was no such practice as he evolved, as that of using together all sorts of different lights in different ways at the same time. The development of the use of colored lights for stage purposes was altogether his own doing.

Completeness of Detail and Artistic Finish, rather than Gain, Were His Aim

When he undertook a play he not only obtained the best expert archæological experience possible, but he himself studied the subject in his own way, always with an eye to stage effect and its bearing on the development of the play. He was so earnest in his work that other great artists were willing to help him—to devote their own talents and experience to the work he had in hand—and the fees which he paid for such services were frequently very great indeed. It might be truly said that all the arts rallied round him at his call. Such painters as Sir Lawrence Alma Tadema, Sir Edward Burne-Jones, Seymour Lucas, R. A., Edwin A. Abbey, R. A. Keeley Hasewell, and Charles Cattermole—such musicians as Sir Arthur Sullivan, Sir Charles Villiers Stanford, Sir Alexander Mackenzie, Sir Julius Benedict, and Edward German—all were eager contributors to the general effect. In addition were the scene painters who did the actual work—great men, these, in their own art: Hawes Craven, William Telbin, Joseph Harper, and Walter Hann. There was also the regular staff of various artists who were employed by him all the year round.

It is not too much to say that Henry Irving devoted his life to Art. He never wearied in her service; he never faltered or hesitated at any sacrifice necessary in her cause. For her he spent the fortune which he made; for her he exhausted the great strength of brain and body with which he was gifted. I worked for him and with him for seven and twenty years— ever since he took into his own hands the management of a theater and a company. In all that long time I never knew him to scamp or skimp anything. The artistic result and completeness were what he sought for, and nothing else would satisfy him. He did not aim at making money. I do not believe that ever, during his whole life, did he consider the ultimate substantial gain to arise from any work he took in hand. Money came and went; with him it was always only a means to an end. I have myself received for him, and pass through my hands in the expenditure incidental to his work, more than ten million dollars. His personal wants were simple, so that all he made was available for further work.

Devotion like this to an art could not fail of great achievement. The public was quick to acknowledge it, and the acknowledgement of the public is not only a stimulus, but also a means to further and loftier endeavor. In 1878, when he took over the management of the Lyceum Theater, he was known as a great actor. When he left it, in 1899, having transferred his rights to a company, the Lyceum had become known all over the world as the foremost theater anywhere—the home of the loftiest ideals and of the most thoughtful and artistic productions. His management was the most revered and respected of theatrical enterprises. The assistance and encouragement given to him by the great American public all through the vast continent from Maine to California, from the Great Lakes to the Gulf of Mexico, aided and encouraged him further in his work from1883, when he paid his first visit, till 1904, when he left its hospitable shores—for ever. The feeling of the nation for the man, or of the man for the nation, never changed, never lessened, but grew, and grew, and grew.

Of course no man can climb so high as he did into public esteem without being now and again assailed by the shafts of jealousy and envy, but throughout his long artistic life he always won the love and good will of his fellows. By them he was accorded not only the first place, but a place which had no second. When her late majesty, Queen Victoria, conferred on him the honor of knighthood, his fellow players presented him with an address set in a wondrous casket of gold and crystal which alone would cap the honor of any career. It was signed by every actor in the Britannic Kingdom, and is in itself a monument of affection and respect. No man could seek such a honor; few could deserve it. It stands alone in the annals of histrionic craft.

Henry Irving had, in an eminent degree, what has been called the courage of his own convictions. He always knew what he wanted and made his mind up for himself. His time for listening to advice was *before* an event, when he was gathering *data* for the formation of his own opinion. I never knew any other man—especially any other artist—who was so anxious to know how other men before him had acted the same part that he was about to essay: of what value they regarded particular readings of various portions of the text; how they led the intelligence of the audience from one point to another; what effects they produced, and how. And yet, when his time came for playing the part himself, it seemed like a new creation. He was always grateful when anyone could recall from memory of the past distinctive visions of detail: how any one was dressed; how or where on the stage he stood at given times, and the particular modulation or expression of voice with which certain passages were given; and he was being proportionately amazed with an ever fresh amazement at how little of such things he could ever find recalled, for it is an odd thing that very few persons—even actors themselves—can recall the detail of things they have seen and heard—nay, more, even of their own work. He used often, when he talked of such things, to instance that past master of stage knowledge, Dion Boucicault, who could recall nothing of one of the most famous parts of his early life on the stage, except that he "wore a white hat."

There Is Always some Element in the Smaller Nature which Will Resent Help

It is, I have noticed, always with great artists, and with them alone, that there is toleration and respect for the work of predecessors. Little people always want to do it all for themselves. There is some fierce streak of vanity or egoism in the smaller nature which resents help—even from the dead! This is, indeed, the supersublime of folly and every young artist should bear it in mind—whether the instrument of his skill be the pen, the brush, the pencil, the chisel, the string, or bow, or that most gracious of all instruments, the body, with all its graces and powers which God has given him and which he has labored to make perfect to artistic use. Nothing in the whole scheme of creation is independent. Every atom, every vitalized cell, every created entity, is dependent on other matter—on other force. All things are interdependent, and, unless one realizes this early in the life of artistic effort, he is apt to find his inner eyes so full of his own identity that there is neither time, place, nor opportunity for seeking for the great thoughts that precede great doings, or for recognizing them as great when, without his seeking, they float across his intellectual vision.

In his early days, on the stage Irving's qualities of resolution and endurance must have been pretty well tried. Fifty years ago the salaries of actors were poor and work was long and hard. The young men of to-day who stroll to rehearsal in the afternoon, if at all, and who draw salaries varying from twenty dollars to two hundred, would probably consider themselves aggrieved if they had to attend a long rehearsal every day in the week, as well as to play, perhaps several parts at night, and to live on a salary of from five to ten dollars a week. Irving had achieved a large measure of success as an actor after ten years of honest work, and was, in addition, manager of a popular London theater, when he was able to draw a weekly wage of forty dollars. In those days, too, there was little to cheer or enliven an actor's life. He had, practically, no social position at all. Such friends as he had, in addition to his own fellows, were the result of happy chance. Such pleasures as were his, outside his own calling, were walks on lonely hillsides, or late evenings in noisy taverns. The doubtful joys of the latter style of amusement had to be heavily paid for in many ways. It was not a matter of chance that the young, ambitious, self-reliant, resolute boy avoided, when possible, such pitfalls. His pleasures were of the hillside, when obtainable. During the two and one half years of his life in Edinburgh, where he went after a few preliminary months in Sunderland, he made it a practice to walk every day round Arthur's Seat—the mountain which towers picturesquely to the eastern side of the city. In these walks he studied the parts which he had to play at night or on coming nights, and thus contrived to mingle work with pleasure in a healthy way.

There was one special act in Irving's young life on the stage that has a lesson for all young artists. When, in 1859, having then had three full years of experience as a player, he got a three years' engagement in London and made his appearance at the Princess's, he came to the conclusion that his work was not yet good enough for metropolitan favor. So he resolutely bent himself to the task before him, and, with the reluctant consent of his manager, canceled his engagement. He went back to the weary routine and labor and hardship of the provinces, till the time should come for a more worthy effort. When we remember that a London engagement was, and is, the goal of an ambitious actor's hopes, and that it means regular work and regular pay and an ever increasing opportunity for distinguishing oneself, we can understand that his self-denying resolution was little less than heroic. When, however, he did come again, seven years later, he had his reward. He came to stay. He knew his work then, and knew that he knew it. His record from that on was an unbroken one of success and honor. His fight was won.

Thenceforward his success was that of the stage of his time. He won a place for acting, and the stage had only to act worthily to hold it. It might almost be said of his relation to the stage of his time, "He found it brick and left it marble."

The honors which crowned the later years of his life were many. He was given honorary degrees in three great universities, in the three nations of the kingdom of Britain. Dublin led the way, in 1892, with the degree of doctor of letters—Litt. D. Cambridge followed, in 1898, with the same degree, and Glasgow, in 1899, added that of doctor of laws—LL. D. In 1895, he was knighted by Queen Victoria, the first time that this honor or anything of the same kind was conferred on an actor in any country. This officially removed a long-standing grievance on the part of players;

up to the second decade of last century their calling was classed amongst others in the vagabond statutes.

And now he has been given the supreme honor which can only come after the end of life. He was accorded a public funeral and burial in Westminster Abbey. He lies in Poet's Corner, to the east of the south nave of the cathedral. His grave lies between those of Charles Dickens and David Garrick, and where he would have lain, I am right sure, had he been granted his choice—at the foot of the monument of Shakespeare.

PART VI

PERIOD WRITINGS ABOUT BRAM STOKER (1896–1913)

Figure 19.1   Photograph of Bram Stoker (*ca.* 1893), by Walery.

(From Laurence Irving, *Henry Irving: The Actor and His World* [London: Faber and Faber, 1951])

Chapter Nineteen

TO BRAM STOKER
(1893)[1]

HALL CAINE

W hen in dark hours and in evil humours my bad angel has sometimes made me think that friendship as it used to be of old,
friendship as we read of it in books, that friendship which is not a jilt
sure to desert us, but a brother born to adversity as well as success, is now
a lost quality, a forgotten virtue, a high partnership in fate degraded to
a low traffic in self-interest, a mere league of pleasure and business, then
my good angel for admonition or reproof has whispered the names of a
little band of friends, whose friendship is a deep stream that buoys me
up and makes no noise; and often first among those names has been
your own.

Down to this day our friendship has needed no solder of sweet words
to bind it, and I take pleasure in showing by means of this unpretending
book that it is founded not only on personal liking and much agree-
ment, but on some wholesome difference and even a little disputation.
"The Last Confession" is an attempt to solve a moral problem which

we have discussed from opposite poles of sympathy—the absolute value and sanctity of human life, the right to fight, the right to kill, the right to resist evil and to set aside at utmost need the letter of the sixth commandment. "The Blind Mother," is a somewhat altered version of an episode in an early romance, and it is presented afresh, with every apology, because you with another friend, Theodore Watts, consider it the only worthy part of an unworthy book, and also because it appears to be at all points a companion to the story that goes before it. Of "Cap'n Davy's Honeymoon," I might perhaps say that it is the complement of the other two—all three being stories of great and consuming love, father's, mother's and husband's—but I prefer to confess that I publish it because I know that if any one should smile at my rough Manx comrade, doubting if such a man is in nature and now found among men, I can always answer him and say "Ah, then, I am richer than you are by one friend at least—Capt'n Davy without his ruggedness and without his folly, but with his simplicity, his unselfishness and his honour—Bram Stoker!"

Hawthorns, Keswick, 1892

Chapter Twenty

GREEN ROOM GOSSIP (1896)[1]

[…]

By the way, "The Spirit of the Times," a most influential New York newspaper, pays this handsome tribute to Mr. Bram Stoker, Sir Henry's business manager. If Mr. Stoker has ever blushed, let him blush now— but I am told that business managers never do such things.

> Bram Stoker is Hercules among managers. Only those behind the scenes know how much he does, for he accomplishes it so easily that he always has time to write a book, to chat with a friend, to promptly rectify anything of which the public might complain. He seems omnipresent, indefatigable, indispensable. The difference in Abbey's Theatre when he is there and when he goes away is like that between sunshine and shadow, and we express the sentiment of all the members of the Press in thanking him most cordially for his courtesies and consideration.

[…]

Figure 20.1   Illustration of "Mr. Bram Stoker" (1897).

(From Walter Calvert, *Sir Henry Irving and Miss Ellen Terry: A Record of Over Twenty Years at the Lyceum Theatre* [London: Henry J. Drane, 1897], 40)

Chapter Twenty-One

NIGHT WITH SIR HENRY IRVING: WITH INTIMATIONS THAT BRAM STOKER WAS ALSO IN THE NEIGHBORHOOD (1900)[1]

R. M. FIELD

Do you mind, Bram, my boy, that a man's chiefest joy
He may whisper the priest when he comes to confess him
Is the thought, when all's done and his life race is run,
"I have sat up all night with Sir Henry. God bless him!"

There were nights. It is true, and, I fear, not a few—
Cleopatra had some and Lacullus had others—
When revels from 1 to the rise of the sun
Were resented by wives and detested by mothers.

But, Bram, do you mind that a night of our kind
Disturbs neither wife nor the parent maternal?
Our proceedings, I think—barring only the drink—
Might be safely inscribed in the Ladies' Home Journal.

Yet the things that we do, known to me and to you,
Shalt remain to the curious public a fable;
And still we betray no great trust when we say:
Where Sir Henry sits down is the head of the table.

What cares he who sups that the smile in the cups
May become in the morning a leer to distress him?
And who would not scorn—not the rose, but the thorn
Who has sat up all night with Sir Henry? God bless him!

Wisdom centered, 'tis said, at historic Turk's Head.
When Johnson, Sir Joshua, Boswell, and Davy
Sat down to partake of a chop or a steak
And Johnson dropped pearls somewhat spattered with gravy.

Great pleasure, perhaps, for such pompous old chaps.
Though I fancy that time has improved on the story;
And Bram, do you mind, I am half-way inclined
To believe the Turks Head cannot steal all the glory.

The wine is as sweet, just as toothsome the meat;
The cook is as honest and true to his labors;
The wit is as keen, though, perchance, not so mean,
As when Johnson grew famous reviling his neighbors.

If you only knew, Bram, how sore prompted I am—
Did ever man have such temptation possess him! —
You would bid me let go and tell all that I know
Of the night we sat up with Sir Henry. God bless him!

And yet I can see that for you and for me
And the others who shared in the happiness festal.
It is better by far to leave things as they are,
For that night was a virgin, the virgin a vestal.

And when in the gray of the coming of day
Our eyes to the wide-rolling lake were directed,
We recognized then, as should all sober men,
The one unsafe liquid we wisely neglected.

'Tis well that we know not the hour that we go.
For this we are careless, for this we are merry.
But, early or late, we must yield to our fate,
And cross the dark flood on the Stygian ferry.

And whether, old friend, I am first at the end,
Or whether your summons must leave us in sadness.
I know we shall meet, and together our feet
Shall press the soft meads of Elysium's gladness.

And when we have met there is one to come yet—
Ah, long may Time linger and gently caress him!—
But, coming at last, we shall think of the past,
And sit up all night with Sir Henry. God bless him!

("Chicago Evening Post")

Figure 21.1 Illustration, "Whitelaw Reid Welcomed to England by the Pilgrims" (1905) in which are pictured, among other notable attendees, "Mr. Bram Stoker," Sir Henry Irving, and "Mr. Kipling."

(From *The New York Times* [July 16, 1905]: 4)

Chapter Twenty-Two

ACTING-MANAGER AND AUTHOR: BRAM STOKER FINDS RECREATION IN WRITING ROMANCES (1902)[1]

Figure 22.1   Photograph of Bram Stoker (*ca.* 1904) at his craft, used to help promote the publication of *The Jewel of Seven Stars* (1903).

(From *The San Francisco Call* [March 13, 1904]. California Digital Newspaper Collection, Center for Bibliographic Studies and Research, University of California, Riverside, htttp://cdnc.ucr.edu)

There are few better known figures in the theatrical circles of England than the almost herculean one of Bram Stoker, Sir Henry Irving's acting-manager, and during the 19 years that the Irving tours of his country have covered Stoker has become nearly as familiar here. It may be as well to explain that the term "actor-manager," which has been imported from England and is now in general use, does not imply that the bearer has anything to do with the acting. On the contrary, his duties are usually confined to the business end, and the hyphenated-words show that he is acting for the manager and is not the pecuniarily responsible proprietor or manager.

Our theatre-going public always sees Bram Stoker near the ticket-taker from the time the doors are opened till the great majority of the audience is seated. His ruddy face, bright eyes and beaming smile are sufficient to placate even the most cross-grained visitor, and should any little difficulty or mistake occur, he can smooth it out with most diplo-matic skill and with that unvarying gentle courtesy which characterizes all the Irving company and is inspired by and reflected from "the chief" himself.

But if, as often happens, there is an unmanageable crowd and an ugly rush at the gallery entrance, Bram Stoker will surely be found in the thick of the scrimmage, giving convincing evidence that he has not for-gotten his early football training.

Bram Stoker was born in Dublin, Ire., a little over 50 years ago, and is the son of a late Abraham Stoker, who was in the British civil service, his duties lying in the chief secretary's office in Dublin. Young Bram was first sent to a private school in that city, and later entered the famous Trinity College. He graduated from there and subsequently took his M. A. degree.

While at the university Stoker took honors in science (pure math-ematics), was president of the philosophical society and silver-medalist of the historical society. With these intellectual occupations he combined great devotion to athletic sports, and was the university champion in that field.

In 1866 he was appointed a clerk in the Irish civil service, and remained in the government employ till 1878, during the last year filling the important position of inspector of petty sessions.

When Henry Irving visited Dublin, under the late Col. Bateman's management, he met Bram Stoker, and a friendship began which has lasted unbroken till today. A promise was then given by Irving that when he should become a manger on his own account, Stoker should be associated with him.

A more fortunate and happy connection has rarely, if ever, been made. Stoker has always entertained the most unbounded admiration for Irving's talents, and has been his most faithful, loyal, and indefatigable assistant, while Irving has reposed absolute confidence and implicit reliance not only on Stoker's business ability, but also on his literary and artistic taste and discernment.

There can be little doubt that much of Irving's pecuniary success has been due to his acting-manager's ability. We all know that no matter how great may be the artistic impulse and how eminent its achievements the adroit exploitation of them is necessary to the public patronage. It is only necessary to recall the terribly expensive failure Edwin Booth made at his own theatre, although giving superb productions with splendid casts, to emphasize this fact.

Bram Stoker's capacity for work is the envy and despair of all his associates. He never seems to know fatigue, and his only recreation appears to be a change of occupations. When he moves it is with extraordinary rapidity and apparently oblivious of all obstacles. On one of the earlier tours he rushed through a plate glass door in the lobby of the Chestnut Street Opera House, Philadelphia, and fortunately escaped without anything more than a scratch.

"An Irishman's luck" he calmly remarked in his usual rather high voice, and with that delicious Dublin brogue, which is almost identical with that which Dion Boucicault made so familiar and enjoyable.

During his work at the London Lyceum Stoker found or made time to "eat his terms," and became registered as a barrister-at-law of the Inner Temple. It is a mystery to most people to know when he gets time to write his books but the secret is that this is his principal amusement during his holiday.

His first book, although he had for several years previously been a contributor to newspapers and magazines, was a technical one on "The Duties of Clerks of Petty Session." Then he branched out into fiction, with "Under the Sunset," "Snake's Pass," "The Wather's Mon'" [*sic*] in 1894; "The Shoulder of Shasta," 1896; "Dracula," 1897, and "Miss Betty," 1898.

Of these "Dracula" is by far the best known here. It was published by the Harpers and in a serial form by the *New York Sun*, and more than a year later by a syndicate of newspapers. The story is that of a human vampire, and the author's power to make the impossible seem real is extraordinarily convincing. Some descriptions of scenery in the wildest country of the Danubian banks are written with a true painter's insight.

Bram Stoker married Florence Anne Lemon, daughter of the late Lieut. Col. Balcombe. Mrs. Stoker, who was famed as one of the most beautiful women in England, has accompanied her husband on some of his tours to America.

In London Stoker lives in St. Leonard's terrace, Chelsea, and, though he has little time for club life, he is a member of the Authors', National, Liberal, and Greenroom.

[...]

Chapter Twenty-Three

STORY OF SENATOR QUAY (1904)[1]

Figure 23.1   Illustration appearing with "The Story of Senator Quay."
(From *Oswego Daily Palladium* [New York] [June 27, 1904]: 3)

Politicians who knew Senator Quay are familiar with the little kegs of sauerkraut he sent to them every year between Thanksgiving and Christmas, says the New York Times. He was as regular with them as Rhode Island senators are with their turkeys. Nothing pleased Senator Quay more than to have somebody praise his sauerkraut. He superintended the making of it himself on his Beaver county farm and always had a supply at his home in Philadelphia. Thus it happened that he sent a keg to Bram Stoker, who was in that city at the time with Sir Henry Irving. The senator did not say in his note that the keg contained sauerkraut. He wrote simply, "A little delicacy from my farm I hope you'll enjoy."

Bram Stoker produced the keg at an after theater supper. "I wonder what's in it?" he said to his guests.

"Scrapple, perhaps," suggested Willie Collier, who knows the weakness of Philadelphians.

"Scrapple be blanked," said a German named Wundt, who was there at the time looking after Herr Conried's interests. "Don't you know that you have one of Senator Quay's famous kegs of sauerkraut? Man, it is worth its weight in gold."

Wundt was told he could have the sauerkraut provided he did not eat it on the premises. Something else was ordered for supper. Wundt went home with the prize greatly rejoicing.

Chapter Twenty-Four

BRAM STOKER (1912)[1]

Figure 24.1 Painting of an aging Bram Stoker (*ca.* 1911).

(From *The Bookman: A Magazine of Literature and Life* 32, no. 5 (January 1911): 456)

The fidus Achates of Henry Irving, perhaps the greatest influence on the theater in the history of stage affairs, has just died in London, and although he was a talented novelist, historian and journalist, Bram Stoker is known only as the "personal representative and business manager" of the great English actor. Meeting with Stoker early in life wrought a great change in Sir Henry's career. Up to that time he had devoted himself entirely to his art and had cared nothing for the publicity or business ends, which were later placed entirely in Stoker's hands thereafter, and cared for in such excellent manner that they had much to do with Irving's success at home and abroad.

In 1878 Irving met Hall Caine and Bram Stoker as newspaper men. "Old Shakespeare," Irving always called Caine, and in Stoker he quickly recognized a man whose services he needed. Stoker willingly accepted an offer from him, and they traveled together until Irving's death, and it was Stoker who has written the most attractive life of the master producer. Irving altered his opinion of newspaper men after viewing Stoker and Caine as representatives of the craft, and thereafter he was courteous and amiable whenever he was asked for an interview by one representing a newspaper.

Stoker was 64 years of age when he died, but he retained the buoyancy of youth in a remarkable manner and his closest friends declared he would live to be 90 and then appear to be a young man. His most famous novel was "Dracula," a blood curdling tale which was the more remarkable to all who knew that it had been written by a mild, gentle Irishman and man of the world, who went about his way peacefully, never raising his voice in argument. Lately he published a book of strange footnotes to history that caused some comment, but it is as Irving's partner in gigantic enterprises that he will be remembered.

BRAM STOKER, IRISHMAN (1913)[1]

Figure 25.1 Bram Stoker modeling as William II in 1911 for the Mural Panel, "William II Building the Tower of London," by G. Goldsborough Anderson, in the Royal Exchange, London.

(From *History Stories of Other Lands*, book 4, ed. Arthur Guy Terry [Chicago: Row, Peterson & Co., 1915], 51)

The announcement was made the past week on the "Book" pages of the daily press, of the sale by auction of the library of Bram Stoker, the "'English author and scholar" who died recently. English forssooth! Someone once said that when an Irishman did anything creditable he was English; when he did the opposite, then he was Irish. Constantly is the effort made to rob Irish brains and genius and courage of the credit their due, Bram Stoker was a fine Dublin man, six feet three and as brainy as he was big. He was a really rabid home ruler and keenly sensitive of the good name of his native land, which he loved, with a rare devotion. He was for years Henry Irving's business manager and it is no secret that he wrote all of that talented actor's speeches and letters, [mana]ged all of his business affairs, and made many, if not all of the changes in the plays which Irving produced. In short Mr. Stoker did all of the literary work of the friendly co-partnership which existed for years with Mr. Irving. Mr. Stoker never let anybody, when the occasion called for a declaration, forget that he was Irish through and through without one title of Angloism in his make-up. He had a superb collection of rare books manuscripts, paintings and miniatures. He would be the first to declare that he was an Irishman, Irish educated, too, and that whatever talents he possessed were due to his Irish birth and Irish environment.

"Boston Pilot, Philadelphia Catholic Standard and Times"

PART VII

CATALOGUE OF VALUABLE BOOKS, AUTOGRAPH LETTERS, AND ILLUMINATED AND OTHER MANUSCRIPTS, INCLUDING THE LIBRARY OF THE LATE BRAM STOKER, ESQ. AND ASSOCIATED PRESS (1913)

Figure 26.1   Death mask of President Lincoln "without the disfiguring beard," in bronze, from the original mould by Leonard W. Volk.

(From Isabel Moore, *Talks in a Library with Laurence Hutton* [New York: G. P. Putnam's Sons, 1907], 112–113)

Chapter Twenty-Six

FIRST DAY'S SALE: THE PROPERTY OF BRAM STOKER, ESQ. (DECEASED) (1913)[1]

CATALOGUE

OF

VALUABLE BOOKS,

AUTOGRAPH LETTERS,

AND

Illuminated and other Manuscripts.

FIRST DAY'S SALE.

The Property of Bram Stoker, Esq. (DECEASED).

OCTAVO ET INFRA.

LOT 1.

UDGE (E. A. Wallis) History of Egypt from the End of the Neolithic Period to the Death of Cleopatra VII, 9 vol. *illustrations*   1902

2.

Budge (E. A. Wallis) Egyptian Ideas of the Future Life, Egyptian Magic, Easy Lessons in Egyptian Hieroglyphics, 3 vol. *illustrations*, 1899-1902—The Mummy, Chapters on Egyptian Funereal Archæology, 88 *illustrations, Cambridge*, 1893 : etc.   (7)

3   Guhl and Koner: Life of the Greeks and Romans, translated by F. Hueffer, *illustrations, n. d.* — Legge (Wm.) History of the Administration of the Earl of Dufferin in Canada, *Montreal*, 1878— Raumer (F. von) America and the American People, translated by W. W. Turner, *New York*, 1846 ; etc.   (5)

B

First Day   2   OCTAVO

4   Browning (E. B.) Poetical Works, 6 vol. *portraits*   1890

5   Jefferson (Joseph) Autobiography, *portrait, character portraits and
    plates, red cloth, uncut, t. e. g. with inscription on title : " To Bram
    Stoker, with kind regards from the Author's daughter, Margaret
    J. Farjion "*   1890

6   Jefferson (Joseph) Autobiography ; another edition, *portrait, etc. white
    cloth, uncut, t. e. g. presentation copy " To Bram Stoker "*
                                                      New York, 1890

7   Shakespeare (Wm.) Works, edited by Howard Staunton. ÉDITION DE
    LUXE, 15 vol. *portrait, and illustrations by Sir John Gilbert,
    original cloth, uncut*   *imp. 8vo.* 1881

8   MEREDITH (GEORGE) Works, with Poems, Essays, Miscellaneous
    Prose, etc. ÉDITION DE LUXE, 35 vol. *and the illustrations prepared
    for this edition in a case, portrait on Japanese paper, original
    linen boards, uncut, with autograph signature of Author on fly-leaf
    of vol. I*   1896-1911

9   Herriot (Edouard) Madame Récamier, translated by Alys Hallard,
    2 vol. 15 *portraits in photogravure, blue cloth, uncut, t. e. g.* 1906

10 Shelley (P. B.) Life, by Edward Dowden, 2 vol. *portrait, brown cloth,
    uncut*   1886

11 Blauchan (N.) Nature's Garden, an Aid to Knowledge of our Wild
    Flowers and their Insect Visitors, *coloured plates and illustrations,
    green cloth, uncut*   *imp. 8vo. New York*, 1900

12 Carleton (Wm.) Traits and Stories of the Irish Peasantry, edited by
    D. J. O'Donoghue, 4 vol. *portrait and illustrations, green cloth,
    uncut, t. e. g.*   1896

13 Ruskin (J.) Works, 12 vol. *blue cloth*   *New York*, 1887

14 Ruskin (J.) Works, vol. XVI–XX (Arrows of the Chace, Miscellanea,
    and Fors Clavigera), 5 vol.   *ib.* 1886

15 Sherman (Gen. Wm. T.) Memoirs, 2 vol. *portrait and maps, New York,*
    1887—MacMullen (J.) History of Canada, *morocco, g. e.* 1868—
    Lossing (B. J.) The Hudson, from the Wilderness to the Sea,
    frontispiece, engravings, cloth gilt, g. e. n. d.   (4)

16 Burton (Isabel) Arabia, Egypt, India, 2 *maps and* 15 *illustrations,
    presentation copy, with autograph inscription : " Bram Stoker,
    with Isabel Burton's kind regards, Feb. 21st, 1879 "*   1879

17 Newfeld (Chas.) A Prisoner of the Khaleefa, Twelve Years' Captivity
    at Omdurman, *portraits and plans*, 1899—Macquoid (G. S.) Up
    and Down Sketches of Travel, 29 *illustrations by T. R. Macquoid,
    presentation copy, with autograph inscription : " To Bram Stoker,
    Esq. with the kind regards of Gilbert S. Macquoid, April, 1890,"
    brown cloth, t. e. g.* 1890   (2)

18 America. The George Catlin Indian Gallery in the U.S. National
    Museum, with Memoir and Statistics by Thomas Donaldson, *maps
    and numerous illustrations*   *Washington*, 1887

19   Craik (G. L.) History of English Literature and the English Language
     from the Norman Conquest, 2 vol. 1866—Molloy (J. F.) The
     Faiths of the Peoples, 2 vol. *presentation copy, with autograph
     inscription:* "*To Mrs. Bram Stoker, with kind regards from J.
     Fitzgerald Molloy,*" 1892   (4)

20   Bernhardt (Sarah) Memoirs, *portraits and illustrations, blue cloth,
     uncut, t. e. g.* 1907—Fitzpatrick (W. J.) Life of Charles Lever,
     portrait, presentation copy, with autograph inscription: "*To Bram
     Stoker, Esq. with the Author's kindest regards,*" *n. d.* — Ernst
     (W.) Memoirs of the Earl of Chesterfield, *portrait,* 1893   (3)

21   Hibbert Journal (The), vol. I, no. 1-3, vol. III, no. 1 and 4, vol. IV,
     vol. V, no. 2 and 3, vol. VI, no. I; together 12 parts, *as issued*
                                                                 1902-7

22   Cervantes (M. de) History of Don Quixote, translated by Thomas
     Shelton, with Introductions by J. Fitzmaurice Kelly, 4 vol. *half
     buckram, uncut, with inscription:* "*Bram Stoker, with very kind
     regards of W. B. Blaikie, Edinburgh,* 16 *June,* 1896 "   1896

23   Shakespeare (Wm.) Works, New Variorum Edition, edited by H. H.
     Furness, vol. II–V, etc. 5 vol. *portrait, cloth, t. e. g. presentation
     copy, with autograph inscription:* "*Bram Stoker, in return for
     many courtesies and with the regards of Horace Howard Furness,
     Jr. September,* 1908 "   *Philadelphia,* 1874-1908

24   Gallup (Mrs. E. W.) Bi-literal Cypher of Sir Francis Bacon discovered
     in his Works and deciphered, *portraits and facsimiles,* 1900—
     Marston (E.) After Work Fragments from the Workshop of an
     old Publisher, *portraits and plates, presentation copy, with auto-
     graph inscription:* "*Bram Stoker, with the kind regards of E.
     Marston, March* 15/05," 1904   (2)

25   Herkomer (Prof. Sir Hubert von) My School and my Gospel, *illustra-
     tions, uncut, presentation copy, with pencil autograph inscription*
     "*To Bram Stoker, from the Author,* 1908 "   *imp. 8vo.*   1908

26   Barrie (J. M.) The Little Minister, "Maude Adams Edition," *illustra-
     tions, some extra included, white buckram, uncut, t. e. g. in case*
                                                         New York, 1898

27   Caine (Hall) The Manxman, a Novel, LARGE PAPER, 2 vol. *one of 250
     copies, illlustrations selected by the Author, and portrait, vellum,
     uncut, t. e. g. presentation copy from the Author, with autograph
     inscription:* "*To my dear friend Bram Stoker, with love and
     greeting, Hall Caine, New York, Dec.* 3*rd,* 1895," *in case*
                                                         New York, 1895

28   Blackburn (Henry) Randolph Caldecott: a Personal Memoir of his
     Early Art Career, *portrait and illustrations,* 1887—Blackburne
     (E. Owens) Illustrious Irishwomen from the Earliest Ages to the
     Present Century, 2 vol. *presentation copy, with autograph inscrip-
     tion:* "*Bram Stoker, Esq. with E. Owens Blackburne's Compts.
     London, Oct.* 1877," 1877   (3)

First Day   4   OCTAVO

29   Ellwanger (G. H.) The Pleasures of the Table. Account of Gas-
      tronomy from Ancient Days to Present Times, *illustrations, uncut,*
      t. e. g. New York, 1902—Wilson (A.) Glimpses of Nature, *illus-*
      trations, presentation copy from the Author, with autograph in-
      scription, 1891 ; etc.   (3)

30   Ward (H.) Five Years with the Congo Cannibals, *illustrations by the*
      Author, etc., presentation copy, 1891—Hatton (F.) North Borneo,
      with Biographical Sketch and Notes, *portrait and illustrations,*
      presentation copy, with autograph inscription: " *Bram Stoker,*
      M.A., from his friend Joseph Hatton, 1886 "   (2)

31   Walker (F. A.) History of the Second Army Corps in the Army of the
      Potomac, *portraits and map*   *New York,* 1886

32   Winter (Wm.) Shakespeare's England, *illustrations, presentation copy,*
      with autograph inscription: " *To Mr. and Mrs. Bram Stoker,*
      from their old friend William Winter, September, 1910," *New*
      York, 1910—Life and Writings of William Law Symonds, *portrait*
      and plate, 1908   (2)

33   Sikes (W.) British Goblins : Welsh Folk-Lore, Fairy Mythology, etc.
      illustrations, 1880—O'Donnell (E.) Byways of Ghost-Land, 1911
      —MacRitchie (D.) Fians, Fairies and Picts, *illustrations,* 1893 ;
      etc.   (6)

34   Waliszewski (K.) Story of a Throne (Catherine II of Russia), *portrait,*
      1895—Romance of an Empress, *portrait,* 1895—Cushman (Char-
      lotte) Her Letters, and Memories of her Life, edited by Emma
      Stebbins, *portrait, Boston,* 1878 ; etc.   (5)

35   Clemens (S. L.) A Connecticut Yankee in King Arthur's Court, *illus-*
      trations, New York, 1891 — Willson (B.) The New America,
      presentation copy from the Author, 1903—Hickey (W.) Constitu-
      tion of the United States of America, *half morocco, Philadelphia,*
      1851 ; etc.   (4)

36   Clemens (S. L.) The Man that Corrupted Hadleyburg, etc. by Mark
      Twain, *frontispiece, presentation copy, with autograph inscription :*
      " *To Bram Stoker, from his friend the Author, London, Aug.* 24/00,"
      1900—Tom Sawyer, Detective, *portrait, presentation copy* " *To*
      B. S. from M. T. with warm regards, London, December, 1896,"
      1897 ; and others by the same author   (7)

37   Dibdin (Thos. *of Theatres Royal, Covent Garden, etc.*) Reminiscences,
      2 vol. *portrait,* 1827—Garrick (David) Life, by Percy Fitzgerald,
      2 vol. *portrait,* 1868—Murphy (A.) Life of David Garrick, *uncut,*
      Dublin, 1801   (5)

38   American Statesmen, edited by John T. Morse junior, 16 vol. 1896, *etc.*

39   Shakespeare (Wm.) Works, reduced facsimile of First Folio, with
      Introduction by J. O. Halliwell-Phillipps, 1876—Bormann (E.)
      The Shakespeare Secret, *illustrations, roy.* 8*vo,* 1895—Shakespeare's
      Garden of Girls, *frontispiece,* 1885—Donnelly (I.) The Cipher in
      the Plays and on the Tombstone, 1900, *two copies ;* and others
      relating to Shakespeare   (12)

OCTAVO 5 *First Day*

40 Brereton (Austin) Henry Irving, a Biographical Sketch, 17 *portraits imp. 8vo. New York*, 1884

41 STEVENSON (ROBERT LOUIS) WORKS, EDINBURGH EDITION, including his Letters to his Friends, Appendix, etc. 30 vol. *portrait, etc. red cloth, uncut Edinb*. 1894-9

42 Stevenson (R. L.) Misadventures of John Nicholson, *New York, n. d.;* The Merry Men, *ib.* 1887; A Footnote to History, *ib.* 1892; Across the Plains, FIRST EDITION, *buckram, uncut*, 1892 (4)

43 Stevenson (R. L.) Father Damien, an Open Letter to the Reverend Doctor Hyde of Honolulu, pp. 30, *original wrappers, uncut* 1890

44 Tennyson (A.) Ode on the Death of the Duke of Wellington, FIRST EDITION, 1852; another edition, 1853—Corbet (W. J.) Battle of Fontenoy, *Dublin*, 1871; etc. *some presentation copies to Bram Stoker from the authors* (20)

45 Tennyson (A.) Maud and other Poems, FIRST EDITION, *original cloth*, 1855; Gareth and Lynette, FIRST EDITION, *original cloth, initials on title*, 1872 (2)

46 Dibdin (C.) Complete History of the English Stage, vol. I-II, 2 vol. *uncut, n. d.*—Calcraft (J. W.) Defence of the Stage, *uncut, Dublin*, 1839—Senior (Wm.) The Old Wakefield Theatre, *frontispiece, uncut, Wakefield*, 1894; and others (14)

47 Stirling (E.) Old Drury Lane, Fifty Years' Recollections, 2 vol. 1881 —Hazlitt (W.) Criticisms and Dramatic Essays of the English Stage, 1854; and others relating to the Stage, etc. (24)

48 Cibber. Theophilus Cibber to David Garrick, Esq. with Dissertations on Theatrical Subjects, with Appendix, *frontispiece and plates, one inserted*, 1759—Shaw (A.) Theatrical World of 1894, with Introduction by G. B. Shaw, 1895—Brereton (A.) Dramatic Notes, *half morocco*, 1885; and others, Plays, etc. *a parcel*

49 Shakespeare (W.) Maude Adams' Acting Edition of Romeo and Juliet, *illustrations, New York*, 1899—Talfourd (T. N.) Ion, a Tragedy, 1836—Beecher (H. W.) Eulogy on General Grant, *autograph signature of Ellen Terry on wrapper and title, New York*, 1885— Falconer (E.) Francesca, a Dream of Venice, 1865; etc. (14)

50 Shipman (L. E.) A Group of Theatrical Caricatures, 12 *plates by W. J. Gladding, New York*, 1897—Jones (H. A.) Triumph of the Philistines, a Comedy, 1895—Brereton (A.) Some Famous Hamlets, with Appendix, 1884—Fargus (F. J.) Bound Together, vol. I, *presentation copy, with autograph inscription: " To Florence Bram Stoker from Hugh Conway, Aug.* 12 /84," 1884 (4)

51 Hilles (Malcolm W.) A Queen's Love, a Drama, FIRST EDITION, *presentation copy, with autograph inscription: " Presented to Henry Irving, Esq. with the Author's Compts.* 13 *Jan.* 1880," *Keighley*, 1879—Long Island Publications, No. 1, The Battle of Brooklyn, a Farce in Two Acts, *presentation copy to " Mr. Bram Stoker," only a few copies reprinted for private distribution, New York*, 1776, *reprinted Brooklyn*, 1873 (2)

First Day 6 OCTAVO

52 Fargus (F. J.) Called Back, by Hugh Conway, FIRST EDITION, *morocco, g. e. presentation copy, with autograph inscription:* "*To Bram Stoker from Hugh Conway, F. J. Fargus, Aug.* 1, 1884"
Bristol, 1884

53 Wilkins (Wm.) Songs of Study, FIRST EDITION, *presentation copy, with autograph inscription:* "*Bram Stoker, Esq. with the Author's kind regards*"
1881

54 Field (Eugene) A Little Book of Western Verse, New York, 1893; Second Book of Verse, *ib.* 1893—Eugene Field, a Study in Heredity and Contradictions, by Mason Thompson, 2 vol. *portraits, views and facsimile illustrations, uncut,* New York, 1901 (4)

55 Bancroft. Mr. and Mrs. Bancroft on and off the Stage, written by themselves, 2 vol. *portraits, half calf gilt, m. e. presentation copy, with autograph inscription:* "*To Bram Stoker from S. B. Bancroft, Christmas,* 1889"
1888

56 Watson (Wm.) Lachrymæ Musarum and other Poems, 1892; Poems, 1892; The Eloping Angels, 1893; Excursions in Criticism, 1893 (4)

57 Caine (Hall) The Mahdi, or Love and Race, a Drama in Story, *no.* 66 *of* 100 *copies, privately printed for copyright, uncut, inscription on title:* "*Private Copy, Hall Caine*"
1894

58 Lloyd (John Uri) The Right Side of the Car, *illustrations on Japanese paper, buckram gilt, uncut, presentation copy, with pencil autograph inscription:* "*Will Mr. Bram Stoker accept this little token of the Author's regard, with the Author's best wishes? sincerely John Uri Lloyd, Cincinnati, March 5th,* 1904"
Boston, 1897

59 Lloyd (J. U.) Red Head, *illustrations and decorations by R. B. Birch, white cloth gilt, uncut, t. e. g. presentation copy, with autograph inscription:* "*To Mr. Bram Stoker, with kind regards and best wishes of John Uri Lloyd, Thanksgiving,* 1903"
New York, 1903

60 Lloyd (J. U.) Scroggins, *illustrations and decorations by R. B. Birch, linen boards, uncut, t. e. g. presentation copy, with pencil autograph inscription:* "*To my friend Mr. Bram Stoker, with many happy recollections and pleasant hours spent together, John Uri Lloyd*"
ib. 1904

61 Lloyd (J. U.) Warwicks of the Knobs, *illustrations of Knob County, presentation copy, with pencil autograph note on fly-leaf:* "*My dear Mr. Stoker. Should you read this book I beg you to bear in mind that I consider it my best (excepting Red Head) study of Kentucky character, sincerely yours John Uri Lloyd. To my friend Mr. Bram Stoker*"
ib. 1901

62 Jacobi (C. T.) Some Notes on Books and Printing, *uncut,* 1903— Winter (Wm.) The Press and the Stage, *linen boards, uncut, presentation copy, with autograph inscription:* "*To Mr. and Mrs. Bram Stoker, with the regards of their old friend, William Winter, June 24,* 1889," New York, 1889 (2)

OCTAVO   7   *First Day*

63   Stoker (Bram) Under the Sunset, *illustrations by W. Fitzgerald and*
     W. V. Cockburn, vellum, g. e.   1882

64   Walton and Cotton. The Complete Angler, edited by G. W. Bethune,
     with Notes, Bibliographical Preface, etc. *portraits, plates, etc. calf*
     gilt, g. e.   *roy. 8vo. New York,* 1880

65   Jacobs (W. W.) A Master of Craft, 12 *illustrations,* 1900 ; Light
     Freights, 12 *illustrations,* 1902 ; The Lady of the Barge, *illustra-*
     tions, 1902; Captains All, *illustrations,* 1905; and other Novels (12)

66   Churchill (Winston) Richard Carvel, *illustrations, presentation copy,*
     with autograph inscription : " To Bram Stoker, October 31, 1899.
     Another Gentleman who belongs to both sides of the Atlantic,
     W. C." 1889—Moore (F. F.) According to Plato, *presentation copy,*
     with autograph inscription : " To Florence A. L. Stoker, with
     affectionate regards from F. Frankfort Moore," New York, 1901 (2)

67   Molloy (J. Fitzgerald) Romance of the Irish Stage, 2 vol. 2 *portraits,*
     presentation copy, with autograph inscription : " To Bram Stoker.
     with best wishes from Fitzgerald Molloy," 1897 ; Life and
     Adventures of Edmund Kean, Tragedian, 2 vol. *autograph*
     inscription : " To Bram Stoker, Esq. with Fitzgerald Molloy's kind
     regards," 1888   (4)

68   Cunningham (Peter) Story of Nell Gwyn and the Sayings of Charles
     the Second, with Index, *uncut, New York,* 1883—Bowker (Alfred)
     King Alfred Millenary, *illustrations, presentation copy, " Bram*
     Stoker, Esq. from Alfred Bowker," 1902   *imp. 8vo.* (2)

69   Caine (Hall) The Deemster, a Romance, FIRST EDITION, 3 vol. 1887 ;
     The Little Manx Nation, 1891 ; Fate of Fenella, 3 vol. *illustra-*
     tions, 1892 ; etc.   (9)

70   Ordnance Survey of Great Britain, with Index, 110 *folding sheets on*
     linen, in 19 solander cases   1848, *etc.*

71   Clarke (Jos. I. C.) Mâlmoida, a Metrical Romance, *vellum, uncut, t. e. g.*
     presentation copy, with autograph inscription : " To my good friend
     Bram Stoker, Esq. in souvenir of many gracious acts, with the
     hearty good wishes of Joseph I. C. Clarke, New York, March 19,
     1894 "   1893

72   Braddon (M. E.) Rough Justice, *presentation copy, with autograph*
     inscription : " To Bram Stoker, with kindest regards from M. E.
     Braddon, Richmond, March 22nd, 1898," 1898—Parry (Judge)
     England's Elizabeth, *presentation copy, " Bram Stoker, with all*
     good wishes from Edward A. Parry, June 1st, 1904," 1904   (2)

73   Tayler (Jeremy) Rule and Exercises of Holy Living, *presentation copy,*
     with inscription : " To my kind friend Bram Stoker, a souvenir of
     some of my happiest hours at the dear Lyceum, M. E. Braddon,
     December, 1892 "   Bickers, 1873

74   Hoffman (E. T. W.) Weird Tales, translated by J. T. Bealby, 2 vol.
     portrait, New York, 1885—Campbell (J. G.) Superstitions and
     Witchcraft and Second Sight in the Highlands and Islands of
     Scotland, 2 vol. *Glasgow,* 1902 ; etc.   (5)

75 Goddard (Arthur) Players of the Period, Both Series, in 1 vol. *illustrations*, 1891—Cook (Dutton) Nights at the Play, 2 vol. 1883—Wills (W. G.) and Hon. Mrs. Greene, Drawing Room Dramas, 1873 (4)

76 Landon (L. E.) Complete Works, 2 vol. in 1, *Boston*, 1859—Figaro Programme and Sketch Book, no. XXVI-LXXVI, in 1 vol. *portraits*, 1875 *roy. 8vo.* (2)

77 Watson (John, Ian Maclaren) Beside the Bonnie Brier Bush, 1894 ; The Days of Auld Langsyne, 1895 ; Kate Carnagie and those Ministers, 1896 ; Church Folks, *presentation copy with autograph inscription, "Bram Stoker, Esq. from the Author with kind regards, Nov. 9, 1900,"* 1900 (4)

78 Millet (F. D.) The Danube, from the Black Forest to the Black Sea, *illustrations, presentation copy " To Bram Stoker, Esq. with regards of F. D. Millet,"* New York, 1893 ; Egyptian Tales, second series, edited by W. M. Flinders Petrie, *illustrations*, 1895 ; etc. (4)

79 Donaldson (Thos.) The House in which Thomas Jefferson wrote the Declaration of Independence, *illustrations, presentation copy with autograph note on fly-leaf, " My dear Mr. Stoker this is father's last book and please accept it as a remembrance, Thomas Blaine Donaldson,"* 1898 —Whittle (J. L.) Grover Cleveland, *two portraits*, 1896 ; etc. (4)

80 Ruskin (John) Sesame and Lilies, revised and enlarged edition, *calf, g. e. autograph letter of the author inserted* 1871

81 Ruskin (J.) Plates to the Stones of Venice, in 1 vol. *some coloured, New York*, 1880—Dickens (C.) The Battle of Life, *illustrations, half calf gilt*, 1846 (2)

82 Beeton's Christmas Annual. Edward the Seventh, a Play, etc. *illustrations, presentation copy with autograph inscription, " To Bram Stoker from Henry Irving,"* 1876—Mayall's Celebrities of the London Stage, *photographic portraits in character* (1867-8) *imp. 8vo.* (2)

83 Shelley (P. B.) Queen Mab, with Notes, *calf gilt* W. Clark, 1821

84 Haggard (H. Rider) Mr. Meesom's Will, FIRST EDITION, 16 *illustrations*, 1888—Strange (T. B.) Gunner Jingo's Jubilee, *illustrations, presentation copy from the author to Col. Reginald Hennell, with interesting autograph inscriptions*, 1893 (2)

85 Kipling (Rudyard) Traffics and Discoveries, 1904 ; Out of India, *New York*, 1895—Field (R.) The Bondage of Ballinger, *portrait, presentation copy with autograph inscription of the author*, 1903 ; etc. (6)

86 Kipling (R.) The Jungle Book, 1896, and The Second Jungle Book, 1895, 2 vol. *illustrations by J. Lockwood Kipling, etc. blue cloth, g. e.* 1895-6

87 Gaskell (Mrs.) Cranford, with Preface by Anne T. Ritchie, *illustrations by Hugh Thomson, presentation copy with inscription, " To Bram Stoker, Esq. as a faint acknowledgment of his kindness, Hugh Thomson "* 1891

88   Pinero (A. W.) Trelawny of the "Wells," *illustrations, New York,*
      1899 ; His House in Order, a Comedy, *portrait and illustrations,*
      1907—Barlow (G.) An Actor's Reminiscences, and other Poems,
      1883 ; etc.   (8)

89   Becke (L.) The Ebbing of the Tide, *presentation copy to "Bram*
      Stoker, with the author's sincere regards," 1896—Evans (R. D.)
      A Sailor's Log, *illustrations, New York,* 1901—Matsell (G. W.)
      Vocabulum, or, The Rogue's Lexicon, *portrait, etc. ib.* 1859 ;
      etc.   (8)

90   Jennings (L. J.) Field Paths and Green Lanes, *illustrations,* 1878 ;
      Rambles among the Hills, *illustrations,* 1880—Fiske (S.) Holiday
      Stories, *presentation copy "To Bram Stoker, with a Happy New*
      Year, Stephen Fiske," St. Paul, 1891 ; etc.   (5)

91   Dowden (Edward) Poems, *presentation copy with autograph signature*
      of the author, 1876—Armstrong (G. F.) A Garland from Greece,
      1882—Veley (M.) A Marriage of Shadows, with Preface by Leslie
      Stephen, 1888, and others, *all presentation copies with autograph*
      inscriptions   (8)

92   Caine (Hall) My Story, *presentation copy with autograph inscription,*
      "To my dear Bram, to whom this book owes much, Hall Caine,
      10 *Oct.* 1908," 1908—Baker (James) The Cardinal's Page, *pre-*
      sentation copy with autograph inscription, "To Bram Stoker, in
      pleasant remembrance of many a famous First-night at the Lyceum,
      from James Baker," 1899 — Moore (F. F.) A Nest of Linnets,
      illustrations, presentation copy "from F. Frankfort Moore," 1901,
      and others, *all presentation copies*   (10)

93   Reid (Capt. Mayne) The Wild Huntress, *illustrations, presentation*
      copy with autograph inscription, "Bram Stoker, Esq. with Compts.
      of Mayne Reid, March 21, 1879," *n. d.*—Law (James D.) Dreams
      o' Hame, and other Scotch Poems, *portrait, "To Bram Stoker,*
      Esq. with the compliments of the author, James D. Law," 1893—
      Becke (Louis) Pacific Tales, *portrait, "To Bram Stoker, from*
      Louis Becke, with kind regards, London, May 26, 1897," 1897 ;
      and others, *all presentation copies to Bram Stoker*   (12)

94   Harte (Bret) The Heritage of Dedlow Marsh and other Tales, *pre-*
      sentation copy with autograph inscription, "To Bram Stoker from
      Bret Harte, London, January, 1891," 1890 — O'Brien (Wm.)
      Irish Ideas, *presentation copy, "To Bram Stoker, Esq. with all*
      best wishes, William O'Brien, July, 1894," 1893   (2)

95   Clifford (Mrs. W. K.) The Last Touches and other Stories, *presentation*
      copy with autograph inscription, "With Mrs. W. K. Clifford's
      very kind regards, to Mr. Bram Stoker, Dec. 1, 1892," 1892 ;
      A Wild Proxy, 1893 ; Mere Stories, 1896 ; Plays, 1909   (4)

96   Shelley (P. B.) Poetical Works, with Memoir by Leigh Hunt, 4 vol.
      n. d.—Shelley (Mary W.) Frankenstein, the modern Man-Demon,
      n. d.—Sheridaniana, or, Anecdotes of the Life of R. B. Sheridan,
      etc. *portrait,* 1826 ; etc.   (10)

First Day 10 OCTAVO

97 Bohn's Extra Volumes, 6 vol. *portraits* 1846-55

98 Harley (Geo.) The Life of a London Physician, edited by Mrs. A. Tweedie, *portrait,* 1899—Wicks (F.) Golden Lives: The Story of a Woman's Courage, *illustrations,* 1891; The Veiled Hand, *illustrations,* 1893; and others, *all presentation copies with inscriptions* (10)

99 Macaulay (T. B.) Lays of Ancient Rome, *with autograph signature and initials of the author,* 1848—Marston (E.) Days in Clover, *frontispiece, uncut, presentation copy, " To Bram Stoker with the compliments and kind regards of E. Marston,"* 1892—Matthews (B.) Vignettes of Manhattan, *illustrations, presentation copy from the author, New York,* 1894; etc (5)

100 Omar. Rubáiyát of Omar Kháyyám, in English Verse, translated by Edward FitzGerald, with notes, etc. *half vellum, uncut, New York,* 1888—Federalist (The), reprinted from the Original Text, edited by H. B. Dawson, *presentation copy to Bram Stoker from Henry Ward Beecher, with autograph inscription, ib.* 1864 (2)

101 Barnes (Wm.) Poems of Rural Life in the Dorset Dialect, 1879—Fergusson (Jas. R.) Poems and Ballads, *presentation copy with autograph letter of the author inserted,* 1876—Le Fanu (J. Sheridan) The Watcher and other Weird Stories, 21 *illustrations by Brinsley Sheridan Le Fanu,* 1894; etc. (8)

102 Yeats (W. B.) The Countess Kathleen and various Legends and Lyrics, *frontispiece, half vellum, uncut, presentation copy with autograph inscription, " To Bram Stoker with the compliments and best regards of W. B. Yeats, Sept.* 1893," 1892—Cochrane (A.) Collected Verses, *frontispiece, half morocco, uncut, t. e. g. presentation copy, " To Bram Stoker, with the author's best regards, April,* 1904," 1903 (2)

103 Smith (Goldwin) Lectures and Essays, *Toronto,* 1881—Verey (Jos.) Poems, Grave and Gay, 1880—Bell (Mackenzie) Charles Whitehead, a Forgotten Genius, 1894; Spring's Immortality and other Poems, 1893; and others, *all presentation copies to Bram Stoker* (15)

104 Faustus, his Life, Death and Descent into Hell, translated from the German, *coloured frontispiece, linen boards, uncut* 1825

105 Heinemann (Wm.) The First Step, a Dramatic Moment, 1895; Summer Moths, a Play, 1898, *original boards, uncut, presentation copies to Bram Stoker, with autograph inscriptions of the author* 1895-8

106 Hatton (Jos.) By Order of the Czar, a Drama, *presentation copy, " In Auld Lang Syne, Bram Stoker from his friend Joseph Hatton, July,* 1904," 1904—Page (T. M.) Santa Claus' Partner, *coloured illustrations, New York,* 1899—Daskam (J. D.) Fables for the Fair, 1901; etc. (8)

107 Alden (H. M.) God in His World, *presentation copy with autograph letters of author inserted, New York,* 1894—Miller (E.) The Yoke, a Romance, 1904—Scott (Clement) Poppy Land, *presentation copy, " To Bram from Clem,* 17 *April,* 1886," 1886; etc. (24)

108   Gabbitas (P.) Heart Melodies, for Storm and Sunshine from Clif-
       tonia the Beautiful, *portrait*, 1885—Wiggin (Kate D.) Diary of a
       Goose Girl, *illustrations, Boston*, 1902—Caster (Eliz. B.) "Boots
       and Saddles," or, Life in Dakota with General Caster, *portrait,
       presentation copy, New York, n. d.* ; etc.   (4)

109   Patterson (E.) The Mermaid and other Pieces, FIRST EDITION, *pre-
       sentation copy with autograph inscription, " To Bram Stoker, Esq.
       with the author's humble compliments, his sincere good wishes and
       his honest desire for further acquaintance, Cardiff, Sep.* 22/97,
       E. Patterson," published by the author   *Cardiff*, 1897
     *** The first book published by the author, only 300 copies of the book
       were printed.

110   Clapp (H. A.) Reminiscences of a Dramatic Critic, with Essay on
       the Art of Henry Irving, *portraits on Japanese paper, Boston*,
       1902—Mead (Thos. Comedian) Lady of the Rose and other Poems,
       *portrait, uncut, " To Mr. B. Stoker, with the kind regards of T.
       Mead,"* 1881   (2)

111   Garrick. Catalogue of the Library, Splendid Books of Prints,
       Poetical and Historical Tracts of David Garrick, Esq. with prices
       and purchasers' names, *half russia*   1823

112   Winter (Wm.) Shadows of the Stage, 3 vol. *New York*, 1892-5—
       Smalley (G. W.) Studies of Men, *autograph letter of author inserted,*
       1895—Todminter (J.) True Tragedy of Rienzi and Alcestes, a
       Dramatic Poem, 2 vol. *presentation copies to Bram Stoker, " with
       the author's kind regards,"* 1879-81 ; etc.   (8)

113   Dodgson (C. L.) Sylvie and Bruno, FIRST EDITION, 46 *illustrations
       by H. Furniss, red cloth, g. e.*   1889

114   Aldrich (T. B.) Ponkapog Papers, *presentation copy, Boston*, 1903 ;
       Judith of Bethulia, a Tragedy, *portrait, presentation copy, " To
       Bram Stoker with affectionate regards from Thomas Bailey
       Aldrich, Boston, September*, 1906," *ib.* 1905 ; Mercedes and Later
       Lyrics, FIRST EDITION, *presentation copy, ib.* 1884   (3)

115   Mayhew Bros. Whom to Marry and how to get Married, *illustra-
       tions by G. Cruikshank*, 1854 — Anstey (F.) Lyre and Lancet,
       illustrations, presentation copy to Bram Stoker, 1895   (2)

116   Benson (Robt.) Sketches of Corsica, *plates, one coloured*, 1825—
       Baker (J.) Imperial Guide, with Picturesque Plans of the Great
       Post Roads, *plates, half calf*, 1802—Collection of Proverbs, Ben-
       gali and Sanscrit, with their Translation, etc. by W. Morton,
       Calcutta, 1832   (3)

117   Le Gallienne (Richard) The Book-Bills of Narcissus, *buckram, uncut,
       t. e. g.* 1892—Arnold (Sir E.) Gwen, a Drama, 1880—Jacobi (C. T.)
       Gesta Typographica, 1897 ; another copy, *one of 50 copies printed
       on Japanese vellum, uncut*, 1897   (4)

118   Remembrances for Order and Decency to be kept in the Upper House
       of Parliament by the Lords when His Majesty is not there, MANU-
       SCRIPT, *old red morocco, g. e. autograph signature of J. Britton on
       fly-leaf*   SÆC. XVIII

119   Toole (J. L.) Reminiscences, chronicled by Jos. Hatton, *portrait and
      illustrations, autograph inscription :* "*With J. L. Toole's kind
      regards to his Friend Bram Stoker, May* 13/92," 1892—Jones (S.)
      The Actor and his Art, 1899—Wallace (Wm.) The Divine Sur-
      render, *uncut,* 1895 — Betty (W. H. West, *the Young Roscius*)
      Memoirs of his Life, *half morocco, Liverpool,* 1804 ; etc.   (5)

120   AUTOGRAPHS.   Collection of interesting Autograph Signatures, etc. in-
      cluding famous Actors, etc. : Charles Dickens, with original sketch,
      W. C. Macready, J. P. Harley, J. A. Van Amburg, with original
      sketch, John Braham, Anna Mordaunt, Drinkwater Meadows,
      G. Y. Bennett, E. W. Elton, Fra Diavolo, Mark Lemon, M. W.
      Balfe, A. E. Betts, E. Vestris, with pencil sketch, W. H. Oxberry,
      W. Farren, Charles Peake, R. Keeley, Geo. Lefanu, C. J. Mathews,
      H. J. Wallack, Fanny Stirling, etc. with Index, in a vol. *half roan*

121   Fitzgerald (Wm.) Collection of Original Pencil Sketches, in a vol.
      half roan

122   Riley (Jas. Whitcomb, *the Hoosier Poet*) Sketches in Prose, 1891 ;
      Rhymes of Childhood, 1891 ; Pipes O'Pan at Zekesbury, 1891 ;
      Old-Fashioned Roses, 1891 ; Flying Islands of the Night, 1892 ;
      Green Fields and Running Brooks, 1893 ; A Child-World, 1897 ;
      Home Folks, 1900 ; Book of Joyous Children, 1903 ; His Pa's
      Romance, 1903 ; etc. together 11 vol. *portraits, etc. all presentation
      copies to Bram Stoker, with autograph inscriptions, some with
      original lines by the author, and an Autograph Letter*
                                                 Indianapolis, etc. 1891-1903
   ₊ "Irving," says Bram Stoker in his Reminiscences of the great actor,
      "like all who had ever known him, loved the 'Hoosier' Poet.
      We saw a great deal of him when he was in London, and when-
      ever we were in Indianapolis, to meet him was one of the expected
      pleasures.   Riley is one of the most dramatic reciters that live, and
      when he gives one of his own poems it is an intellectual delight."

WALT WHITMAN.

*For many years Mr. Bram Stoker was an intimate friend of Walt
Whitman.   He first became acquainted with his works through
the volume of Selections, issued in 1868 by Mr. W. M. Rossetti,
which, as he observes in his "Reminiscences," provoked his ardent
admiration, in spite of the hostility and ridicule with which it
was generally received.*

123   WHITMAN (WALT) Leaves of Grass, Author's Edition, with Inter-
      calations, *half calf gilt, g. e. presentation copy, with autograph
      inscription :* "*Bram Stoker, from his friend, the Author*"
                                                 Camden, New Jersey, 1876

124   Whitman (Walt) Leaves of Grass, Author's Edition, *green cloth,
      presentation copy from the author, with autograph inscription :*
      "*Bram Stoker, from the Author W. W.*"   *ib.* 1882

125 Whitman (Walt) Leaves of Grass, *portrait, brown cloth*
Philadelphia, 1884

126 Whitman (Walt) Leaves of Grass, including Sands at Seventy, Goodbye my Fancy, *green cloth, uncut, with autograph signature of Bram Stoker* *ib.* 1894

127 Whitman (Walt) Two Rivulets, including Democratic Vistas, Centennial Songs, and Passage to India, Author's Edition, *portrait (inserted) with autograph signature, half calf gilt, presentation copy, with autograph inscription: " Bram Stoker from his friend the Author "* *Camden, New Jersey,* 1876

128 Whitman (Walt) Complete Prose Works, *green cloth, uncut, t. e. g. autograph signature of Bram Stoker inside cover*
Philadelphia, 1892

129 Whitman (Walt) As a Strong Bird on Pinions Free, and other Poems, *autograph signature of the author on title, presentation copy, with inscription: " Bram Stoker Esq. with compliments of Thos. Donaldson, July* 31/85 " *Washington,* 1872

130 Whitman (Walt) November Boughs, *portrait of the author in his 70th year, red cloth, t. e. g. with autograph receipt from author : " Camden, New Jersey, U. S. America. Received from Bram Stoker, Twenty-five Dollars (Deepest thanks and remembrances), Walt Whitman," and Autograph Letter,* 4 *pp. from Thomas Donaldson to Bram Stoker, having reference to Walt Whitman*
1889

131 Whitman (Walt) Specimen Days and Collect, *brown cloth*
Philadelphia, 1882-83

132 Whitman (Walt) Drum-Taps, FIRST EDITION, *brown cloth, presentation copy, with note and inscription by Thomas Donaldson : " Given me by Walt Whitman May* 31, '85, *Thos. Donaldson July* 31 – '85," *" Bram Stoker, with regards of Thos. Donaldson "* *New York,* 1865

133 Whitman (Walt) After All, Not to Create only, recited at the American Institute Sept. 7, 1871, *Boston,* 1871—Trimble (W. H.) Walt Whitman and Leaves of Grass, *presentation copy to Bram Stoker from the Author,* 1905
(2)

134 Whitman. Donaldson (Thomas) Walt Whitman the Man, *portrait, illustrations and facsimiles, buckram, uncut, Autograph Letter from the author to Bram Stoker enclosed* *New York,* 1896

135 Whitman (Walt) In re Walt Whitman : edited by his literary Executors, Horace L. Traubel, Richard Maurice Bucke, Thomas B. Harned, *original cloth, uncut* *Philadelphia,* 1893

136 WHITMAN (WALT) A COLLECTION OF FRAGMENTS OF WALT WHITMAN'S WRITINGS, all in his Autograph, consisting of Eighteen various Pieces, some written in ink and some in pencil, together with his portrait, containing his autograph signature, *all mounted or inlaid* in a vol. *given to Bram Stoker by Thomas Donaldson*

⁎⁎ " He sometimes wrote on scraps of paper, on the inside of envelopes addressed to him, on the backs or on unwritten portions of letters

LOT 136—*continued.*
received by him, and on paper received around packages, in fact on anything that would carry ink. His manuscript was like Joseph's coat, of many colours. Sometimes he used half a dozen kinds of paper on which to complete one poem,—a verse or two on each, and then he would pin them together. His poems he worked over and over again. He would roll a completed poem, or a book, or an article up, wrap it about with a piece of twine, and throw it in the corner of his room. In his bedroom were packages of manuscript in baskets, in bundles, or in piles. Some of them were mixed up with lot of short-cut pine wood, which he kept to fire up his sheet iron stove. He used the crook on his cane to hook out what he wanted from the pile on the floor. Usually before sending a poem or a manuscript to a paper, or away, he had it set up in type and sent it to the publisher printed."—*Thomas Donaldson in his "Walt Whitman the Man," 1896, pp. 73-74.*

137 WHITMAN (WALT) Lecture by Walt Whitman on Abraham Lincoln, THE ORIGINAL PRINTED NOTES, with autograph emendations and corrections, as given to Thomas Donaldson by Walt Whitman, Aug. 11/86; a Portrait of Walt Whitman, with his autograph signature; a Portrait of Abraham Lincoln; and an exceedingly interesting Autograph Letter to Thomas Donaldson (author of "Walt Whitman the Man"), *mounted on cardboard and enclosed in a cover, with autograph notes of Thos. Donaldson*

⁎⁎ "A Message from the Dead." "We did not reach Philadelphia till towards the end of January 1894. In the meantime Walt Whitman had died, March 26, 1892. On 4th February I spent the afternoon with Donaldson in his own home. Shortly after I came in he went away for a minute and came back with a large envelope which he handed to me. 'That is for you from Walt Whitman, I have been keeping it till I should see you.' The envelope contained in a rough card folio pasted down on a thick paper the original notes from which he delivered his lecture on Abraham Lincoln at the Chestnut Street Opera House on April 15, 1886. With it was a letter to Donaldson in which he said 'Enclosed I send a full report of my Lincoln Lecture for our friend Bram Stoker.' This was my message from the dead."—*Bram Stoker in his "Henry Irving," 1906, vol. II, p. 3.*

138 WHITMAN (WALT) An exceedingly interesting Autograph Letter from Walt Whitman to Bram Stoker, with Introductory Note, 1 p. 4to, 24 lines, *dated from Camden, N. Jersey, U. S. America, March 6/76*: "My physique is entirely shatter'd, doubtless permanently from paralysis and other ailments. But I am up & dress'd & get out every day a little—live here quite lonesome but hearty & good spirits. Write to me again. Walt Whitman," *mounted within covers*

⁎⁎ One evening in 1876 at the "Fortnightly Club," a club of Dublin men who met occasionally for free discussions, a violent attack was made on Walt Whitman, which drew forth a most impassioned

LOT 138   *continued.*
protest from Edward Dowden. Bram Stoker followed on the same side, and together they carried the question. Stoker, excited by the stress of the meeting, went home, and, before he went to bed, poured out his heart in a long letter to Walt Whitman. Bye and bye came the characteristic letter from the Poet described above.

139   FIELD (EUGENE) "Willie," an Autograph Poem from Eugene Field to Bram Stoker, written in black and red and signed by the author, Jan. 11, 1888, *inserted in a cover, with explanatory note*
*** Bram Stoker, who knew Eugene Field well, and greatly admired his delightful poems for and about children, one day expressed a wish for the poet's autograph. Shortly afterwards, to his amusement and delight, he received the accompanying dainty verses, entitled "Willie." As far as is known, and it is obviously unlikely, they have never been printed.

140   Riley (James Whitcomb) Armazindy, *presentation copy, with autograph inscription*   1894
*** This volume contains the poem Leonainie, with which many literary critics were successfully hoaxed in the early seventies. It was supposed to be an hitherto unknown poem by Edgar A. Poe, which had been found written on a fly-leaf of a book once in the possession of Poe.

141   Whistler (J. McNeil) Exhibition of Etchings, with a Note on the Etchings of Whistler by F. Wedmore, *frontispiece, uncut*   1903

142   Whistler (J. McNeil) Etchings and Dry Points. Venice, Second Series, *n. d.* ; "Notes," "Harmonies," "Nocturnes," Second Series, 1886, *uncut*   (2)

143   LINCOLN (PRESIDENT) A Death Mask and Hands, closed, of President Lincoln, in bronze, and a plaster cast of the left hand, opened (4)
*** The death mask and closed hands were cast by the celebrated sculptor Augustus St. Gaudens in 1886 from the original moulds made by Volk before Lincoln went to Washington for his first Presidency, and were found by Volk's son twenty-five years later. Twenty men joined to purchase the moulds and present them to the American nation, two of the twenty being Henry Irving and Bram Stoker, and each of the subscribers received casts in bronze of the face and hands with his name in each case cut in the bronze (*see Bram Stoker's* "*Henry Irving,*" 1906, *vol. II, pp.* 108-9).

144   Lincoln (President) THE ORIGINAL MANUSCRIPT of Bram Stoker's Lecture on Abraham Lincoln, First Notes and Variantes, *in a solander case*   (1)

145   Lincoln (President) Reminiscences, by distinguished Men of his Time, edited by A. T. Rice, *portraits, etc. New York*, 1886—Stoddard (W. O.) Abraham Lincoln, the True Story of a great Life, *portrait, illustrations, etc. ib.* 1885—Arnold (I. M.) Life of Abraham Lincoln, *portrait, half morocco, Chicago*, 1885   (3)

First Day   16   OCTAVO

146   Lincoln (President) The Lincoln Memorial, Album Immortelles, etc.
       collected and edited by O. H. Oldroyd, *portrait and illustrations*,
       1882—Holland (J. G.) Life of Abraham Lincoln, *portrait, Spring-
       field, Mass*. 1866—Nicolay (J. G.) Short Life of Abraham Lincoln,
       portrait, New York, 1906   (3)

147   Lincoln (President) Life, drawn from original Sources, by Ida M.
       Tarbell, 2 vol. *portraits and illustrations, red cloth, t. e. g. presen-
       tation copy with autograph inscription " To Bram Stoker, from
       Henry Irving, Chicago*, 1900 "   *New York*, 1900

148   Lincoln (President). Barrett (J. H.) Life of Abraham Lincoln,
       portrait, 1865 — Curtis (W. E.) The True Abraham Lincoln,
       portrait and illustrations, 1903—Brooks (Noah) Abraham Lincoln,
       a Biography, *portrait and illustrations*, 1888 ; etc.   (8)

148A   Hope (A.) Adventure of the Lady Ursula : a Comedy, *illustrations*,
       New York, 1898—Days with Sir Roger de Coverley, *illustrations*,
       1886; etc.   (5)

QUARTO.

149   Lavater (J. C.) Essays on Physiognomy, translated by Henry Hunter,
       5 vol. *numerous portraits and plates, by T. Holloway, blue morocco
       gilt, ornamental borders on the sides, silk linings, g. e.*   1789

150   Budge (E. A. Wallis) The Book of the Dead. The Papyrus of Ani, in
       the British Museum, the Egyptian Text, with Translation, etc.
       half morocco, uncut, t. e. g.   1895

151   Shakespeare (Wm.) Works, " Henry Irving Edition," edited by Henry
       Irving and F. A. Marshall, with Notes and Introductions, EDITION
       DE LUXE, *one of* 150 *copies*, 8 vol. *numerous illustrations by Gordon
       Browne, linen boards, uncut, t. e. g.*   1888-90

152   Quasi Cursores. Portraits of the High Officers and Professors of the
       University of Edinburgh, *drawn and etched by William Hole, uncut,
       presentation copy " Bram Stoker, Esq. in memory of a very pleasant
       visit, W. B. Blaikie, Edinburgh, 2nd Nov. 1894 "*   *Edinb.* 1884

153   History of the Two Americas, 2 vol. *portraits and illustrations, half
       morocco, m. e. New York*, 1880—Young (L. R.) Around the World
       with General Grant, 2 vol. *illustrations, half morocco, m. e. New
       York, n. d.*   (4)

154   Irving (W.) Rip Van Winkle, *illustrations by F. T. Merrill, linen
       boards, g. e. Boston*, 1888—Walsh (W. S.) Faust, the Legend and
       the Poem, *etchings by H. Faber, Philadelphia*, 1888 ; etc.   (4)

155   Smith (Adam) Inquiry into the Nature and Causes of the Wealth of
       Nations, Second Edition, 2 vol. *calf, presentation copy " From the
       Author "*   1778

156   Byron (Lord) Childe Harold's Pilgrimage, Cantos I-II, FIRST EDITION,
       binding broken   1812

157   Thackeray (W. M.) Orphan of Pimlico, FIRST EDITION, *illustrations,
       half morocco*, 1876—Archer and Barker : A National Theatre,
       Scheme and Estimates, 1907 ; etc.   (4)

158   Leather (R. K.) and Ricd. le Gallienne.   The Student and the
      Body Snatcher, etc. LARGE PAPER, *one of* 50 *copies, buckram,
      uncut,* 1890 ; The Hardships of Publishing, *one of* 120 *copies,
      uncut, privately printed,* 1873   (2)

159   Caldecott (R.) Some of Æsop's Fables with Modern Instances,
      illustrations   1883

160   Greey (E.) The Golden Lotus and other Legends of Japan, *presentation
      copy " Bram Stoker San, with compliments of the Author, Edward
      Greey," Boston,* 1883 ; The Royal Ronins, translated from the
      Japanese of Tamenaga Shunsai, by E. Greey, etc. *illustrations,
      presentation copy " with the compliments of Edward Greey,"* 1884 ;
      etc.   (5)

161   Kipling (R.) Verses written for Nicholson's Almanac of Sports for
      1898, with the Almanac, *illustrations,* 1897-98—Smith (Pamela C.)
      Annancy Stories, *illustrations, presentation copy " Mr. Bram
      Stoker, with compliments of Pamela Colman Smith,"* 1899—Garcia
      (G.) The Actor's Art, *illustrations by A. Forestier,* 1882 ; etc. (4)

162   Calmour (Alfred C.) Fact and Fiction about Shakespeare, with Notes,
      *illustrations, presentation copy from the author to Bram Stoker,
      with autograph note on fly-leaf,* 1894—Berg (A. E.) The Drama,
      Painting, Poetry and Song, *illustrations, New York,* 1884—Yellow
      Book (The), vol. IV, *illustrations,* 1895   (3)

163   Balfour (A.) Second, Third and Fourth Reports of the Wellcome
      Research Laboratories at the Gordon Memorial College, Khartoum,
      3 vol. *map and illustrations, some coloured, Khartoum,* 1906-11 ;
      etc   (4)

164   Le Gallienne (Ricd.) Volumes in Folio, *one of* 50 *copies, signed by the
      author, uncut*   1889

165   Green Sheaf (The), edited by Pamela Colman Smith, nos. I-VI and
      no. IX, *illustrations, some coloured by hand by the editor, autograph
      letter and receipt of the editor inserted*   1903-4

166   Hawks (F. L.) Narrative of the Expedition of an American Squadron
      to the China Seas and Japan under the Command of Commodore
      M. C. Perry, 3 vol. *maps, numerous illustrations, plates of costumes,
      etc.   Washington,* 1856

167   Powell (J. W.) First and Second Annual Reports of the Bureau of
      Ethnology, 1880-1, *numerous plates, Washington,* 1881-3 ; Second
      Annual Report, another copy, 1883   (3)

168   Blake. Blair (Robert) The Grave, a Poem, *portrait of W. Blake,
      and 12 etchings from Blake's original designs by Schiavonetti
                                                    Bensley,* 1813

169   Wiley (W. H. and S. K.) The Yosemite, Alaska and the Yellowstone,
      portrait and illustrations, 1893 ; Collection of Newspaper Cuttings
      relating to the Drama, etc. in a vol.   (2)

170   Whistler (J. M.) Gentle Art of Making Enemies, FIRST EDITION, *one
      of the* 15 *special large paper presentation copies, uncut, t. e. g. with
      autograph letter of W. Heinemann inserted*   1890

C

171 Whistler (J. M.) Memorial Exhibition, Catalogue of Paintings, Drawings, Etchings and Lithographs, EDITION DE LUXE, *portrait and illustrations, uncut, t. e. g.* 1905

172 Whistler (J. M.) Catalogue of Paintings, etc. 1905—Page (The), vol. I, in 12 parts as issued (*wanting nos. VIII, IX and X*), *portraits, woodcuts, etc. only* 140 *copies printed*, 1898 (10)

173 Febure (Nic. de) Compleat Body of Chymistry, rendred into English by P. D. C. *plates, covers gone*, 1670—Temple (Sir J.) The Irish Rebellion, FIRST EDITION, *old calf*, 1646 (2)

174 [Mathews (C. J.)] Catalogue Raisonnée of Mr. Mathews's Gallery of Theatrical Portraits, *calf, presentation copy with autograph inscription*, "*John.Pritt Harley Esq. from his great Admirer and Friend Anne Mathews, Saturday September* 16, 1848" 1833

175 Dryden (John) An Evening's Love, or the Mock-Astrologer, 1671; The Rival Ladies, a Tragi-Comedy, 1675; The Assignation: or Love in a Nunnery, 1678; Secret Love, or the Maiden Queen, 1679; Marriage a-la-Mode, a Comedy, 1684; The Wild Gallant, a Comedy, 1684; The Indian Emperor, or the Conquest of Mexico, 1686; The Conquest of Granada, 1687; The Spanish Fryar, 1690; The Kind Keeper, or Mr. Limberham, A Comedy, 1690; Amphitryon, or the Two Sosias, 1691; and others by the same Author, some FIRST EDITIONS, in 1 vol. *old calf* 1671-91

176 Play-Bills. Collection of Play-Bills of the Theatre-Royal, Edinburgh, ranging from Nov. 25, 1820, to Aug. 17, 1824, in 1 vol. 1820-24

The following Six Manuscripts are mainly in the autograph of the Author, but some passages appear to be in the handwriting of an Amanuensis. They are all sold subject to the copyright being reserved.

177 STOKER (BRAM) Personal Reminiscences of Henry Irving, "THE ORIGINAL MANUSCRIPT" 1906

178 Stoker (B.) Lady of the Shroud, "THE ORIGINAL MANUSCRIPT," with the outline of the Story 1908

179 Stoker (B.) Snowbound, the Record of a Theatrical Touring Party (the last four chapters only), "THE ORIGINAL MANUSCRIPT" 1908

180 Stoker (B.) Under the Sunset, "THE ORIGINAL MANUSCRIPT" 1882

181 Stoker (B.) Lair of the White Worm (the last Book written by the Author), "THE ORIGINAL MANUSCRIPT" 1911

182 Stoker (B.) Original Notes and Data for his "Dracula," *in a solander case* (1)

FOLIO.

183 Harris (John) Complete Collection of Voyages and Travels in Europe, Asia, Africa and America, 2 vol. *maps and plates, calf* 1744

184 Norden (F. L.) Travels in Egypt and Nubia, enlarged by P. Templeman, 2 vol. *plates, old calf* 1757

185   Lightning Sea-Column (The) or Sea-Mirrour, discovering all the Coasts
      and Islands of Europa, Africa, America, and Asia, with a plain
      description thereof : translated from the Dutch, printed, ingraved,
      and sold by Jacob Robyn, *numerous curious old maps and plans,
      old calf binding, broken, a few leaves torn, and some mended, sold
      not subject to return*   *Amst.* 1689

186   Jansson (I.) Novus Atlas sive Theatrum Orbis Terrarum, in quo
      Magna Britannia seu Angliæ et Scotiæ nec non Hiberniæ regna
      exhibentur, *numerous maps, binding broken*   *ib.* 1659

187   Hamilton (Sir W.) Collection of Vases mostly of pure Greek Work-
      manship, discovered in Sepulchres in the Kingdom of the two
      Sicilies, 3 vol. *numerous engravings, calf, y. e.*   *Naples,* 1791-95

188   Hay (Robt.) Illustrations of Cairo, *lithographs, half morocco*
                                                      imp. folio. 1840

189   Budge (E. A. Wallis) Book of the Dead.   Facsimile of the Papyrus
      of Ani, in the British Museum, *coloured plates, half morocco* 1894

190   Bourgeois (É.) Century of Louis XIV, its Arts, its Ideas, translated
      by Mrs. Cashel Hoey, *numerous portraits and illustrations* 1895

191   Walter (Jas.) Shakespeare's Home and Rural Life, *illustrations,
      presentation copy from the author,* 1874—Tennyson (A.) Vivien
      and Guinevere, in 1 vol. *illustrations by G. Doré, morocco, g. e.*
      1867   (2)

192   Chaucer (G.) Works, with the Story of the Siege of Thebes, by
      J. Lidgate, and Life of Chaucer, 𝖇𝖑𝖆𝖈𝖐 𝖑𝖊𝖙𝖙𝖊𝖗, *frontispiece, half calf,
      stained, and wants last leaf*   1687

193   Chaucer (G.) Works, edited by John Urry, with a Glossary, Life of
      Author, etc. LARGE PAPER, *portrait inserted, calf*   1721

194   Barnes (J.) History of Edward III, and of the Black Prince, *portrait,
      calf, Cambridge,* 1688—Denon (V.) Egypt Delineated, *portrait,
      plates, etc. calf, binding broken,* 1825   (2)

195   Omar.   Rubaiyat of Omar Khayyam, rendered into English Verse
      by Edward Fitzgerald, *engravings from drawings by Elihu Vedder,
      brown cloth gilt, t. e. g.*   *Boston,* 1884

196   Crane (W.) Mrs. Mundi at Home, *outline engravings by Walter
      Crane, oblong, n. d.*—Wood (L.) Prehistoric Proverbs, 12 *coloured
      illustrations, n. d.*   (2)

197   Statutes made and established from the time of Kyng Henry the
      thirde, unto the fyrste yere of the reigne of Henry the VIII, 𝖇𝖑𝖆𝖈𝖐
      𝖑𝖊𝖙𝖙𝖊𝖗, *old calf, r. e.*   1543

198   Rastall (Wm.) Collection of Statutes now in force from Magna
      Charta, untill the reigne of Queene Elizabeth, 𝖇𝖑𝖆𝖈𝖐 𝖑𝖊𝖙𝖙𝖊𝖗, *old calf,
      2 leaves of old vellum MS. as fly-leaves*   *C. Barker,* 1588

199   Sadeler (M.) Vestigi delle Antichita di Roma, *engraved title and* 50
      engravings, vellum   *oblong. Roma, n. d.*
                              C 2

200 Brereton (Austin) Henry Irving, a Biographical Sketch, LARGE PAPER, *one of* 100 *copies*, 17 *portraits on india paper, vellum, uncut, t. e. g.*
1884

201 Brereton (A.) Henry Irving, another copy, *vellum, uncut, t. e. g. ex-libris of Richard D'Oyly Carte* 1884

202 Report from Select Committee on Dramatic Literature, with Minutes of Evidence, *Mr. Bram Stoker's copy, with MS. notes, etc. in his handwriting* 1832

203 Theatre (The) A Weekly Critical Review, vol. I, 1877—Players (The), vol. I–III in 1 vol. *portraits, wanting no.* 1, 1860—Newspaper cuttings, in 1 vol. (3)

204 Stirling (Wm.) Some Apostles of Physiology, Account of their Lives and Labours, *numerous portraits, etc. vellum*
Privately printed, 1902

205 Fourcand (L. de) Maîtres Modernes, Bastien-Lepage, sa Vie et ses Œuvres, *fine engravings, india proofs, etc.* *Paris*, 1884

206 Harvey (F.) List of Portraits, Views, Autograph Letters, and Documents contained in an Illustrated Copy of the Princess Marie Liechtenstein's History of Holland House, *only 25 copies printed. coloured frontispiece, etc. blue morocco* *n. d.*

207 Newspaper Cuttings, relating to America, the Drama, Eminent Persons, etc. in 5 vol. 1885-87, etc. (6)

208 Play-Bills. Miscellaneous, in 3 vol. and case (4)

209 Play-Bills. Three of Drury Lane Theatre, 1804, *in gilt glazed frames*, and seven of the Theatre Birmingham, including Mrs. Jordan's Last Night, and Mrs. Siddons' Benefit, 1805-6

210 Ballads, Songs, etc. Collection of, *in portfolio*—Stevenson (R. L.) The Body Snatcher, as it appeared in the Pall Mall Gazette, Jan. 31, 1895 (2)

211 Boston Theatre. Plans for the Boston Theatre, by Edward C. Cabot, *drawn on linen, in roll* (1)

Chapter Twenty-Seven

BRAM STOKER'S VALUABLE LIBRARY TO BE SOLD (1913)[1]

B ook collectors and all other book lovers will be interested in the announcement of the sale by auction of the library of Bram Stoker, the English statesman, author and scholar, who died recently. The sale, which will take place in London, will be held on Monday and Tuesday, July 7 and 8, under the management of Messrs. Sotheby, Wilkinson & Hodge.

Besides the hundreds of valuable autographed books there are a great many autographed letters and manuscripts. Some of the latter are illuminated as in early days of the printing art.

Among the treasures which will go to the highest bidder are a very important collection of letters and manuscripts of David Garrick, as well as letters of celebrated persons to him. Also the Dryden copy of the first folio Shakespeare, a copy of the second folio, expurgated by the Spanish inquisition: Hazlitt's "Life of Napoleon" with nearly 2,000 extra illustrations, and copyrights of many distinguished authors of the eighteenth century will be sold under the hammer.

The collection is of tremendous historical value, for besides the collection of armorial bindings of French monarchs from Henri II. to Napoleon

III. there are scores of historical works, including a large number of rare pamphlets about George Washington. The paintings and miniatures are another interesting feature of the sale.

The American writers are well represented, and perhaps one of the most interesting collections is that of Walt Whitman's works. Mr. Stoker was a close friend of Whitman's and besides the many rare and autograph copies of Whitman's works there are several autograph letters.

Also there is an autograph poem entitled "Willie" by Eugene Field, which has been printed only once and then privately.

Another of the American collections that would draw very large prices in this country and which doubtless will be equally well approached at the English sale is that of the eleven volumes of James Whitcomb Riley. All are presentation copies with autograph inscriptions and some have original lines written in by the author.

In the Whitman collection one of the features which will be of exceptional interest is the sheaf of original notes of Walt Whitman's lecture on Abraham Lincoln. But this is not all about Lincoln in the library, for Mr. Stoker and Henry Irving joined with eighteen others in the purchase of moulds of the death mask and hands of Abraham Lincoln from the son of the sculptor Volk. Augustus Saint Gaudens cast these in bronze and the twenty subscribers each received a copy. Doubtless Mr. Stoker's will sell for very high prices.

Chapter Twenty-Eight

LOW PRICES FOR AMERICANA: LIBRARY OF LATE BRAM STOKER SOLD IN LONDON (1913)[1]

Special Cable Dispatch to *The Sun*

LONDON, July 7—The printed books, autograph letters and illuminated and other manuscripts and the library of the late Bram Stoker, who was for years manager for the late Sir Henry Irving, were sold at Sotheby's to-day. The prices were not very high and many of the articles brought only a few shillings each. The total for the day was only $3,630.

Mark Twain's "The Man Who Corrupted Hadleyburg," a presentation copy with the author's autograph, and "Tom Sawyer," also a presentation copy, sold together for $60. Robert Louis Stevenson's works, Edinburgh edition, fetched $305. Several poems by James Whitcomb Riley, all presentation copies, sold together for $230.

An important collection of letters and manuscripts of David Garrick in his autograph, together with letters from theatrical and other celebrities, was sold privately, and the prices were not announced.

A collection of Walt Whitman's works, of which Mr. Stoker was a great admirer, brought $217.50. A collection of fragments of Walt Whitman's writings, all in his autograph, fetched $82.50. Several works and portraits of Abraham Lincoln and the original manuscript of Mr. Stoker's lecture on Lincoln sold for a few shillings each.

Chapter Twenty-Nine

WHITMAN WRITINGS SOLD: LECTURE ON LINCOLN BRINGS $25 AT BRAM STOKER LIBRARY SALE (1913)[1]

Special Cable to *The New York Times*

LONDON, July 7—At the sale at Sotheby's to-day of the Bram Stoker library, a collection oif [*sic*] fragments of Walt Whitman's writings was sold for $82.50. Whitman's lecture on Abraham Lincoln was sold for $25, and a letter from Whitman to Stoker for the same price.

Eleven volumes of the works of James Whitcomb Riley, with autograph inscriptions and a letter, brought $230.

AFTERWORD

DACRE STOKER

This collection is a treasure trove of Stoker material, least of which an invitation to consider Bram Stoker in a new light. 2012 is a landmark year. Not only is it the centenary of Bram's death, but the publication of this collection and Bram's own *Lost Journal*[1] will add significantly to modern interpretations of the man and his work.

The *Lost Journal* presents a cipher of the very kind Bram himself enjoyed, and I continue to puzzle through the significance of its entries. So, finding a few connections between short stories in the present collection and Bram's *Lost Journal*, which was written between 1871 and 1881, has been for me very satisfying. Like Jonathan Harker in *Dracula*, Bram kept notes as reminders to himself in his *Lost Journal*, but in Bram's case many of the jotted ideas or phrases were intended for later use in stories or speeches. For example, in the *Lost Journal* he noted "a howling piece" as a "Yankee name for a dog," and more than 20 years later he would use "howling piece" to describe the baby in "A Baby Passenger." Neatly penned in the margin next to the entry, "Heard a man today speak of his wife as 'my mother-in-law's daughter'," we found "Old Hoggen," a reminder to himself (added later) that he had used the phrase "mother-in-law's daughter" in his story "Old Hoggen: A Mystery" (1893). At the time we edited the *Lost Journal*, we missed the implication, not having read the story.

This collection helps to reaffirm the idea that Bram's writing was as varied and interesting as his life. *The Times* (London), for example, wrote of Bram in 1912:

> A fluent and flamboyant writer, with a manner and mannerisms which faithfully reflected the mind which moved the pen, Stoker managed to find time, amid much arduous and distracting work, to write a good deal. He was the master of a particularly lurid and creepy kind of fiction, represented by "Dracula" and other novels; he had also essayed musical comedy, and had of late years resumed his old connexion with journalism.[2]

During his lifetime, Bram, a prolific writer, wrote children's stories, short stories, and full-length novels in the gothic horror, fantasy, mystery, and romance genres. He also wrote poetry, theatrical reviews, news articles, and essays on various subjects, published a legal manual, and having trained as a barrister, drew up publishing contracts for himself and others. Most of his writing was done in his "spare time" during his tenure as Sir Henry Irving's business manager, a job that required he write thousands of business letters. Bram truly was "Hercules among managers," wrote a London newspaper in 1896, yet "Only those behind the scenes know how much he does, for he accomplishes it so easily that he always has time to write a book, to chat with a friend, to promptly rectify anything of which the public might complain."[3]

Unfortunately, whether a deliberate attempt by Bram to keep his life private, or a modest (and mistaken) belief that his life would be of little interest to others, the absence of a contemporary biography or autobiographical work by Bram has left much open to speculation. I—and countless others—continue to scour the archives and the attics (both proverbial and real) in an effort to better understand the man who wrote *Dracula*. Piecing together, bit by bit, every biographical sliver that comes my way, I have come to better understand Bram within the framework of his family and his friends. However, questions raised about him during his lifetime concerning the seemingly contradictory nature of his life as a gentleman and his Gothic sensibilities are still floating around today. In Boston, *The Sunday Herald* wrote in 1902 that

> His most famous novel was *Dracula*, a blood curdling tale which was the more remarkable to all who knew that it had been written by a mild, gentle Irishman and man of the world, who went about his way peacefully, never raising his voice in argument.[4]

One can tell much about a person by the company he keeps, in particular those friends to whom he is closest. Bram extols the virtues of his friends in a theatrical souvenir on Miss Ellen Terry (and Irving) in 1899, in "Sir Henry Irving: An Appreciation" (1904), and "Henry Irving's Fight for Fame" (1906), and in a lengthy piece on Sir Henry Hall Caine in 1908, while Caine's own heartfelt obituary of Bram returns the favor. These three were his closest friends as well as his long-time business associates, and Bram was clearly a man who valued and was valued by his circle of friends.

As Bram remained in the employ of the Lyceum for nearly 30 years, his life was inextricably entwined with both Irving and Terry. Just as Bram's career under Irving came to define their relationship as a monument to mutual understanding and respect, so too was it obvious that, in addition to appreciating each other's professional acumen, Bram's relationship with Ellen Terry was filled with warmth, admiration, and true fondness.

Bram was not alone, however, in his recognition of Terry's talents and beauty; the actress was greatly admired by the public and her colleagues alike. According to playwright George Bernard Shaw, "every celebrated man of the last quarter of the nineteenth century had been in love with Ellen Terry."[5]

In "The Art of Ellen Terry" (1901), Bram paints her as not only beautiful, but as a beautiful person, whose depth of character and life experiences gave her much on which to draw.[6] He sees "the sincerity of her regard for the essential truthfulness of things" as a component of her success, and writes that even as a child actor, "Her parts came naturally to her, and she never departed from the truth as she felt it to be in her portrayal of even the most conflicting emotions."[7]

Bram and Terry shared Irving, for better and for worse. Surely an understanding (mostly unspoken) of the rewards and demands of their respective positions with "the Gov'nor" served to strengthen their own bond of friendship. In her memoirs, Ellen noted somewhat bitterly Irving's use of Bram as a buffer to shield him from any unpleasant details of theater life:

> For years he has accepted favours, obligations to, etc, *through* Bram Stoker! Never will he acknowledge them himself, either by business-like receipt or by any word or sign. He "lays low" like Brer Rabbit better than anyone I have ever met.[8]

However, an article in *The Boston Sunday Herald* describes how the world at that time saw their symbiotic relationship:

> A more fortunate and happy connection has rarely, if ever, been made. Stoker has always entertained the most unbounded admiration for Irving's talents, and has been his most faithful, loyal, and indefatigable assistant, while Irving has reposed absolute confidence and implicit reliance not only on Stoker's business ability, but also on his literary and artistic taste and discernment.[9]

The complex alliance that was theirs had more layers than an onion; both were mutually beneficial to and dependent upon each other. Their liaison began in Dublin in 1876, when Irving, 38, impressed then university student Bram, 29, first with his talent on the stage, then with his desire to elevate "the stage" to social acceptability—a dream Bram, too, shared. Each saw in the other a means to an end: to provide theater patrons with intellectually stimulating productions. I contend that this is the tie which bound them through thick and thin.

It is oft-noted that Bram's association with Irving and the Lyceum brought him into contact with leading ladies and gentlemen of the day:

artists, writers, politicians, statesmen, and noblemen; and that rubbing elbows in this way was so fine a perk that Bram was willing to subjugate himself completely to Irving. But in reality, as we learned from his *Lost Journal*, in Dublin it was Bram's friends who were the movers and shakers, the artists and intelligentsia. Undoubtedly Irving, who never made an uncalculated move, realized Bram's Dublin associations were of great value to his own plans. Irving saw Bram not only as a kindred spirit, but also as a well-educated student of the stage. Bram had grown up attending Dublin theaters with his father, critiquing performances, discussing possible improvements, as well as writing theater reviews for a Dublin newspaper. With his attention to detail, a mathematics degree from Trinity, and charming demeanor, Bram seemed perfectly suited for theater management.

If, however, Bram had any doubt of his father's opinion on the matter, it was clarified in a letter to Bram, warning him that, as a profession, "theater life" was beneath him:

> I don't think they are altogether desirable acquaintances to those not connected with their own profession (if I may call it), because it may involve expense and other matters which are not at all times advantageous. Under all the circumstances I believe such acquaintanceship is better avoided.[10]

Abraham Stoker, Sr.'s attitude was typical of the nineteenth century, and it was this attitude that Bram and Irving poised themselves to change through their extensive preparations for Lyceum productions. As Bram noted in "Sir Henry Irving: An Appreciation by His Longtime Friend":

> Periods of history have to be studied; at times literature and the records or art ransacked for guiding hints. Experts must be found who can undertake various branches of the work. Painters and musicians, costumers, peruquiers, armorers and the producers of that comprehensive list of items, otherwise unclassified, called "properties"—all these people have to be found and arranged with. Add to these troubles the cares of the exchequer and it can be imagined how great is the strain on one man.[11]

Notably, Bram described this "one man," Irving, with the pride of a parent. Indeed, Terry's pet name for Bram was "Mama" or "Ma."[12] Yet, although Bram refers, in his "Sir Henry Irving: An Appreciation," to Irving's "single-handed venture" as the element which "made his theatre as well as himself illustrious and known all over the civilized world,"[13] the article is at the same time a wonderful account of all that Bram *and* Irving accomplished together toward elevating actors from "players" to artists, from alleyways to society parlors.

Although Bram would certainly have borne the brunt of Irving's artistic temperament, I know of no instance in any of his writings hinting at the sort of behavior described by costume designer Alice Comyns Carr, who wrote:

> I realized the existence of two distinct and separate Irvings. Gone was the debonair, cheery holiday companion, and in his place was a ruthless autocrat, who brooked no interference from anyone, and more than a little rough in his handling of everyone in the theatre—except Nell.[14]

While I believe Bram derived great pleasure from his position at the Lyceum, the Stoker/Irving friendship must have worn thin after so many years. But, one would never have known it from Bram.

In contrast, Bram's friendship with Hall Caine seems to have run deep and true to the end. In his obituary of Bram in 1912, Caine spoke of fallen friend's selflessness:

> In one thing our poor Bram, who had many limitations, was truly great. His was indeed the genius of friendship. I speak as perhaps the oldest of his surviving associates, outside the immediate circle of his family, when I say that never in any other man have I seen such capacity for devotion to a friend.[15]

In *The New York Times* article, "Where Hall Caine Dreams Out His Romances" (1908), Bram seems slightly amused by his friend's fame and popularity, as crowds of summer tourists on the Isle of Man invade Caine's otherwise quiet island home. Caine was a wildly successful novelist, and although he enjoyed his adoring fans, unlike Irving Caine did not seem to expect the same devotion from his friends. Caine wrote:

> There were moments during the last twenty-odd years when I felt ashamed that anybody should give me his time, his energy, and his enthusiasm as Bram gave them, and the only way in which I could reconcile myself to his splendid self-sacrifice was to remember that he loved to make it. I can think of nothing—absolutely nothing—that I could have asked Bram Stoker to do for me that he would not have done.[16]

The high regard they shared for each other is articulated in the dedications printed in two of their novels: Caine's *Capt'n Davy's Honeymoon* (1893), whose lengthy dedication is reprinted in the present collection; and *Dracula* (1897), in which Bram writes, simply, "to my dear friend Hommy-Beg" (Caine's Manx nickname). But Caine goes so far as to say, "Cap'n Davy without his ruggedness and without his folly, but with his simplicity, his unselfishness and his honour" is Bram Stoker.[17] Written 9 years before Bram's death, this beautiful ode to their friendship, "a deep stream that buoys me up and makes no noise,"[18] indeed brings tears to my eyes. In his obituary to Bram, Caine closed with, "It is only once in a man's life that such a friendship comes to him, and when the grave is closed on the big heart which we are to bury to-day, I shall feel that I have lost it."[19]

We who strive to know Bram so long after his death will savor the long-lost works collected in this volume. It is my hope that family, scholars, and fans of Bram Stoker will continue to uncover even more material, and that they—like Noel Dobbs with Bram's *Lost Journal* and John Edgar Browning with this collection—will share their finds with the world.

NOTES

Introduction

1 Two of the works collected here, "Bengal Roses" (1898) and "The Wrongs of Grosvenor" (1892), as well as parts of this introduction (in slightly different form), will appear concurrently with the present collection in the *Journal of Victorian Literature and Culture* (accepted and forthcoming). I am grateful to Abigail Bloom (CUNY-Hunter College) for her helpful comments.

2 Richard Dalby, "Quest for Bram Stoker," in *Bram Stoker: A Bibliography*, by Richard Dalby and William Hughes (Southend on Sea, UK: Desert Island Books, 2004), 12.

3 See Carol A. Senf, *Bram Stoker (Gothic Authors: Critical Revisions)* (Cardiff, Wales: University of Wales Press, 2010).

4 See Lisa Hopkins, *Bram Stoker: A Literary Life* (New York: Palgrave Macmillan, 2007).

5 With the exception of a laudatory letter addressed to Stoker from his friend Arthur Conan Doyle (reprinted in Elizabeth Miller's [ed.] *Bram Stoker's Dracula: A Documentary Journey Into Vampire Country and the Dracula Phenomenon* [New York: Pegasus Books, 2009], 267, and John Edgar Browning's *Bram Stoker's Dracula: The Critical Feast, An Annotated Reference of Early Reviews and Reactions, 1897-1913* [Berkeley, CA: Apocryphile Press, 2011], 75) and a parenthetical reference by Hall Caine in his obituary, "Bram Stoker: The Story of a Great Friendship" (*The Daily Telegraph* [London] April 24, 1912, reprinted in Miller's [ed.] *Bram Stoker's Dracula*, 24-26), little else is mentioned about *Dracula* by Stoker's friends.

6 As Miller points out, the only substantive comments Stoker is recorded to have made about *Dracula* may be found in a personal letter he addressed to former British prime minister William Gladstone (reprinted in Miller's

[ed.] *Bram Stoker's Dracula*, 274), in an interview by Jane Stoddard ("Mr. Bram Stoker: A Chat with the Author of *Dracula*," *British Weekly* [July 1, 1897]: 185, reprinted in Miller's [ed.] *Bram Stoker's Dracula*, 275-278, and Browning's *Bram Stoker's Dracula*, 60-64), and in the preface he wrote to the 1901 Icelandic edition of *Dracula*, entitled, *Makt Myrkranna* ("Powers of Darkness").

7 Nina Auerbach, *Ellen Terry: Player in Her Time* (New York: W. W. Norton & Company, 1987), 199.

8 William Hughes, "'*Dracula* and Other Novels': Reviewing Stoker's Fiction, 1882–1912," in *Bram Stoker: A Bibliography*, by Richard Dalby and William Hughes (Southend on Sea, UK: Desert Island Books, 2004), 18.

9 Ironically, Minnie Blackstone Douglas's "Aggie," which was awarded the prize in The Midland April Competition and published subsequently in the August 1896 issue of the *Midland Monthly*, was attacked for its striking similarities to Stoker's *The Watter's Mou'*. To this claim, Douglas, a Scotswoman, responded in a letter to the editor saying that "Mr. Bram Stoker is, I fancy, a countryman of my own, and therefore it is not strange that we should express ourselves in those peculiarly pathetic tones so much a part of true Scottish nature" ("The Prize Story 'Aggie' Under Fire," 575).

10 "A Gallant Act," *The Journal of the County of Surrey, Wandsworth & Battersea District Times, and Putney, Roehampton, and Wimbledon News*, no. 670 (September 23, 1882): 3.

11 See Christopher Craft's "Just Another Kiss: Inversion and Paranoia in Bram Stoker's *Dracula*," *Representations* 8 (Fall 1984): 107–133.

12 Bram Stoker, *Dracula: Authoritative Text, Contexts, Reviews and Reactions, Dramatic and Film Variations, Criticism*, ed. Nina Auerbach and David J. Skal (New York: W. W. Norton & Company, 1997 [1897]), 266.

13 Ibid., 42.

14 See, among other works, "The Boy Who Refused to Die," the first chapter in Harry Ludlam's *A Biography of Bram Stoker*, as well as David Skal's *Hollywood Gothic* (20), and Barbara Belford's *Bram Stoker and the Man Who Was Dracula* (13).

15 Whether or not Stoker was ever approached about a stage adaptation of *Dracula* has long eluded researchers, but an obscure notice I located in the "Musical and Dramatic Notes" column of the *Kansas City Journal* (Sunday, December 3, 1899) sheds new light on this riddle, lending itself not only to

the possibility that Stoker may have been actively pursuing a stage version, but that he was public about it as well, perhaps in an attempt to generate interest:

"Since arriving in Boston, Bram Stoker, manager of Sir Henry Irving, has received a proposition to dramatize his latest book, 'Dracula.' If it is put on the stage 'Dr. Jekyl [*sic*] and Mr. Hyde' in comparison will, it is said, become a pleasant memory." (18)

16 See, for example, *Publishers' Weekly* (September 30, 1899): 552; *Detroit Free Press* (November 18, 1899): no pagination; *The Annual American Catalogue, 1889* (1900): 207; *New York Times* (March 17, 1900): 169; *State* [Columbia, SC] (August 4, 1901) Sunday morning ed.: 10; and *Book News* (October 1902): 125.

17 The complete story of *Dracula*'s serialization is forthcoming in the latest of Skal's *magna opera*, *Bram Stoker: The Final Curtain*, due out soon.

18 "The Vampire" [advertisement], *Fitchburg Daily Sentinel* [Fitchburg, MA] 49, no. 19 (May 27, 1921): 18; "The Vampire" [advertisement], *Lowell Sun* [Lowell, MA] (May 28, 1921): 7.

19 Katharine Tynan Hinkson, ed., *The Cabinet of Irish Literature: Selections from the Works of the Chief Poets, Orators, and Prose Writers of Ireland*, vol. 4 (London: The Gresham Publishing Company, 1906), 338–342.

20 *The Fielding Star* [Manawatu-Wanganui, New Zealand] 13, no. 3144 (January 18, 1917): 4. In an article entitled, "Reviews for Readers," under "The Latest Magazines," the January 1917 issue of *Short Stories* gives the following, rather cryptic listing: "A Bram Stoker Dracula story appears."

21 *The Supplement to the South Bourke & Mornington Journal* [Richmond, Victoria, Australia] 27, no. 3 (May 3, 1882): 1.

22 See the *Western Mail* [South Glamorgan, Wales], 712, no. 6 (November 21, 1890): 1.

23 Paul McAlduff, "The Snake's Pass," *Bram Stoker*, accessed June 1, 2012, www.bramstoker.org. McAlduff also notes that the novel reportedly appeared in *The People* [London] from late 1889 to early 1890.

24 *Current Literature: A Magazine of Record and Review* 6 (January–April 1891): 148–152.

25 Justin McCarthy, ed. et al., *Irish Literature*, vol. 8 (Philadelphia: John D. Morris and Company, 1904; New York: P. F. Collier & Son, 1904), 3228–3237.

26 *Current Literature: A Magazine of Record and Review* 18 (July–December 1895): 438–441.

27 See the *Northampton Mercury* 168, no. [illegible] (January 16, 1903): 1.

28 The publication dates for the American editions of *The Gates of Life* and *Lady Athlyne* are given by Dalby in "A Bibliography of First Editions" (67, 72).

29 Hughes, "*Dracula* and Other Novels," 23.

30 I am grateful to Paul McAlduff of bramstoker.org for supplying this information.

31 E. L. Blanchard, "A Chain of Memories," in *The Theatre Annual*, ed. Clement Scott (London: Carson & Comerford, 1887), 48.

32 McAlduff, "Our New House," *Bram Stoker*, accessed August 15, 2012, www.bramstoker.org.

33 Dalby and Hughes, "Short Fiction in Periodicals and Anthologies," in *Bram Stoker: A Bibliography*, 117.

34 *The Boston Sunday Herald* (May 7, 1899): 42.

35 McAlduff, "A Yellow Duster," *Bram Stoker*, accessed June 1, 2012, www. bramstoker.org.

36 Dalby and Hughes, "Interviews and Journalism," in *Bram Stoker: A Bibliography*, 121.

37 *Daily Kennebec Journal* [Augusta, ME] (September 2, 1907): 6; *The Daily News* [Perth, Western Australia] 26, no. 10,136 (November 23, 1907): 6; *The Star* [Auckland, New Zealand] no. 9104 (December 9, 1907): 2; *Examiner* [Launceston, Tasmania] 67, no. 1 (January 1, 1908): 2.

38 Dalby and Hughes, "Interviews and Journalism," in *Bram Stoker: A Bibliography*, 121.

39 *Evelyn Observer and Bourke East Record* 35, no. 1789 (February 28, 1908): no pagination.

40 *The Daily News* [Perth, Western Australia] 27, no. 10,383 (September 10, 1908): 6.

41 Paul Murray, *From the Shadow of Dracula: A Life of Bram Stoker* (London: Jonathan Cape, 2004), 239.

42 *Supplement to the Poverty Bay Herald* [Gisborne, New Zealand] 33, no. 10,830 (November 24, 1906): 5; *The Mt. Sterling Advocate* [Mt. Sterling, KY] 26, no. 28 (January 23, 1907): 15; *The Montgomery Tribune* [Montgomery City, MO] 25, no. 13 (January 04, 1907): 3.

43 F. A. L. Bram (Florence) Stoker," Foreword," *Dracula*, by Bram Stoker, in *Argosy: The World's Best Stories* 1 (June 1926): 16

44 Murray, *From the Shadow of Dracula*, 153.

45 See "Short Stories," bramstoker.org.

46 Florence A. L. Bram Stoker, "Preface," in *Dracula's Guest and Other Stories*, by Bram Stoker (Hertfordshire, UK: Wordsworth Editions Limited, 2006 [1914]), 16.

47 Albert Power, "Bram Stoker and the Tradition of Irish Supernatural Fiction," in *Bram Stoker's Dracula: A Documentary Volume (Dictionary of Literary Biography 304)*, ed. Elizabeth R. Miller (Detroit: Thomson Gale, 2005), 110.

Chapter One

1 This poem is reprinted from *Judy: Or The London Serio-Comic Journal* [London] (January 8, 1890): 14. It appeared under the following prefatory title and remark:

OUR HARMONIC CLUB
Thirty-third Meeting.

"You have all heard the report gentlemen," said the Ever Young and Lovely, "that Mr. Henry Irving is about to woo parliamentary honours as candidate for the Strand. Who, I asked myself, when the news reached my ear, is likely to be able to tell me the "true inwardness" of the matter better than Mr. Irving's indefatigable assistant, Mr. Bram Stoker? So off I went forthwith to call upon Mr. Bram Stoker, and here Mr. Bram Stoker is, ready to contribute to the harmony of an evening that is never anything but harmonious, a song, entitled—

Chapter Two

1. This poem is reprinted from *The Speaker* [London] 5 (June 18, 1892): 741.

Chapter Three

1 This short story is reprinted from *The Boston Sunday Herald* (January 15, 1893): 24.

2 It was probably Stoker's intention, for comedic effect, that the ship's name should bear striking resemblance to "Tamar Indien Grillon," a drug used

in the 1890s to treat "Constipation, Hæmorrhoids, Bile, Headache, Loss of Appetite, Gastric and Intestinal Troubles." See "Tamar Indien Grillon," *Grace's Guide: British Industrial History*, accessed May 5, 2012, http://www. gracesguide.co.uk/Tamar_Indien_Grillon.

Chapter Four

1 This short story is reprinted from *The Boston Sunday Herald* (August 5, 1894): 20 [chapter 1], and *The Boston Sunday Herald* (August 12, 1894): 28 [chapter 2]. It was kindly donated to this collection by Paul McAlduff of bramstoker.org.

Chapter Five

1 This short story is reprinted from *Lloyd's Weekly Newspaper* [London] (July 17, 1898): 16 [chapter 1], and *Lloyd's Weekly Newspaper* (July 24, 1898): 16 [chapter 2].

Chapter Six

1 This short story is reprinted from *The Boston Sunday Herald* (March 26, 1899): pagination illegible.

Chapter Seven

1 This short story is reprinted from the earliest American edition I have been able to locate, the *Daily Iowa State Press* [Iowa City] 1, no. 175 (April 26, 1899): no pagination. A British edition predating the American edition appeared in *Lloyd's Weekly Newspaper* [London] (February 19, 1899): 17. However, the latter edition, although "first," resembles more its much later off-shoot, "Chin Music," which Stoker publishes in *Snowbound: The Record of a Theatrical Touring Party* (London: Collier & Co., 1908), whereas the American edition includes extended passages not present in the British edition or "Chin Music," and it is the more prolific of the two, appearing in multiple newspapers across not only the United States but Australia and New Zealand as well. Thus have I chosen to reprint it in lieu of the British version.

Chapter Eight

1 This fictionalized self-narrative is reprinted from *The St. Paul Globe* [Minnesota] 23, no. 121 (May 1, 1900): 4.

Chapter Nine

1 This short story is reprinted from *Lloyd's Weekly News* (December 27, 1908): 15. It was kindly donated to this collection by Paul McAlduff of bramstoker.org. "What They Confessed" seems to be a variant version of Stoker's short story "In Fear of Death," which, curiously, he publishes the same year in *Snowbound: The Record of a Theatrical Touring Party* (London: Collier & Co., 1908).

Chapter Ten

1 This obituary article is reprinted from *The Graphic: An Illustrated Weekly Newspaper*, no. 1151 (December 19, 1891): 722. It was kindly donated to this collection by Paul McAlduff of bramstoker.org.

Chapter Eleven

1 This article is reprinted from the *New-York Daily Tribune* (November 20, 1904): 3.

Chapter Twelve

1 This eulogy is reprinted from the earliest edition I have been able to locate, *The Des Moines Daily News* (November 18, 1906): 11.

Chapter Thirteen

1 This article is reprinted from *The New York Times* (September 6, 1908): 3.

Chapter Fourteen

1 This interview is reprinted from *The Boston Herald* (November 1, 1886): 1.

Chapter Fifteen

1 This interview is reprinted from *The New-York Daily Tribune* (November 1, 1886): 5.

Chapter Sixteen

1 This interview is reprinted from *The Era* [London] (October 11, 1890): 10.

Chapter Seventeen

1 Stoker, Bram, *Sir Henry Irving and Miss Ellen Terry in* Robespierre, Merchant of Venice, The Bells, Nance Oldfield, The Amber Heart, Waterloo, *etc.* Illustrated by Pamela Colman Smith (New York: Doubleday & McClure Co., 1896).

Chapter Eighteen

1. This article is reprinted from *Success Magazine* 9, no. 141 (February 1906): 87–88, 126.

Chapter Nineteen

1 This dedication appears in Hall Caine's *Capt'n Davy's Honeymoon* (London: William Heinemann, 1893): no pagination.

Chapter Twenty

1 This article is reprinted from the *Daily Mail* [London] (June 3, 1896): 3.

Chapter Twenty-One

1 This poem is reprinted from *The Brooklyn Daily Eagle* (March 4, 1900): 6.

Chapter Twenty-Two

1 This article is reprinted from *The Boston Sunday Herald* (April 6, 1902): 36. The review of Bram Stoker's *The Mystery of the Sea* (New York: Doubleday, Page & Co., 1902), which accompanied this article, has been omitted.

Chapter Twenty-Three

1 This short short story is reprinted from the *Oswego Daily Palladium* [New York] (June 27, 1904): 3.

Chapter Twenty-Four

1 This obituary is reprinted from the *Cleveland Plain Dealer* (April 25, 1912): 8.

Chapter Twenty-Five

1 This article is reprinted from *The Irish-American* 65, no. 30 (July 26, 1913): 4.

Chapter Twenty-Six

1 These pages are reproduced from the *Catalogue of Valuable Books, Autograph Letters, and Illuminated and Other Manuscripts, Including the Library of the Late Bram Stoker, Esq.* (London: Dryden Press: J. Davy and Sons, 1913), 1–20. The first day's sale occurred on Monday, July 7, 1913.

Chapter Twenty-Seven

1 This article is reprinted from *The Sun* [New York] (July 27, 1913): 6.

Chapter Twenty-Eight

1 This article is reprinted from *The Sun* [New York] (July 8, 1913): no pagination.

Chapter Twenty-Nine

1 This article is reprinted from *The New York Times* (July 8, 1913): no pagination.

Chapter Thirty

1 Elizabeth Miller and Dacre Stoker, *The Lost Journal of Bram Stoker: The Dublin Years* (London: The Robson Press, 2012).

2 "Mr. Bram Stoker," *The Times* [London] (April 1912): no pagination.

3 "Green Room Gossip," *Daily Mail* [London] (June 3, 1896): 3.

4 *The Boston Sunday Herald* (April 6, 1902): no pagination.

5 Forrest Izard, *Heroines of the Modern Stage* (New York: Sturgis & Walton Company, 1915), 116.

6 Bram Stoker, "The Art of Ellen Terry," *The Cosmopolitan* 31, no. 3 (July 1901): 241–250.

7 Ibid., 250.

8 Ellen Terry (Dame), Edith Craig, and Christopher St. John, *Ellen Terry's Memoirs* (1932; New York: Benjamin Blom, 1969), 270.

9 "Acting-Manager and Author: Bram Stoker Finds Recreation in Writing Romances," *The Boston Sunday Herald* (April 6, 1902): 36.

10 Harry Ludlam, *A Biography of Dracula: The Life Story of Bram Stoker* (London: W. Foulsham & Co., Ltd., 1962), 39.

11 Bram Stoker, "Sir Henry Irving: An Appreciation by His Longtime Friend," *New-York Daily Tribune* (November 20, 1904): 3

12 Daniel Farson, *The Man Who Wrote Dracula: A Biography of Bram Stoker* (London: Michael Joseph, 1975), 49

13 Stoker, "Sir Henry Irving: An Appreciation," 3.

14 Laurence Irving, *Henry Irving: The Actor and His World* (London: Faber and Faber, 1951), 467.

15 Hall Caine, "Bram Stoker: The Story of a Great Friendship," *The Daily Telegraph* (April 24, 1912): 16.

16 Ibid.

17 Hall Caine, "To Bram Stoker," in *Capt'n Davy's Honeymoon* (London: William Heinemann, 1893), no pagination.

18 Ibid.

19 Caine, "Bram Stoker: The Story of a Great Friendship," 16.